D1300738

WHEN NOVELS WERE BOOKS

When Novels Were Books

Jordan Alexander Stein

Harvard University Press

Cambridge, Massachusetts
London, England
2020

First printing

Library of Congress Cataloging-in-Publication Data
Names: Stein, Jordan Alexander, author.
Title: When novels were books / Jordan Alexander Stein.
Description: Cambridge, Massachusetts : Harvard University Press, 2020. |
Includes bibliographical references and index.
Identifiers: LCCN 2019011192 | ISBN 9780674987043 (alk. paper)
Subjects: LCSH: Fiction—History and criticism. | Books—History. | Printing—History. |
Early printed books. | Books and reading—History.
Classification: LCC PN3491 .S68 2020 | DDC 808.3—dc23
LC record available at https://lccn.loc.gov/2019011192

for Teresa Toulouse

Contents

Tout ceci doit être considéré comme dit par un personnage de roman.

—*Roland Barthes*

WHEN NOVELS WERE BOOKS

Introduction

Form and Format

In January 1759, Samuel Johnson acquired a book. He was at work on a fictional tale, to be published several months later as *The History of Rasselas, Prince of Abyssinia,* and needed to do some research. From his house on Gough Square, Johnson made a request to his friend, publisher, and fellow Londoner William Strahan.[1] No record remains of exactly which book Strahan sent, but all the probable candidates—such as a volume of the English translation of Giovanni Paolo Marana's *The Letters Writ by a Turkish Spy, Who Liv'd Five and Forty Years Undiscover'd at Paris* (1741), or *The History of the Marchioness de Pompadour* (1758)—would have been small-format books.[2] All eight volumes of the *Turkish Spy,* for instance, were published in duodecimo.[3] Neither does any record remain of whether Johnson paid for the book, though it is apparent that Johnson was paid for his. The author received £75 for the manuscript of *Rasselas,* which was printed and published that April by R. and J. Dodsley and William Johnston.[4] Readers of the first edition of *Rasselas* would have beheld two octavo volumes, similar in format to whichever book Strahan sent Johnson for inspiration.[5]

The format of *Rasselas* raises a question. By the time that work appeared in print, Johnson had already established his literary reputation with *A Dictionary of the English Language,* published four years prior by Strahan and others. The latter work's two volumes, however, were printed in the larger format of a folio. It's well known that the physical properties of a book—its size, its binding, its overall appearance of quality—are presumed by booksellers and book buyers alike to designate a book's importance.[6] In the case of the *Dictionary,* its large format signaled not only the prestige and significance of the work, but also that of the author—or, as he appeared credentialed on its title page, "SAMUEL JOHNSON, A.M."[7] But if Johnson was by 1759 accomplished enough as a literary man to be paid respectable sums for his writing and to have his credentials flaunted, and if the size of a book was one indication of its importance, then why wasn't *Rasselas* printed in a large format? Why print the work of a respected writer and well-known author of the *Dictionary* in such a way as to make it look less like the latter work and more like the *Turkish Spy?*

While the format in which an individual literary work is printed surely indicates something about its *significance*, the argument of the following chapters is that, into the early nineteenth century, format also indicates something about the work's *genre*. This point is easily neglected in the twenty-first century where it is, simply, far less true, because single works so often appear simultaneously in multiple formats. Should you wish to buy a copy of *Rasselas,* for example, your bookshop might stock a small-format paperback marketed to college classrooms and middlebrow readers (say, a Penguin Classics imprint), a medium-format hardbound library edition (like a volume from the Yale University Press *Works of Samuel Johnson*), or a cheap out-of-copyright reprint (such as a Dover Publications edition). If you shop for books at an online superstore, you may be a few clicks away from a choice among not only any of these editions but also a number of digital versions formatted for an e-reader. If you go to an antiquarian bookshop, or if you have access to a rare books library, you may be able to put your hands on an edition from Johnson's lifetime. Meanwhile, my own copy, purchased in my student days and reread over many years, is sandwiched in a medium-format textbook anthology of Johnson's writings.[8] All this variation begins to tell us a lot about how contemporary book publishing and bookselling segments readers as consumers, but it tells us little about the published work itself. And, more to the point, in telling us little about the work itself, these multiple competing formats obscure something that would have been comparatively obvious to eighteenth-century readers perusing a bookseller's catalog or browsing among shelves and tables in a shop where books were conventionally ordered, not by subject or alphabet, but by size.

As book ownership became increasingly commonplace among Anglophone readers in the course of the seventeenth century, and as this expanded market for books developed over the next hundred-plus years, a book's format continued to indicate its genre. Situated squarely in this historical period, the mid-eighteenth-century appearance of *Rasselas* as an octavo classed this work among fictions, tales, adventure stories, and belles lettres. The format in which *Rasselas* was initially printed made that book, as a physical object, resemble a number of other books with which its genre at least partially overlapped. We have already seen that the small format of *Rasselas* likened it to orientalist tales like the *Turkish Spy*, but that format would also have likened *Rasselas* to works that are now recognized as early novels and that tended to appear in duodecimo, such as *Pamela; or, Virtue Rewarded* (1741) printed in two volumes, *Clarissa; or, the History of a Young Lady* (1748) printed in seven volumes, or *The History of Tom Jones, a Foundling* (1749) printed in four volumes. Its format would also have likened *Rasselas* to adventure stories printed in a single octavo volume, such as *A General History of the Pyrates* (1726), or those printed in a single duodecimo, such as *The Adventures of a Kidnapped Orphan* (1767). The same small format would further have located *Rasselas* on a bookshop or library shelf next to spiritual narratives like *Grace Abounding* (1666), initially printed in duodecimo, or *The Life of David Brainerd* (1749), first printed in octavo.

If, as I am arguing, format indicates genre for many books in the handpress period, already this relationship between format and genre might seemed strained by two facts. First, not all the above-mentioned books are the same size. Though octavo and duodecimo are both smaller formats, they are not identical; and it might further be objected that the attempt to connect the significance of a work with its printed format makes sense only at the more prestigious large-format end of book publishing. Certainly, anyone who has read through seventeenth- or eighteenth-century book or library catalogs knows that they begin by enumerating folios, then quartos, and usually lose steam thereafter, lumping the majority of books under a heading like "Octavo and Lesser." Small-format books matter less in the eyes of printers and collectors than their larger cousins, and so the generic connections I'm positing between different small-format books might seem only approximate. Second, and following on the first objection, while a text like *Rasselas* bears physical similarities to many other texts, literary historians presume that these many texts nonetheless bear few similarities to one another. In what sense can an octavo of *Pamela,* one of the most important early novels, be related to another octavo like the missionary diary *The Life of David Brainerd?*[9] To make the kind of claim on which I'm insisting—that small-format books were printed with designed generic aspirations—may feel tenuous as it seeks to impose a broad logic on a diverse and too large range of books.

Let me then be the first to insist that if book format was indicative of genre, it nonetheless remains the case that "genre" with regard to seventeenth- and eighteenth-century books means something trickier than our contemporary literary historical categories tend to presume. Rather than indicate a kind or type of literary writing—what Lisa Gitelman helpfully defines as "a mode of recognition instantiated in discourse"— many genres in the seventeenth and eighteenth centuries were still gradually assuming their modern discursive shape.[10] Of course some *were* well established (such as the tragic or the georgic, which stemmed respectively from classical drama and poetry), but prose genres in particular showed much greater flux. Genres do not emerge well defined and fully formed; rather, they are developed by trial and error, though practices of iteration, citation, and recognition. The meaning of any generic category—whether the tragicomic, the bildungsroman, or the noir film— depends on the human activities of identifying it, maintaining it, challenging it, circulating it, and otherwise *using* it. Generic emergence deserves to be understood, in Carolyn R. Miller's phrase, as a kind of social action.[11] Moreover, the categorical integrity of most genres is built not only on social recognition but also by material practices of articulation and instantiation, including editing, circulation, and reprinting, by which, as Meredith L. McGill has argued, "literary culture and its audiences are constituted."[12]

Few examples better serve these observations than the novel, a genre that arguably emerges with European print in about the sixteenth century, but in the Anglophone world begins to consolidate under the sign "novel" much later, in the 1790s, from which point it was retroactively projected onto a number of earlier fictional prose narratives. Only when the genre was clearly established through a network of texts that imitated, cited, debated, mutated, or otherwise mutually developed one another was "the novel" able to claim recognition *as* a genre. This work of gradual development and belated naming, however, entails more than a few classificatory frustrations. That literary historians now recognize the progress of the novel in the eighteenth century and after does not mean, for example, that we can pinpoint its origins, and this long-standing critical interest in the origins of the novel—which itself dates to the eighteenth century—has never been conclusively resolved. The variety of candidates for the origin of the novel in English depends instead on which formal qualities of the novel one prizes and has accordingly included works as different as *The Pilgrim's Progress* (1681), *Oroonoko* (1688), *Robinson Crusoe* (1719), and *Pamela*. The formal features of these texts are various, with different structures of plot, narration, point of view, and dialogue—to say nothing of the considerable differences of theme. The fact remains, moreover, that none of these works calls itself a novel in its preface or title; nor did that term circulate in any of their initial critical reception. All this formal variation has made novels seem, as Henry James once designated them, "large, loose, baggy monsters, with their queer elements of the accidental and the arbitrary."[13]

Yet this looseness in one direction might feel considerably tightened in another if it were acknowledged that all four of the above-mentioned candidates for first novel in English were initially printed in duodecimo. While I concede that this fact hardly determines all that we might need to know about the history of the novel, the supposition of the following chapters is that there is something to be gained if scholars of the novel stop treating these features of format as largely irrelevant to our understanding of genre. Indeed, the wager of *When Novels Were Books* is that works scholars now recognize to be novels—like *Pamela*—and works we don't—like *Brainerd*—may, in the moments of their initial printing, publication, and circulation as books, have had more in common for

eighteenth-century readers than contemporary critics' retroactive generic designations have allowed us to see.

I

Novels were also books. For the first three centuries of their history,
novels came into readers' hands predominantly as printed sheets ordered into a codex of successive gatherings (usually of eight or twelve
pages) and bound along one edge, typically between boards or paper
wrappers.[14] Though a thoughtful book historian might observe that considerable variation exists among printed novels (including differences in
page size, typeface, paper quality, numbers of volumes, and technologies of illustration, for example), many equally thoughtful novel readers
have ignored these physical differences in the material text, in favor of
attention to the formal features of plot, setting, and characterization.[15] For
these latter readers, the novel is first and foremost a genre, and the idea
that this genre is packaged in book form has often seemed a mere point of
fact, too obvious to merit serious—let alone scholarly—consideration.

As an increasing number of digital platforms coexist with the codex
format in the twenty-first century, however, novels are no longer always
books.[16] This media shift has made many readers newly aware of how
specificities of platform and format may contribute to the phenomenology of our reading experiences. Yet what has proven true for the experience of reading has not substantially been tested on the history of
the novel as such. Studies of the novel as a genre are only beginning to
consider the media platform of the book, and studies of media are equally
incipient in their considerations of genre.[17] It remains to be seen whether
the fact that, historically speaking, novels have also been books stands to
revise the scholarly history of the eighteenth-century phenomenon that
Ian Watt so influentially described as "the rise of the novel."[18] The following chapters therefore undertake this work of revision.

Pursuing a long view of the historical development of novels in the
Anglophone world since the seventeenth century, *When Novels Were
Books* argues that the novel as a genre shares a mutually informing his-
tory with that of the development of the book as a media platform. This

argument contravenes histories that imagine "the rise of the novel" to be exclusively or even primarily a story of innovation in literary form, however historically grounded, politically inflected, or even ethical we may find "form" to be.[19] Tilting my argument away from form may seem like an unwonted move, at least insofar as the long-standing dominance of formalist interpretation has not staunched the field-wide flow of new attention to novelistic formalism—such that, for example, upstarts like the "Manifesto of the V21 Collective" can ask "How can we further develop formalist interpretations that are politically astute and intellectually supple?" even as established critics like Nancy Armstrong and Leonard Tennenhouse are simultaneously arguing that early American novels "simply must have observed a different formal standard than their British counterparts."[20] Form appears not only central to the ways scholars conceive of the novel as a genre; it also appears to be an ever-renewing source for analysis. Parting ways with this assumption, the critical intervention of *When Novels Were Books* is to show that methodologies drawn from book history can supplement the formalist analyses on which literary historians and theorists of the novel have for the last six decades typically relied.

While supplanting the *dominance* of formalist analyses for the study of the novel is one of this study's chief aims, it would be a significant misreading of the following pages to suppose that they argue against formalist analyses themselves. Indeed, my keenest interest is to synthesize scholarly conversations in an interdisciplinary spirit and to show how the history of the novel and the history of the book belong, and have always belonged, together. Scholarly attention to novelistic form is not and should not be divorced from the material contexts by which those forms circulate. To a certain extent, then, the ambitions of this study are fairly modest: to relate different parts of a story that we already know. Readers of these pages will, accordingly, find few unheard-of discoveries and fewer smoking guns. However, as I hope the same readers will see, once a large number of things we already know are lined up, they illuminate circumstances we may not have appreciated, and they lead to conclusions we may not expect.

Following from the argument that the novel as a genre shares a mutually informing history with the development of the book as a media platform, *When Novels Were Books* advances three theses. The first thesis concerns literary form. If novels, in a historically significant way, are also books, it follows that the formal features by which the development of the novel have been studied should also pertain in some meaningful way to the development of the book. Subsequent chapters test this idea by focusing on the literary figure most thoroughly associated with the novel: character, or the figural representation of persons.[21] These chapters demonstrate that in the seventeenth century, character was not proprietary to the novel or its prototypes, and that indeed the figural techniques for representing persons that became most associated with early novels—representing persons in terms of their vulnerability—developed previously in Protestant confessional and soteriological writings.[22] The circulation (in both manuscript and printed books) of these Protestant writings worked gradually to conventionalize this figure, which later found articulation in the early novelistic fictions of the 1740s and after. Subsequently, novels became a major flashpoint in the dissemination of character, and changes in Anglophone book publishing in the last quarter of the eighteenth century helped to create conditions where novels and other kinds of Protestant narratives were increasingly printed, circulated, marketed, and recognized as distinct from one another. Nonetheless, I argue that the long-standing formalist association between novels and character mistakenly credits novels with developing a figure that in fact incubated elsewhere.

The second thesis concerns reading. If novels and books share a history, and if character gradually came to be understood as a proprietary feature of eighteenth-century novels, it would follow that this formal evolution coincided with an evolution in the ways that readers used books. The subsequent chapters register that evolution in two related historical changes. On the one hand, prior to the eighteenth century, readers often engaged the random-access feature of the codex (the fact that, unlike a scroll or a website, a reader need not start at the beginning of a book and can instead instantly open it to any page). Early Anglophone printed books were often collections of ideas and information, organized into some order, but designed to be read discontinuously, to be "dipped into at need," rather than read from cover to cover.[23] The increasing reliance on character in the design of Protestant-inflected Anglophone texts toward the end of the seventeenth century coincides with a gradual increase in continuous, or cover-to-cover, reading. On the other hand, as the eighteenth century progresses, this tendency toward continuous reading seems also to generate an upswing in reading for identification—the process by which readers relate their experiences of the world with those of characters, and vice versa. I argue that character, figuring both fictional and biographical persons, becomes increasingly central to the ways that eighteenth-century readers read all kinds of texts, including but not limited to novels.

The third thesis concerns secularization. If novels, historically speaking, were also books, then they presumably coexisted with other books that were not novels. Several of the following chapters accordingly pair Protestant writings in a range of subgenres with texts that are indisputably now recognized to be novels. One aim in doing so is to demonstrate throughout the formal and material similarities among these texts. Another aim is to show how frequently historical readers could have found these (now) generically diverse books in the same bookshops, libraries, piles, shelves, and armloads. However, these pairings make historical sense only until about the last quarter of the eighteenth century. By that point, with the efficacy of print for disseminating ideas well established, many Protestant organizations (including voluntary associations, outlying religious factions, missionary societies, and emergent tract societies) begin to control their own printing presses, circulating printed materials at lower cost to their producers and often at no cost to their consumers, thus effectively subtracting themselves from the economics of the London print market (which remains the largest print market in the Anglophone world for the entire two centuries under discussion). This economic subtraction branches Protestant writings off from novels by about the 1790s, around which point the creators of these two types of printed materials recognize one another—for the first time in their history—as real competitors. Put differently, novels were not historically secular, and the fact that they came to be so has more to do with changes in religious publishing than in novel publishing. It has long been presumed that the history of the novel was part and parcel of a history of secularization—that the novel, in Georg Lukács's apocalyptic phrase, was "the epic of a world that has been abandoned by God."[24] I argue that any conception of novels as fundamentally secular refracts their history through a tardy historical development.

Over four chapters, *When Novels Were Books* braids these three theses together into a roughly chronological narrative. Chapter 1, "Paper Selves," examines the confessional narratives that Reformed Protestants developed as a criterion for church membership, first in New England in the 1630s, and later in England after the deposition of Charles I. These narratives assumed an idiomatic consistency, whereby speakers figure themselves negatively: as weak, impure, vile, corrupted, or otherwise vulnerable before God's judgment. Such figuration draws on the model of Augustine's fourth-century *Confessions,* but achieves rapid conventionalization through circulation of testimonial narratives in the form of manuscript books, two of which survive from Thomas Shepard's Cambridge, Massachusetts, congregation. This chapter identifies the formal features of this characterological figuration and details how, a century before the emergence of the Anglophone novel, and without entirely relying on printing, ancient Christian strategies for pious self-representation find new life among Reformed Protestants in both England and New England.

Moving from manuscript to print, Chapter 2, "The Character of Steady Sellers," examines the class of Protestant devotional books that, in addition to Bibles, were among the few books that Anglophone common readers might have owned in the seventeenth century. Designed like Bibles to be read discontinuously, "steady sellers" were predominantly nonnarrative works. Though they were, thereby, not character-driven texts, many steady sellers nonetheless did figure characters, describing piety in the same negative idiom as confessional writings, including humility, self-effacement, and subjective vulnerability before God. While retaining this negative figuration of character, toward the end of the seventeenth century steady sellers begin to assume a deliberately narrative shape. The final section of the chapter turns to *The Pilgrim's Progress* and *Robinson Crusoe,* two enduring Anglophone narratives usually taken to be early novels, and demonstrates their debts to, and significant formal and material continuities with, the steady sellers of the seventeenth century.

Chapter 3, "The Rise of the Text-Network," follows the emergent textual pairing of negatively figured characters and continuous narratives as they migrate around the Atlantic world. Considering the multiple texts of, and responses to, *Pamela* (first published in London in late 1740, but revived with immense popularity in New England in the 1780s) and the many different editions of the missionary diaries of David Brainerd (first published in Philadelphia in 1746, but reedited by Jonathan Edwards in 1749, and widely circulated and reprinted in England and Scotland through the 1760s and 1770s), this chapter demonstrates the abundant similarities between the figurations of the fictional Pamela and the nonfictional Brainerd in their respective stories. These texts share not only a similarly negative means of figuring characters, but also similar material processes of dissemination (including abridgment, anthologization, translation, and reprinting). Their mirrored transatlantic receptions indicate that as late as the mid-eighteenth century both early novels and Protestant autobiographies could achieve the kinds of high-volume, short-term sales that book historians have otherwise argued distinguish the novel from the reliable returns of the steady seller.

The material similarities between eighteenth-century novels and Protestant narratives break down toward the end of the eighteenth century, a story detailed in Chapter 4, "Printers, Libraries, and Lyrics." One overwhelming force in the ultimate generic differentiation of novels and Protestant narratives is the series of changes, described in the third thesis above, by which the printing of "books of piety" effectively subtracts itself from the London print market. Consequent upon this subtraction, the 1790s mark a burst of religious antinovelism in the Anglophone Atlantic, not because novels were new in this decade, but because for the first time novels and Protestant narratives were recognized as being in competition. Though a predominant force in the secularization of the novel, these economic circumstances are by no means the only cause. Accordingly, this chapter pays attention to some of the emergent ways that books were being used in the last quarter of the eighteenth century: in the context of voluntary associations, circulating libraries, and in the increasingly divergent cultural values of prose and poetry. Chapter 4 concludes with an analysis of the ways that early nineteenth-century editions of *The Pilgrim's Progress* materially repackage this text as a novel, whereas late seventeenth-century editions had published it like a steady seller.

Finally, the brief Conclusion, subtitled "The Retroactive Rise of the Novel," attempts to answer the difficult question that all revisionist histories face: If the history of the novel and the history of the book are indeed related, as the previous chapters say, why don't scholars already know this story? My answer is located in the retrospective critical judgments of nineteenth-century critics (and their twentieth-century inheritors), who emphasized the formal properties of the novel over its material manifestations. The Conclusion summarizes some of the ways that the appearance of literary criticism in nineteenth century begins to invent traditions for the British and American novel by collecting eighteenth-century prose narratives into a prehistory of the novel.

For better or for worse, the four central chapters of this study are not independent essays, and each does not readily stand on its own. Still, readers with particular interest in the development of the novel as such should focus on Chapter 3, which provides the core of the argument and the most extended engagement with a novel this study has to offer. Chapters 2 and 4 position novels more explicitly in relation to the books of piety with which they were most often associated in the seventeenth and eighteenth centuries, respectively, and readers eager to think about religious print and attendant practices of reading should focus here. Chapter 1, meanwhile, takes the widest step away from printed books, considering instead other media (such as manuscript and performance) in order to situate the concerns of the subsequent chapters—novels, print, Protestantism, and character—in a wide historical and cultural context.

When Novels Were Books aims to synthesize the history of the book and the history of the novel, but, as the above narrative outline already suggests, there is some asymmetry to the way the story is being told. This study's emphasis falls on demonstrating the force of the material history of the book as it bears on the generic history of the novel, rather than the other way around. The implications of the study accordingly push toward an intervention into novel studies, and it certainly has been readers, colleagues, and students working in this field whom I have most often imagined to be the addressees of these pages. Precisely for this reason, however, outside of Chapter 3, readers will find only passing engagements with novels in recognizably literary critical modes, as this study seeks instead to demonstrate its interpretations with recourse to some of the bibliographic, archival, and empirical evidence that books yield. If the result is a history of the novel without close readings of very many novels, the reader will hopefully recognize aspects of my argument reflected in my method.

II

Having explained what the present study does, I should now explain what I understand some of its practical limits to be. One concerns evidence. Though interested in broad patterns for reading, *When Novels Were Books* tends to engage texts—including *The Pilgrim's Progress, Robinson Crusoe, Pamela, The Life of David Brainerd*—whose material histories are not typical of other books. These texts have been read more widely, in more editions, and in more locations than many other texts with which they have coexisted. Because historical reading practices are difficult to reconstruct, the sheer number of permutations of these particular texts makes them especially useful for this study's interpretations. *When Novels Were Books* accordingly treats these texts as case studies, on the theory that they can be taken as pieces of a larger pattern not because they are in any statistical sense representative, but because, as Carlo Ginzburg has so usefully shown, even a limited case can prove representative when "it permits us to define the latent possibilities of something (popular culture) otherwise known to us only through fragmentary and distorted documents."[25] I certainly cannot claim that, within the history of books, there is any text "like" *Pamela*, but I can and do claim that the comparatively exaggerated phenomena of *Pamela*'s production and reception have things to teach us about the history of books in the Anglophone world more generally.

A second point concerns gender. Far and away the most important revision to the study of the novel in the last four decades has been the expansion of a contracted masculine canon and the restoration of women writers (including those who worked anonymously) to the development of the novel.[26] If the following chapters concentrate on male-authored texts and so fail to do sufficient justice to these revisions, that failure reflects no disagreement on my part about the significance of gender to authorship and publishing practices in the seventeenth and eighteenth centuries. Rather, that failure is due in part to the present study's emphasis falling on readers rather than authors, and due in part to a certain archival chauvinism—to say nothing of its cultural counterparts—that enables literary historians to document male readers rather more precisely than female ones. To correct for this chauvinism, where possible I have privileged documentary evidence of female readership and book ownership. As Jan Fergus conclusively shows, however, there is no empirical evidence whatsoever that eighteenth-century women read novels in any greater number than did men.[27] The experiences of women novel readers, difficult as they are to isolate in the historical record, in strictly empirical terms tend to confirm, rather than challenge, what scholars know about patterns for reading practices writ large.

A third point is about where race does and doesn't enter this story. As with the above point regarding gender, where possible, I have tried to include mention of African, Afro-diasporic, Native American, and other readers of British books in the reaches of that empire's colonies; however, unlike the above point regarding gender, evidence of nonwhite readers does not tend to conform to patterns for reading practices writ large. A study that paid explicit attention to the relations among such different readers, or that took race as its central term, would be an entirely different study; moreover, it would be one that I felt, mutatis mutandis, was likely to prove overly complicated in relation to my larger intervention regarding genre. And so, though the chapters that follow do not engage analytically with race, they are written with some awareness that the intersecting histories of the book and the novel in the Anglophone world are profoundly vectored by a history of whiteness that needs to be further exposed and unlearned. A number of scholars have begun this work in the study of seventeenth- and eighteenth-century communications media, but its bearing on the novel largely remains to be seen.[28]

A final point concerns the transatlantic scope of this study. If the novel is a national emblem, the book is an undeniably international one.[29] Where novels have often been taken to represent a national culture, a way of life, or a people, books transmit those representations often well beyond the boundaries of any readerly communities that could plausibly imagine national novels as self-representations.[30] Meanwhile, as Joseph Rezek has shown, by the early nineteenth century, the national fictions (first tales and later novels) of England, Scotland, Ireland, and the United States were all printed, published, and sold in London, with few writers or readers appreciating the contradiction between the ideologies of national narrative and realities of metropolitan printing.[31] The story of how novels came to seem national, while books remain vigorously international, is part of the story the following chapters tell; and so, one of the things the present study asks of its readers is that they suspend the idea that novels are inevitably national, the better to historicize that presumption.[32]

Ideally, *When Novels Were Books* would build on a first wave of scholarship that seriously links the long history of book use to genre, demonstrating a more global orientation to the history there outlined.[33] However, with the possible exceptions of just a few scholarly monographs, there has not yet been a critical movement that properly links genre to material book use in one long national context.[34] Even the major encyclopedic histories of the book in Britain, Ireland, Scotland, France, or America do not give sustained attention to genre.[35] That the present study tries to push past a national orientation for genre and consider novel circulations in multiple national contexts, may, accordingly, seem overstretched. Yet such stretching is necessary, for the question of how novels come to matter to the world in the eighteenth century does not, empirically speaking, have a nationalist answer.

III

Having explained how this study proceeds practically, let me now explain how it works in theory. The intervention of *When Novels Were Books* is to interpret the history of the novel as a genre, by way of the interdisciplinary field of book history. Though the latter field is not guided by a uniform object or a single methodology, the following chapters will demonstrate that book history offers novel studies an opportunity to gather some material and bibliographic data against which to verify, nuance, and specify claims about the novel's development and— what we will see amounts to the same thing—its material distinction from other genres.[36] Attending to the (fairly indisputable, though not usually meaningful) fact that novels are, and though their history most consistently have been, the material objects called books, scholarship on the history of the book can supplement the kinds of formalist and genre-centered literary history typically directed at the novel.

More precisely, scholarship on the history of the book can attend to patterns of textual circulation, including generating both hard empirical data and relevant circumstantial observations about how novels were printed and sold; the other kinds of books and objects with which novels were associated; the routes and networks through which novels circulated; and the occasions where readers might have variously read novels and possibly heard about novels they did not or could not read. Attention to patterns of textual circulation illuminates, in historical and material terms, *how* novels come to distinguish themselves as what one doyen of novel studies calls "a great anthropological force" in human culture.[37]

Bringing the history of the book to bear on the history of the novel supplements many long-standing practices of literary historicism. One does not have to be a scholar of the novel to be aware that attempts to elaborate and specify the significance of novels were tackled aggressively in the 1980s and 1990s by the New Social History, New Historicism, and cultural studies, all of which encouraged literary scholars to make broader claims about the world and the culture. As Stephen Greenblatt and Catherine Gallagher summarize in a retrospective statement about New Historicism, "We wanted to delve as deeply as possible into the creative matrices of particular historical cultures and at the same time we wanted to understand how certain products of these cultures could seem to possess a certain independence."[38] Meanwhile, the editors of the agenda-setting 1992 collection *Cultural Studies* connected literature not just to the world at large but to academic worlds specifically, arguing that "a scholarly discipline, like literature, cannot begin to do cultural studies simply by expanding its dominion to encompass specific cultural forms. . . . Cultural studies involves *how* and *why* such work is done, not just its content."[39]

Yet the contextualizing methodologies of cultural studies and, especially, of New Historicism have provoked objections on the grounds that they are still too little concerned with the more empirical aspects of historical reconstruction—that they are, to put a fine point on it, insufficiently interdisciplinary. Though New Historicism understands texts as historical, it also generally understands history as textual, with the consequence that the methodologies of close reading are reinforced, rather than reimagined, as they are applied to many kinds of texts (such as legal documents, paintings, or medical treatises) that the discipline of English had not typically regarded as literary. This reinforcement of close reading as a cornerstone method for New Historicism led one of its early critics, in a strenuously argued essay, to insist that "it is simply not the case that the New Historicism is essentially different from formalism."[40] Others have more generously tempered their conclusions, observing that the rise of New Historicism in English departments corresponded to a broader intellectual interest in ideas and narratives, evidenced by the rise of cultural history in History departments in the United States in the same decades as New Historicism gained prominence.[41]

But however one wishes to calibrate the point, critiques of New Historicism are correct to observe that even though this methodology seeks to connect texts with contexts, it nevertheless treats the category "context" with far less intellectual energy than historians reserve for the category "history" or anthropologists spend theorizing the category "culture." Thus, as David Kastan writes, "In its often dazzling demonstrations of the circulation of discourses through culture, New Historicism has rarely paid much attention to the specific material and institutional conditions of the discursive exchanges it has explored."[42] Or, as Meredith L. McGill argues, "New Historicist critics are often more interested in the discursive mediation of social relations than they are in the mediation of discourses themselves."[43] Or again, as Matthew P. Brown insists, despite its "its acrobatic movements from anecdotal detritus to canonical work," New Historicism is nonetheless "bedeviled by assumptions of aesthetic value, which still defines most literary studies."[44] To make the point one more way, New Historicism and cultural studies have each done important work teaching us how to put novels into contexts, and those contexts have been excitingly various, depending on field-wide fashions and individual researchers' expertise; yet these bodies of scholarship have nevertheless not yet taught us as much as they might have about the ways that books themselves were for so long the inevitable context for any novel and any act of novel reading.

Whether we concentrate on its New Historicist strains or not, it's hard to deny that studies of the novel are particularly guilty among literary subfields of extrapolating enormous claims about the culture from the close reading of a small handful of texts. Such a conclusion is foregone in the case of *The Rise of the Novel,* and specifically the five Anglophone novels by three (London-based, male) authors on which basis Watt articulated what has become an enduring insistence that the novel as such is an epistemology, a way of understanding the world, and thus "the literary form which most closely satisfies [readers'] wishes for a close correspondence between life and art."[45] But *The Rise of the Novel* is not alone in restricting the epistemology of fiction to the novel while simultaneously emphasizing the novel's reach, and indeed this critical move has been repeated even by scholars who have otherwise disputed Watt's canon and conclusions—including Nancy Armstrong, D. A. Miller, Michael McKeon, and Franco Moretti.[46]

Somewhat paradoxically, then, some of the most influential scholars of the novel have argued for its significance to world history at the same time that their methodology has isolated the novel as a particular kind of reified entity. In so doing, their arguments offer examples of a kind of formalism inclined to far-reaching cultural and historical claims on the basis of formal evidence alone. Little wonder that, following from this line of thinking, scholars have been satisfied by definitions of the novel wherein its generic features resemble "large, loose, baggy monsters."

This grand leap from a claim about a few novels to a claim about the world leaves insufficient room for the subtleties of generic refinement, development, or mutation. And so, as I have said, while the keenest interest of *When Novels Were Books* is synthesis, part of what I would insist that synthesis leads to is an appreciation of history's ironies. Where prior scholars of the novel have expended considerable energy trying to demonstrate that the novel was born secular, or born national, or born middle-class, or born female, the following chapters instead take origins to be a red herring and birth as a considerably misguided metaphor. Novels do not appear in the world as such at one juncture in the British eighteenth century; rather, novels gradually evolve and only retrospectively come into recognition, from which latter point they, as objects, come to be made and remade in the image that names them. That making, like that retrospective recognition, is a historical and cultural activity, subject to decades of considerable variation and trial and error before achieving the generic consistency for which scholars have been inclined to hunt at its putative origin. *When Novels Were Books* presents a history of the novel that proceeds through what, following Gilles Deleuze and Félix Guattari, we can call "mutations"—spontaneous changes and perversions that attain gradual refinement and differentiation.[47] Mutations figure history ironically, at least insofar as the undeniable changes they represent cannot be said to follow from anything resembling efficient causality or individual intention.[48]

Reframing "the rise of the novel" as ironic rather than progressive, *When Novels Were Books* aligns itself with other scholarly attempts that marshal empirical evidence to challenge and reframe some of the conclusions associated with New Historicism, and in particular with the efficiencies this body of work sometimes demonstrates between what literature or representation proposes and what the culture accordingly disposes—a phenomenon that two different scholars of the novel, Philip Fisher and Jane Tompkins, have each dubbed "cultural work."[49] Critiquing this notion of efficiency, *When Novels Were Books* takes for granted that culture happens in the often quite yawning space between what people say they do and what they actually do.[50] This study accordingly belongs on the shelf with scholarship by Lara Langer Cohen, Trish Loughran, and Ben Kafka, proponents of what sometimes goes by the moniker of "the bummer theory of print culture"—the use of archival and empirical evidence to challenge the theoretical assumption that, as Cohen puts it, "cultural work always *works.*"[51]

When Novels Were Books, then, picks up on the critique of New Historicism outlined by these other book historians, and adds to it a way of thinking about genre, taking seriously the fact that novels long circulated in a specific material format—printed, gathered, and bound. In both subtle and profound ways, the physical properties of a book affect our experience of reading it: how large or small it is, how heavy, how closely printed, how lavishly illustrated, how finely or cheaply made, how it is most likely to be used—and, indeed, in whose fellowship we might find ourselves to be constituted as its audience. The physical properties of books influence the way readers select them from shelves or stacks, how we esteem their contents or authors, where and whether we choose to display them, and many other things besides. Readers judge books by their covers. The idea that we ought not to is an ideological stance that privileges the abstract domain of literature over the inexorable material vicissitudes of experience. My contention is that literary formalism, New Historicism, close reading, or any other methodology requiring that we read what's on the page should not discourage us from reading the page as well, for the page itself is not only a context for the history of novels; it is—and has historically been—*the* context for reading them.

❧ 1 ❧

Paper Selves

N ovels are also books, but scholars typically define novels by their formal figures and features, rather than their material manifestations. An impatience with such claims about formal innovation motivates the argument of this book, and that impatience is due to the fact that, as the Introduction elaborates, the books that novels are, the literacies required to read them, and the imaginings of self and culture that follow from engagements with them, are all complex and dynamic things, which formalist arguments have a tendency to underexplain. Yet because critics so often estimate the novel by its formal features, this and the next two chapters conduct an experiment with form. The experiment will track the progress and development of character—one of the novel's signature formal features—through a series of texts that are and are not novels. The aim here is to demonstrate that the materiality of books, and not just the generic figurations of novels themselves, are what mediate the development, refinement, and mutation of this formal figure. The conclusion toward which this experiment points is not designed to be antiformalist; rather, I hope to show that while form does matter to novels, it at best works in tandem with other material aspects of what novels are, and it should be valued accordingly.

Though character does not originate with the novel, readers commonly find this aspect of the novel, to use E. M. Forster's colloquialism, "more interesting" than the plot or setting by which novels are also most often anatomized.[1] A strong association persists between character and novels, such that readers may tolerate spare settings or plotless plodding as long as these are inhabited by compelling figures.[2] This association, however, is a relatively recent historical development, for if one understands "character" as the figural representation of persons, such figuration indisputably appeared in European writing and performance well before the emergence of the Anglophone novel in the eighteenth and nineteenth centuries.[3]

A common explanation for the association between novels and characters, then, is that the kinds of figures who appear in novels are distinct from other kinds of characters. What is often thought to differentiate novelistic character from its antecedent figures is the degree of psychological depth and detail that novels (and their narrators) tend to elaborate for characters. By this logic, novelistic characters are not just figural representations of persons, but, more specifically, persons figured in terms of their individuality. (Forster, for one, titles his lectures on character in *Aspects of the Novel* "People.") Like many people, characters in novels have opportunities to be more than just figures, and indeed many novels would seem implicitly to correlate characters with Eve Kosofsky Sedgwick's famous axiom about modern personhood: *"People are different from each other."*[4] More than figures, characters in novels are capable of personalities—capable of what Nancy Ruttenburg, with admirable precision, describes as "an individuality which, lacking a transcendent referent, reveals itself in and as a series of representations, each of which might plausibly support the claim to constitute the truth about a self."[5]

The aim of this and the next two chapters will be to show how this kind of character gradually flourishes in the novel. The story fully begins in Chapter 2, which demonstrates how prose narratives come into fashion as book design and reading practices shift toward the end of the seventeenth century, encouraging readers to read in a cover-to-cover fashion that nudges the arc of characterological experience closer to the heart of the purpose and pleasures of reading. Yet because the figure of character is older than the continuous reading practices that track its novelistic version, this chapter takes a chronological step backward to consider the particular emphasis that Reformed Protestants (sometimes inexactly referred to as Puritans)[6] placed on character in the first half of the seventeenth century.

Reformed faith is not usually taken as an origin point for fictional prose narratives, due in no small part to the rejection of iconic representations that Reformed Protestants loudly espoused. Nonetheless, seventeenth-century Protestants expended considerable energies to create figures in a manner that conformed with their beliefs—both about Christian piety and about representation. Many Protestants trained in theology to see with Calvin that literal meanings were preferable to figural ones were the same Protestants trained in rhetoric to see with Quintilian that figural language was emotionally and rhetorically powerful language.[7] Such parallel training generally meant that the use of figurative language for its own sake was to be avoided, but the use of figurative language as a means to point toward divine truth could be effective. As Ann Kibbey argues, "Puritan preachers conceived of literal meaning as a rhetorical construct, as a pliable figure and not a given of language. Even literal meaning was dependent on the interplay of signifiers and the use of tropes, so much so that the function of reference could depend substantially on the relation of words to each other in discourse."[8] Structuralist theories of language in the twentieth century, emphasizing the arbitrary relationship between signifier and signified, cleared the way for the deconstructive insight that language is nonreferential and, in that sense, entirely figural.[9] But transcendent reference had not been similarly jettisoned in the rhetorical theories adopted by seventeenth-century Protestants, despite their interest in linguistic elasticity.[10] Indeed, for all the historical figures under discussion in this chapter, semiotic variety seemed compatible with transcendent meaning. At the same time that transcendent meaning was posited, however, the question of how best to measure it was the subject of much theological debate. Determining the validity of transcendent meaning often turned on whether the right person was the one making that meaning. As T. H. Breen has discussed, across both seventeenth-century Protestant and Anglican discourses, many people believed, and were encouraged by civil and religious authorities to believe, that it was only "few rulers who possessed God's special gifts."[11] And so the definition of character in the figural sense (a representational construct) traversed character in the social sense (a pious reputation).

The following pages will tease out these points with the larger aim of demonstrating that the history of novelistic character owes something to the history of Protestant character. It is important to clarify at the outset of such an argument, however, that the imbrication of these histories is profoundly ironic. Viewed from the orthodoxy of Christian doctrine (or, for that matter, of novel studies), the stakes of characterological figuration in a confessional context have little to do with fiction and everything to do with salvation. As we shall see, confessional narratives, which expound upon the felt experience of the dispensation of grace, are one place where the figuration of character develops powerfully in the late sixteenth and early seventeenth centuries. Nonetheless, many Protestant theories of representation from the period rely on assumptions about language's ability to arrive at truth, which seem naïve to latter-day readers, who are well aware that meanings and the figures that convey them both are capable of what Gilles Deleuze and Félix Guattari have called "mutation," a practical loosening of "the hegemony of the signifier" through ordinary use.[12] The ability of these Protestant figures to inform later novelistic figures is, in my view, a consequence of that relative naïveté. Many seventeenth-century Protestants unwittingly contributed to the mutation of their figures by presuming that even the elastic use of figures will ultimately tend to signify truth, so long as a pious person is the one using them. Such faith, and the ironic mutations that followed, should be understood as the consequence of what happens when, as Gayatri Chakravorty Spivak has put it, "signifiers are left to look after themselves."[13]

Like nearly everything else in this story, mutation as such neither begins nor ends with the seventeenth century texts on which the following pages will concentrate. Nonetheless, concentration on these texts finds justification with the premise they are a significant and immediate incubator for the characterological figures that eventually find their way into print in the late seventeenth century and that will be discussed in

Chapter 2. The present chapter makes a preliminary effort to look back from print to the manuscript context for characterological figuration among seventeenth-century Protestants; it substantiates that choice by considering some of the figures to which seventeenth-century Protestants were themselves looking back. And so this story about New England requires a detour to North Africa.

I

The history of Christianity is rarely considered as the progress of a theory of representation. Considering it as such, however, would harmonize many significant touchstones in Christian theology, spanning at least from the first-century pseudo-Pauline epistle to the Hebrews, which appoints faith as the evidence of things not seen, to the seventeenth-century Westminster Confession, which details the relationship between scriptural authority and pastoral care.[14] Between these points in time, representation emerges as a central, if somewhat tacit, motif in Augustine's fourth-century *Confessions*. This text is better known for its consideration of the role of will in the experience of salvation, in part because Augustine's notoriously pessimistic theory of free will was refused by his contemporary Pelagius (thereby meriting defenses and disquisitions by many subsequent commentators).[15] But in spite of its centrality to Augustine's account of salvation, will does not emerge as a main topic until Book VIII of the *Confessions*. Leading up to—and, significantly, setting the stage for—this discussion of will are numerous considerations of representation.

Recalling his time as a teacher of rhetoric in Book III of the *Confessions*, Augustine expresses a quietly neo-Platonic suspicion toward the very idea of representation, observing, for instance, that

> the art of poetry, by which I composed, does not vary from one line to another: it is the same for all alike. But I did not discern that justice, which those good and holy men obeyed, in a far more perfect and sublime way than poetry contains in itself at one and the same

time all the principles which it prescribes without discrepancy; although, as times change, it prescribes and apportions them, not all
at once, but according to the needs of the times.[16]

[et ars ipsa qua canebam non habebat aliud alibi, sed omnia simul.
et non intuebar iustitiam, cui servirent boni et sancti homines, longe
excellentius atque sublimius habere simul omnia quae praecipit et
nulla ex parte variari et tamen variis temporibus non omnia simul,
sed propria distribuentem ac praecipientem.[17]]

The quasi-universal laws or principles of poetic composition *(ars)* are
always the same, though a poet deploys those universal aesthetic principles variously in order to produce diverse compositions suited to particular times, audiences, and rhetorical needs. For this reason, Augustine
draws the analogy between the universal principles of poetry *(ars)* and
the universal principles of justice *(iustitia),* which are always and every-
where the same even though they are deployed variously to suit times
and circumstances. Also like the art of poetry, the art of rhetoric aims to
persuade an audience, and thus both these species of representation depend on audiences who are in a certain sense malleable, capable of per-
ceptual shifts. Such malleability prompts Augustine to align both rhetoric and poetry with appearance, which can change, and to oppose
them, in this passage and elsewhere, to justice, whose truth is "far more
perfect and sublime."

Crucially, however, Augustine's suspicion of these varieties of representation does not lead him to eschew representation altogether. Indeed,
he cannot reject all forms of representation, because he understands that
one arrives at an immediate experience of faith in a complexly mediated
fashion.[18] As Augustine observes in Book VI of the *Confessions,* "Since
we are too weak to discover the truth by reason alone and for this reason
need the authority of sacred books, I began to believe that you [i.e.,
God] would never have invested the Bible with such conspicuous authority in every land unless you had intended it to be the means by which
we should look for you and believe in you" [ideoque cum essemus in-
firmi ad inveniendam liquida ratione veritatem et ob hoc nobis opus
esset auctoritat sanctarum litterarum, iam credere coeperam nullo modo
te fuisse tributurum tam excellentem illi scripturae per omnes iam terras

auctoritatem, nisi et per ipsam tibi credi et per ipsam te quaeri volu-
isses].[19] Though the Bible is neither poetry nor rhetoric, it is nonetheless
a mediated artifact—*litterarum,* a book or letters, a written message. By
virtue of being written, the Bible bears similarity to a work of poetry or
rhetoric, at least in the sense that its audience has the capacity to change
as they read it and comprehend its meanings with different degrees of
sophistication. Just as "people recognize what is meant by the word 'eloquence' even though they have not mastered the art themselves" [qua-
mvis enim et hoc nomine audito recordentur ipsam rem, qui etiam
nondum sunt eloquentes], so people may read the Bible's truth and not
experience the salvation it promises.[20] Yet it is only through reading the
Bible that salvation becomes possible.

Augustine writes, then, with a cognizance of the limits of writing.
These limits are both the rhetorical limits of a literary form (the meaning
of which, by definition, is not absolute) and the material limits of medium (the experience of which, by definition, is not immediate). A structuring paradox of the *Confessions* is that Augustine represents his own
conversion experience in full awareness that his representation is a
representation, and so it is significantly nonidentical to his own experience. Even though his successful conversion is what motivates Augustine to write, and even though (his stated objections to rhetoric notwith-
standing) the text is written in a mode designed to persuade its reader of
the value of the Catholic faith, the experience of conversion is incom-
mensurate with this scene of writing. "Conversion is the fissure in the
grain of confession," writes Jean-François Lyotard, drawing attention to
the ways that the divine event and the worldly narrative stand, irreducibly, phenomenologically, at odds.[21] A representation of an experience—
even of one's experience with the divine—can never be equivalent to an
experience.

For Augustine just as much as for Lyotard, the incommensurability
between experience and the representation of experience is intrinsic to
the nature of representation itself. It has little to do with what's being
represented. Augustine, indeed, is overwhelmingly unconcerned with
the fact that one person's experience is not another's. The medium of
writing, rather than the biography of the author or reader, is the sticking
point. This emphasis is often underappreciated by readers for whom the

thematic centrality of will and the topical example of Augustine's own life make the *Confessions* into an originary point for thinking about individuality in the Western tradition. Reading in this vein, Charles Taylor, for example, emphasizes the "radical" quality of Augustine's first-person standpoint, in that, by placing emphasis on his individual experience, Augustine makes his own experience an object to be studied.[22] Such an account interprets Augustine's discussion of will as anticipating later notions of individuality, including those that emerge in liberal political theory in the late seventeenth and eighteenth centuries. But where the liberal individual is self-interested and unimpaired in pursuit of "his life, liberty and estate" as John Locke's well-known formulation has it, Augustine's worries about the discrepancy between experience and the representation of experience instead locate a certain kind of impairment or limitation at the center of his notion of the self.[23] Underpinning the representation of the self in the *Confessions* is an exploration of the ways that such a representation, by virtue of being a representation, does not in fact amount to a self.

One of the clearest ways to demonstrate the difference between Augustine's position and that of Locke and his peers would be to observe how relatively disinterested a self Augustine represents in the *Confessions*. At the end of Book VIII, Augustine narrates the moment of his conversion. Overcome with feeling during prayer, he leaves the church to weep beneath a fig tree, where he hears a child's voice say "Take it and read it, take it and read it" [tolle lege, tolle lege].[24] Imagining these words to be a divine command, he proceeds to find his "book containing Paul's epistles" [codicem apostoli] and is converted upon reading a verse from Romans 13.[25] The conversion is narrated with a string of negatives *(nec)*: "I had no wish to read more and no need to do so. . . . I no longer desired a wife or placed any hope in this world but stood firmly upon the rule of faith" [nec ultra volui legere nec opus erat . . . ut nec uxorem quaererem nec aliquam spem saeculi huius, stans in ea regula fidei in qua me ante tot anno ei revelaveras].[26] The saved self, though presumably not diminished from a theological standpoint, is nonetheless represented in linguistically negative terms—not as what it is, has, or is entitled to, but as what it is not or is freed from.

Augustine skirts the difficulties of representation by employing these descriptions of his self in the negative terms of what he is not or is no longer. The descriptions here are significantly less compromised by the incommensurabilities between experience and the representation of experience about which Augustine worries elsewhere, for here the negative rhetoric allows him to represent his saved self with a double negative— rather than claim that he is *saved*, he claims that he is *no longer unsaved*. Previously, Augustine had worried that his readers might recognize something that they have not mastered themselves, and in such mere recognition there would be no real reckoning. But the rhetorical negatives in this later passage allow him to represent the space of salvation not with the recognition of a condition that some readers may not fully comprehend, but with the more pedagogical negation of a state that they might well know. Augustine's concerns about the discrepancy between experience and the representation of experience in the first few books of the *Confessions* help to explain why his conversion episode is narrated in the rhetorically negative terms that it is. And, indeed, Augustine's elegant rhetorical solution offers an enduring model when, centuries later, closely related representational concerns intensify during the Reformation.

II

Sometime in the late 1630s, gathered churches in New England began admitting members on the basis of a public testimony, "to make known unto them the worke of free grace upon their soules."[27] According to Edmund S. Morgan's definitive history of this practice, "It is certain that the new system was fully established in Massachusetts by 1640; yet it is highly probable that it did not exist in 1629."[28] Scholars agree that in the following decades, and especially in the second half of the seventeenth century, such public confessional narratives proliferated across the English-speaking Protestant world.[29] They disagree, however, about the precise origin of confessional narratives.[30] And while one does well to be suspicious of precise origins, the rhetorical features of these narratives nevertheless harken back in significant ways to the representational problem at the heart of Augustine's *Confessions*.

To understand how, we must first observe that the narratives themselves display some clear rhetorical consistencies. Consider the following excerpts:

> *William Hamlet:* And so since my affliction [there is] some presence of God every Sabbath in assurance or affliction and I desire to walk under the feet of God and his people and all men, being more vile than any.[31]

> *Robert Holmes:* And my heart was melted all sermon time and being sacrament time I went home and cried to Him. Still I am doubting but I know I shall know if I follow on and if He damn me He shall do it in His own way.[32]

> *Jane Palfrey:* At last I was left to a discontented frame and I considered with a woeful frame I had distrusting God's providence and so was in a confusion in my spirit and could not speak to my husband. So I went sadly loathing myself.[33]

> *Elizabeth Oakes:* After that, hearing out of John 13 that when Peter denied Christ he went out and wept, and I thought on those words, and I thought I had denied the Lord often, convincing me by his word yet unhumbled, and out of those words, Out of me ye can do nothing, he [i.e., her minister, Thomas Shepard] showed that the soul could do nothing without Christ, and I saw it then, that of myself I could do nothing good. . . . After the Lord giving me a heart to seek him to enjoy him in all his ordinances, I thought I was so unfit and unworthy that I was unfit, and I heard that some might not find God because they did not seek him in all his ordinances, and that the Sacrament was a means wherein the Lord would coming [*sic*] more.[34]

> *Goodwife Stevenson:* And I asked him ["a godly man"] what I should do; if ever he did me good, it must be for his name sake and out of his grace, and hence I saw my own unworthiness more.[35]

> *John Shepard:* Mr. S[hepard] came to open 3 Commandment about preparation, though I sought God, yet I was guilty of

neglect of preparation to seek God [*manicule in margin*] in either for Sabbath or privy duty. And I saw my inability to prepare for any and unfitness to come to God in it.[36]

Robert Browne: And here God hath endeared my heart more to himself, hath showed me more of my vileness and wretchedness, and needing all his love to look upon such a wretch to show me evil of sin and love me.[37]

Elizabeth Dunster: I was assured I was where God would have me, and so I submitted. Since I came, I thought I was not profitable, considering what mercy Lord had shown.[38]

As these excerpts indicate, confessions in New England narrated the self in terms of what it was not. They do so, first of all, by figuring the confessing self in negative terms—in terms of what is absent; in terms of qualities that were lacking or neglected; in terms of fundamental unwillingness, unfitness, inability, doubt, confusion, and self-loathing. Additionally, these narratives pair that negatively figured self with a passive sense of agency. They suppose that God, not people, holds the power to dispense grace, and congregants accordingly speak of their worthiness to have received grace by recognizing that its dispensation can only be a result of God's works upon them, whether evident in assurance or affliction. Throughout these various confessions, a negative rhetoric figures the self as vulnerable before God's judgment, and that rhetoric describes salvation with a grammar that recalls Augustine's double negatives in Book VIII of the *Confessions:* rather than boast that they are saved, New England congregants indicate that they are no longer unsaved.

Though there is little evidence that New England congregants were self-consciously drawing on Augustine's *Confessions* as such, broad links between Augustine and Reformation theology are well established. Charles Hambrick-Stowe summarizes that "the major themes of Calvin's theology were Augustinian, Luther himself had been an Augustinian monk, and the precursors of the Reformation such as the Brethren of the Common Life, John Wycliffe, and John Huss were Augustinian in their theology."[39] Perry Miller, who saw enough theological links between fourth-century Hippo and seventeenth-century Massachusetts to ascribe to the latter an "Augustinian strain of piety," emphasized that these links obtained most observably at the level of intellectual investigation, within which analytic theologians "luxuriated—the word is not too strong—in fine discriminations of preparation from humiliation, of vocation from implantation, and all these from exaltation."[40] Furthermore, though great differences of time and place separate Augustine's thinking about representation in the *Confessions* from the seventeenth-century Protestants who drew on that earlier model, a commitment to rhetorical negation is just one of several features that makes their brand of confession (and the ones they influenced later in the seventeenth century) decidedly Augustinian.

Confessional self-knowledge among influential Reformation Protestants was, additionally, clearly understood to be a gradual process of apprehending the self's depths. John Calvin devoted a chapter of his systematic *Institutio Christianae religionis* (1536; translated into English as *Institutes of the Christian Religion* in 1561) to consideration of the biblical basis for confession and to the refutation of false confession. The *Institutes* argued ultimately in favor of the confessional form as a means to self-knowledge, because one "who will embrace this confession in his heart and before God will without doubt also have a tongue prepared for confession, whenever there is need to proclaim God's mercy among men."[41] Following this lead, William Perkins, in his major theological treatise *A Golden Chain* (1591), located confessional self-knowledge at the heart of Reformed Christianity, on the grounds that "*Theology*, is the science of liuing blessedly foreuer. Blessed life consisteth in knowledge of God. . . . And therefore it consisteth likewise in knowledge of our selues, because we know God by looking into our selues."[42] In his twentieth-century synthesis of Puritan theology, Miller argued that seventeenth-century theologians dilated upon self-examination in a manner that was far more Augustinian even than the likes of Calvin or Perkins proposed, as it involved a slow courtship with salvation rather than "a forcible seizure, a rape of the surprised will."[43] This slow wrestling with faith that occupies Augustine in the *Confessions* thereby distinguishes his conversion from the other great saintly model, that of Paul struck dumb on the road to Damascus.[44] Conversion in New England assumed an Augustinian strain of piety, in other words, not just because it borrowed the rhetorical form of the negative figure, but additionally because it was less a spontaneous experience and more a gradual process that culminated in a public confession.

This gradualism solved social problems. Surely one reason that the Pauline model of immediate revelation was less favored in early colonial New England than the Augustine model of a gradual coming to grace was that the longer *durée* of the Augustinian model allowed for extended social reinforcement and verification of sainthood, beyond the moment of congregational election. The Augustinian model accordingly helped to void bald bids for saintly authority. For instance, when John Underhill attempted to defend himself before a Massachusetts court in September 1638 by arguing that "as the Lord was pleased to convert Paul as he was in persecuting, etc., so he might manifest himself to him as he was taking the moderate use of the creature called tobacco," his Pauline evocation provoked only the ire of a legislature that did not find a smoke break an acceptable means to grace.[45] This regulatory aspect of the Augustinian model has been widely recognized, even by those who discountenance it. Judith Butler, for example, writes that "the very terms by which we give an account, by which we make ourselves intelligible to ourselves and to others, are not of our making. They are social in character, and they establish social norms, a domain of unfreedom and substitutability within which our 'singular' stories are told."[46] Butler's account of confessional unfreedom draws on the even starker one advanced by Michel Foucault, in which the confession "is driven from its hiding place in the soul, or extracted from the body."[47] A particular means of representing ourselves to others, confessions are freighted with the tension of being at once irreducibly individual and ineluctably social. The practicalities of social regulation help to explain why New England confessional narratives represent the path to salvation by way of Augustine's belabored model.

A concern for social regulation also explains why these confessional narratives sound not only like Augustine's, but like one another. Sarah Rivett has called this similar rhetorical structure a New England "testimonial idiom," and Kathleen Lynch has identified its presence across the Protestant Atlantic as a "semiotics of salvation" by which the meanings of inward and outward experience were coordinated by precise hermeneutic schemes.[48] The genuineness of a confessional narrative was measured in part by its accordance to this testimonial idiom, but, practically speaking, its genuineness also would have to have been measured by something transcending the mere rhetorical value of that idiom, or else anyone could simply speak in that idiom and appear to be saved. There are at least two ways to account for that transcendent "something." One would be to develop a theory of language that would definitively account for literal meanings and referential truth. Some Reformed Protestants did attempt to create linguistic systems (including Calvin's commitment to literal representations and Perkins's endorsement of plain style in preaching) but there was no widespread theological agreement on or dissemination of any theory of language as such. And so the second way to account for that transcendent "something" would be simply to presume it.

That is to say, Protestant ministers commonly presumed that the testimonial idiom was more or less an effective measure of its own genuineness. To some extent, this presumption was born of a relative naïveté about language. Sixteenth- and seventeenth-century theories of language are various, though over the course of the seventeenth century in Europe they trend toward a mounting distrust of ordinary language.[49] One source of this distrust was a gradual (and incomplete) recognition that language was social, rather than divine, at its putative origins. But at the opening of the seventeenth century, no significant distinction obtained in Reformed faith communities between the social and the theological. Only into the eighteenth century did the quasi-secular abstraction "the social" begin to have currency in scientific and philosophical writings.[50] Prior to the eighteenth century, distinctions between the social, the theological, the political—distinctions, in other words, of the kind that matter to modern historians—were not much recognized and, when attempted, not consistently made. Instead, salvation was understood to be a zero-sum game, and the only real rule of the game was to stay within bounds. Or, as Morgan argued, the act of confession before a congregation "required both understanding and belief. These, together with good behavior, constituted for the Separatists sufficient proof of the holiness and faith of prospective members."[51] Thus, somewhat tautologically, if the person making a confession of faith was already a trustworthy member of the community, that person could more easily become a member of the congregation.

The idiomatic rhetorical features of confessional narratives helped further glue together the tautological qualities of this rhetorical-cum-social construction. Yet that idiomatic quality accomplished its work more or less invisibly, as the idiomatic features of confessional narratives were unremarked upon in the period. Instead, it seems that New England confessional narratives were regarded less as texts, in the written sense, and more as ritual performances. Testimonies before a congregation were not, according to Michael McGiffert, "impromptu performances; they had been practiced at home, coached by the minister, and vetted by senior saints."[52] In this way, these confessions suspended the tension of being both irreducibly individual and ineluctably social, as they were explicitly crafted in contexts that bridged public and private explorations of piety.

Confessional narratives thus enacted a number of competing assumptions. As a condition of church membership, they answer the question "Am I saved?" and so relate profoundly to individual experience. At the same time, they assume a highly idiomatic quality that makes them nearly unrecognizable as personal expressions of a modern, individualistic sort. They were performances, but ones prized for their rehearsed and ritualized (rather than spontaneous) expressions. Yet that rehearsed and ritualized quality had what scholars now recognize as a social function, though any absolute distinction between its social and its theological value would not have been legible in the seventeenth century. Moreover, to attribute to these confessional narratives an idiomatic quality is to understand them as having a kind of consistency within their rhetorical representation; it is unlikely that educated seventeenth-century ministers would have denied that confessions were rhetorical (recall that Calvin's *Institutes* acknowledges the possibility of false confessions in order to refute worries about them), but it is equally unlikely that they would have considered confessional rhetoric as merely rhetorical.[53] In sum, then, the social function of the Augustinian confession flowered among Protestants in the seventeenth century, and so did many of the formal tensions inherent in that fourth-century model.

Drawing these connections between Augustine and some of his Reformation inheritors, the preceding discussion has relied on the presence of shared rhetorical devices in the writings of each time and place. Despite these clear rhetorical resonances, however, formalist evidence alone may not indicate an ample enough connection between Augustine's *Confessions* and seventeenth-century church confessions for these to seem anything other than coincidental. That is to say, one reason that Augustine's negative figurations of self are not often taken as a point of departure for thinking about seventeenth-century conceptions of character may have to do with some open questions about how the use of such rhetorical devices could have been transmitted to and through seventeenth-century New England. In fact, scholars do not have a standard account of the material transmission of confession narratives at all. The next section accordingly turns in some detail to the material texts in which seventeenth-century confessions resided, in order to extrapolate from them some understanding of their transmission.

III

One additional reason that the above-quoted confessional narratives may evince rhetorical similarities has to do with the fact that they happen to be drawn from the same congregation. The significance of confessional narratives in seventeenth-century Reformed Protestantism, which, as we have seen, many scholars readily recognize, is nonetheless based on preciously scarce evidence. The best records remain from New England, where confession was a prerequisite for church membership (a circumstance that could not obtain in England until the parish system was revised after the English Civil War).[54] But compared to the several thousand church members in Massachusetts and Connecticut in the second quarter of the seventeenth century,[55] just under 100 confession narratives exist from anywhere in New England.[56] The majority (67) of these are preserved in two surviving notebooks, recorded by minister Thomas Shepard from his Cambridge congregation during the periods from 1637 to 1645 and from 1648 to 1649.[57] Another four, during the period from 1653 to 1657, appear in Michael Wigglesworth's diary, presumably from those seeking admission to his Malden, Massachusetts, congregation.[58] And an additional 23 confessions were recorded during the period from 1644 to 1666, at Wenham and Chelmsford, Massachusetts, in John Fiske's congregation.[59] The lion's share of scholarship focuses on these New England narratives, though they are not the only ones to survive in relatively large batches. John Rogers's *A Tabernacle for the Sun* (1653), for example, contains forty relations from his parishioners in Ireland, which also conform with the negative rhetorical idioms discussed above.[60] But what is most striking about the extant narratives from Shepard's congregation in particular—and the reason they merit emphasis in the present discussion—is the material forms in which they have survived. As in Rogers's printed book, the confessions preserved in the hand of Fiske and Wigglesworth are scattered into other kinds of relations. They appear much more like notes or records among other kinds of notes and records. Shepard's relations are preserved in a more unusual manner.

Approximately half the total extant New England confessions from the seventeenth century—fifty-one, all from Shepard's Cambridge church—are preserved in a single volume. Originally created as a blank notebook, the book is a leather-bound sextodecimo, just under six inches tall and four inches wide, containing six gatherings of sixteen leaves, plus two endpapers (for approximately 198 single-sided pages). Its small size and the plain geometric tooling on the edges of its cover suggest that this bound blank notebook was probably of London origin, though it is unknown where, when, or how Shepard would have acquired it. Almost exactly two-thirds (four of its six gatherings) appear to a be fair copy (despite the fact that transcribers of the modern edition undoubtedly earned the right to call it "a calligraphical horror").[61] The text opens with a headnote, "The Confessions of diverse propounded to be received and were entertained as members," and begins with Edward Hall's confession as the first of fifty.[62] The other third of the book begins from the opposite cover (and thus appears upside-down relative to the text of the confessions). This third of the text consists primarily of sermon notes that Shepard took as an auditor in other ministers' churches, as well as the confessional narrative of Wil Ames, which, according to one set of editors, "indicates its addition as an afterthought."[63]

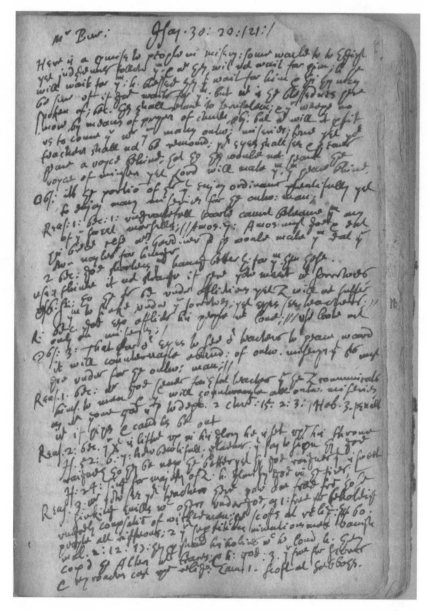

Figure 1.1. "Thomas Shepard's Confessions," manuscript notebook. (New England Historic Genealogical Society)

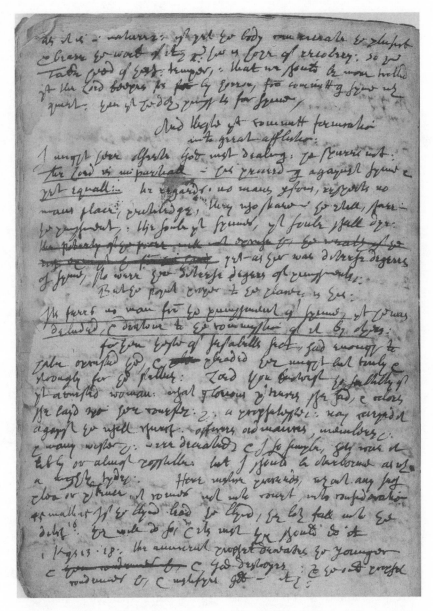

Figure 1.2. Thomas Shepard, sermon notes. Note the heavy editing marks. (American Antiquarian Society)

In contrast to the neatness of the copy of the confessional texts in the same notebook, these sermon notes include a few ink blots and cross-outs, which are far more characteristic of Shepard's other extant manuscript pages.

These confessions are almost certainly edited notes from auditory performances and not verbatim transcripts. That they are edited notes is suggested by the substantial variation in their length and detail: Mrs. Greene's statement takes only six brisk sentences, while Alice Stedman's occupies nearly five manuscript pages.[64] Wil Ames's narrative—the one not included with the fifty others—stops midsentence.[65] Despite the likelihood that these notes are edited, there is every reason to agree with Charles Cohen's observation that "the documents speak primarily in the tones of their subjects rather than in those of their compilers."[66] Attempts by auditors to reproduce the voice and meaning of another speaker, without precisely recording their words, was, as Meredith Marie Neuman has amply demonstrated, common among the various note-taking practices of seventeenth-century Protestant churchgoers.[67] Moreover, the juxtaposing of these confessions—and Ames's confession in particular—in the same notebook with sermon notes suggests practical continuities with these different kinds of notes all taken in church.

What is more obscure, however, are Shepard's reasons for setting the first fifty narratives apart from the other notes. The material form of these confessional narratives does not merely appear as documentary evidence, nor even necessarily what one editor describes as "a formal record kept for a formal parochial purpose."[68] These confessional narratives are set apart from other kinds of notes, beginning at the opposite end of the same blank book, prefaced with a headnote, and written in relatively careful handwriting.[69] Of course these features of the material text do not rule out the possibility that these confessional narratives were notes too; as Ann Blair rightly argues, notes are taken in many different ways and with any combination of the various objectives of "storing, sorting, summarizing, and selecting."[70] With this variety of note-taking practices in mind, however, the features of Shepard's material text still make these confessions seem not just like his other extant notes, which may indeed be documentary records, but rather like the kind of notes that one does not take merely for one's own reference. More than Shepard's other extant notes, these confessions seem preserved in a form conducive to being read by someone other than their notetaker. I am suggesting, in other words, that Shepard may have written these confessions in this form in order to circulate them to other potential candidates for church membership, or to ministers at other congregations.

Copying manuscripts in order to circulate them was an established practice in the Anglophone world well into the nineteenth century—a phenomenon that Harold Love has usefully dubbed "scribal publication."[71] Manuscript has been long identified as a technological and cultural antecedent to print, though many scholars have pinpointed that print initially superseded manuscript only in some domains—much as the invention of ballpoint pen in the twentieth century did not render its antecedent the pencil otiose, so much as it created finer cultural distinctions about where each is appropriate. In the case of seventeenth-century England, manuscript was often aligned with the literary practices at court, which, as part of a capitalist system of literary patronage, produced rarefied texts of limited circulation for small audiences.[72] Print, by corollary, was instead aligned with a broader public (and sometimes a mass) readership, which, as part of a modern capitalist marketplace, produced large numbers of texts for theoretically limitless audiences.[73] Long after the spread of printing in the Anglophone world, however, particular kinds of texts continued to circulate in manuscript. As Arthur F. Marotti summarizes, "It took a relatively long time for poetry anthologies and single-author editions of lyric poetry to become an established feature of print culture in England, as the manuscript system of transmission continued to have a remarkable strength and durability through the first two centuries of English printing."[74] Certainly, some Protestant writings did come into print very early in the history of European printing, indicated not least by the Bible's enduring emblematic status as *the* book. Nonetheless, a vast majority of seventeenth-century Protestant discourse relied on oral and manuscript mediations, rather than printed ones. As George Selement calculates, "A full 66 percent of the practicing clergymen in New England never published anything [i.e., in print], an additional 11 percent of them wrote only a single publication, and a mere 5 percent published ten or more tracts during their lives."[75] The oral and manuscript mediations in which ministers did engage unquestionably aimed for circulation, even if those texts did not achieve (or even neces-sarily seek) the more robust kinds of impersonal circulation that print offered other texts in the same period.[76] While it is impossible to know whether Shepard's text did circulate, there is nothing about the text's material features that indicates it *wasn't* designed to be circulated.

The most likely evidence that Shepard's notebook may have circu-lated, however, is a different book altogether. Gathered under the modern title "Relations of Conversion by Various Members of the Church of Cambridge," sixteen additional confessions from Shepard's Cambridge church are persevered in a small unbound manuscript book, six inches tall and four inches wide, composed of nine sheets folded in half (to create thirty-six pages).[77] The outermost sheet is a wrapper, on the front of which is written in Isaiah Thomas's hand "Memoradums of of ~~Rev. Increase Mather~~ a Minister in Boston or its vicinity 1640. Visits to Criminals, &c," but which is otherwise blank on three sides.[78] The blank pages, along with the cover's mistaken title and the slightly finer quality of the wrapper's paper, indicate that it was likely added to the object in the eighteenth or early nineteenth century, at which point a two-hole stitch binding (no longer extant) may have kept these pages to-gether. Even without a wrapper or a stitch binding, however, these "Re-lations" have the feel of a little book.

Gathering these confessions into this small book gives them a more substantial unity. Though these "Relations" share the testimonial idiom described previously, their unity is more precisely an effect of their ma-terial, rather than rhetorical, shape. Unlike any other extant collection of conversion narratives, this set includes no other text. The narratives in this book stand apart from other notes and details and relations, sug-gesting some sense of their generic specificity. Yet the generic specificity implied by the material properties of the book is, relatively speaking, otherwise absent from the narratives themselves. The differences among these narratives are arguably more pronounced in the "Relations" than in any other collection of confessions—ranging, for example, from that of Daniel Gookin, the most prominent citizen in the Cambridge congre-gation, to that of Abraham Arrington, the only unsuccessful applicant among all of the extant Cambridge confessions. The most curious inclu-sion is also potentially the most deliberate. Leaves 5–10 of the "Relations," covering the substance of Goodwife Jackson's confession, are clearly a separate gathering (evidenced by a different paper quality and slightly smaller paper size) and written in another hand.[79] Goodwife Jackson's confession begins in Shepard's handwriting on the bottom of the verso of the fourth leaf, and, along with three blank pages, makes up the entirety of this inserted gathering. Because this insertion completes a record that was begun in Shepard's hand, it clearly belongs among the "Relations." The inserted gathering may be an attempt to correct errors of transcription or improve readability by being a fairer copy. It may also replace pages that were originally included by subsequently damaged. Mary Rhinelander McCarl speculates that Shepard was merely interrupted in his note-taking and that "another member of the examining committee, who had begun notes on the testimony with the same quotation from Isaiah that Shepard had written down, took extensive notes on her testimony, including the entire question-and-answer session at the end of the formal deposition."[80] Though a more exact reason is unknowable, the inclusion of Goodwife Jackson's confession lends circumstantial weight to the possibility that these confessions were less a verbatim transcription of events, and more a kind of textual construction of different valences of confession. What the inserted gathering corroborates, in other words, is the likelihood that this little book was an intentional construction—a rhetorical and social construction, to be sure, but also a material one.

Unlike the bound notebook containing the majority of Shepard's Cambridge confessions, we can be certain that his "Relations" circulated.[81] This little manuscript book was discovered in June 1985, misfiled for 170 years among the American Antiquarian Society's Mather Family papers. The papers had been acquired by Isaiah Thomas in 1814, a bequest from Hannah Mather Crocker, the great-great-granddaughter of the minister and first-generation Massachusetts settler Richard Mather.[82] Thomas originally (as we have seen, mistakenly) identified them as criminal confessions transcribed by Richard's son Increase Mather. Any exact provenance before 1814 is unknown, as is any motivation for why Shepard (or someone with access to Shepard's papers) might have given this book to someone in the Mather family (or someone who had access to the family's library). Nevertheless, the fact that this

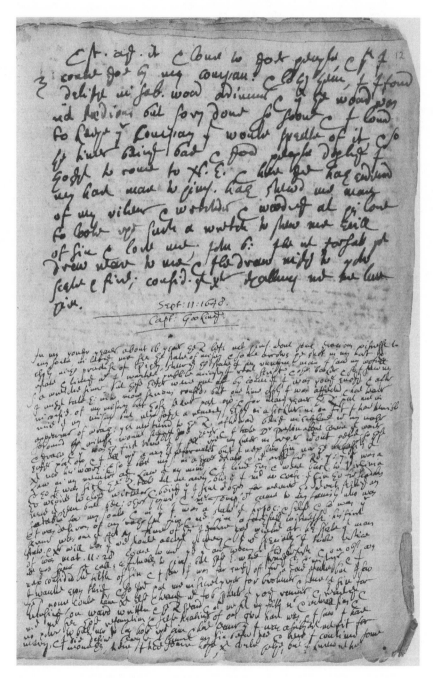

Figure 1.3. Thomas Shepard, "Relations of Conversion by Various Members of the Church of Cambridge." Note the relative cleanness of the copy. (American Antiquarian Society)

little book spent the better part of two centuries folded into the Mather papers suggests what its material properties indicate: not only did it happen to circulate, but it may well have been designed explicitly for that purpose.

To return to an earlier point, then, one reason that the confessions from Shepard's Cambridge congregation share a testimonial idiom is that their general participation in the same discourse may have been amplified by material mediations of that discourse. The material forms into which the extant confessions are gathered would seem to encourage a rhetorical conventionalization, along the broad lines of genre as well as the finer details of figuration. Meanwhile, the probable circulation of these material texts helps to account for the spread and adoption of the testimonial idiom. Congregants learn how to speak in that idiom by absorbing the material mediations—perhaps oral as well as written—of that idiom, including its negative characterological figures. Consideration of the material texts of Shepard's Cambridge confessions begins to account for the idiomatic consistency of their figural practices.

Yet even as applicants for church membership might have used these or similar texts as their models, no records remain that account for this mediation. As we saw previously, in congregations such as Shepard's salvation was often considered a zero-sum game, and, absent a theologically standard theory of language, many Protestant ministers commonly presumed that the testimonial idiom was more or less an effective measure of its own genuineness. The negative figures that populate confessional narratives would have been recognized at least by educated seventeenth-century men as rhetorical constructions, but, again as we have seen, even literal meanings were understood to be rhetorically constructed. To call something *constructed* did not make it fragile in relation to truth. The assurance of literal meaning behind a rhetorical construction simply and presumptively nudged it beyond doubt, in the direction of faith. Thus, the absence of any records of an applicant for church membership drawing on a text like one of Shepard's manuscript collections should be interpreted as the evidence of an ultimate, grand irony: rhetorical form, however constructed, counted more to seventeenth-century Reformed Protestants than the means of its transmission. Provided that one spoke in the language of piety, it mattered much less how one learned that idiom, or indeed by what means other than utterance that idiom was refined. It was this presumption, as we shall see, that allowed the circulating powers of the material text to transmit its rhetorical idiom—its negative figures—well beyond the pious intentions of those who designed them.

IV

Seventeenth-century Reformed Protestants had many competing theories about what representation is and how it should work, but they had almost none about mediation. The concept of media—of being between or moderating two things—was ancient, dating at least to the fourth century, when Augustine uses it in Book VI of the *Confessions* to described Christ as "the Mediator between you and me, who are one, and men, who are many" [mediatore filio hominis inter te unum et nos multos].[83] However, only in early modern Europe does *media* emerge in its modern sense, which Lisa Gitelman helpfully defines as "socially realized structures of communication."[84] The concept of media as means for communications develops slowly, unevenly, and, given the spread of print since the mid-fifteenth century, belatedly. "The concept of a medium of communication," argues John Guillory, "was absent but *wanted* for the several centuries prior to its appearance."[85]

Such wanting meant that any number of seventeenth-century Reformed ministers mediated their ideas about salvation in print, manuscript, and oral performance without any articulated sense that they were engaged in mediation at all. These men saw little distinction between medium and message, yet the fact that they communicated that message via the medium of writing harbors an obvious irony. Nonetheless, that irony could be ignored insofar as the avowed point of ministers' work was to encourage salvation, not to produce texts. And so when their mediations appeared in manuscript or oral performance, the consequences of this irony remained relatively few because the circulation of such texts was mostly restricted to particular communities of the faithful and necessarily limited by the medium of their expression. Were such texts able to get into print, however, their audiences would expand, errors could multiply, and texts might mutate in ways their creators never intended. The amplified scope of print stands in turn to amplify the potential for the ironic consequences of mediation.

And there were consequences. In 1647, the English minister Giles Firmin wrote to Thomas Shepard across the Atlantic for verification of a passage in Shepard's printed book *The Sincere Convert* (1641) that he found "so strange . . . that *I* could not believe that ever Mr. *Shepard* did deliver such Doctrine." Shepard replied, *"That which is called the* Sincere Convert, *I have not the book, I once saw it; it was a Collection of such Notes in a dark Town in* England, *which one procuring of me, published them without my will or privity."*[86] This reply is preserved in Firmin's own printed book *The Real Christian* (1670), which presents these words as Shepard's, "faithfully transcribed," and on which basis concludes that *The Sincere Convert* "is not a book for the unsound heart to delight in, I mean, in those places where he agrees both with Scriptures, and other able Divines, of these make use."[87] Firmin takes for granted the fidelity of his text to Shepard's because both make similar sense of scriptural teachings. His commitments, in other words, are to hermeneutics and to making meaning of scripture, and Firmin evinces a shrewd sense of which kinds of meaning make the most sense. What he ignores, however, is very much the same thing that Shepard had ignored when he let his manuscript out of his hands: the media through which ideas can circulate divorces them from the immediate control of their authors.

On a number of other occasions, Shepard complained about the printing of *The Sincere Convert*. His 1646 spiritual autobiography, for instance, recalls that after a friend's death, Shepard found the strength "not only to speak by me to his people but likewise to print my notes upon the nine principles[;] I intended to proceed on with in Yorkshire but never intended them or imagined they should be for the press. Yet six of them being finished in old England and printed, which I do not glory in (for I know my weakness) that my name is up by this means, but that the Lord may be pleased to do some good by them there in my absence."[88] Though this objection briefly borrows the negative idiom of weakness, Shepard's complaint is ultimately less with the potential vanity reflected by the medium of print than with the comparative loss of control he had with overseas printing, generating errors such as the ones Firmin caught. As late as the mid-nineteenth century, faithful editors worked to correct the text of *The Sincere Convert,* which one of Shepard's biographers, echoing his subject's judgment, found to be "barbarously printed."[89]

The Sincere Convert is not unique in this regard. The scarcities attendant upon New England colonial printing in the seventeenth century compared to the abundance of facilities in London meant that colonial writers who sought to print their works did so most efficaciously by sending manuscripts across the Atlantic. At such a distance, however, they were usually unable to oversee or correct their printed texts, and the consequences of this disadvantage were sometimes greater even than problems of theological interpretation. As Jonathan Beecher Field has shown, colonial writers who were able to travel to London could utilize print to secure advantages—as substantial as royal charters—over their political enemies back home.[90] But if the conditions for the printing of *The Sincere Convert* are not unique for the time, its author arguably is. Unwilling to lose control over any more of his writings, and unable to keep them definitively from the press, Shepard enlisted assistance to prepare two subsequent volumes, *The Sound Believer* (1645) and *Theses Sabbaticae* (1649), for print publication.[91] His stated justification, offered in the preface to *Theses Sabbaticae,* appeals pathetically to his colonial status, bemoaning that *"we are strangers here (for the most part) to the books and writings which are now in Europe"* and yet finishing caustically that, as those who are in Europe *"have with too much tenderness and complyance tolerated Errours, Errour will one day grow up to that head that it will not tolerate or suffer them to speak truth."*[92] Shepard clearly speaks of doctrinal errors, but there is every reason that printing errors may also have been on his mind. In other words, Shepard was growing savvy to the materiality of textual transmission.

Underneath his savvy, however, lie further ironies. Even as he was beginning to appreciate the materiality of textual transmission, Shepard (like his correspondent Firmin) still did not appreciate the range of consequences for textual mediation via print. Some of this failure of appreciation was due to other aspects of Reformed Protestant thinking. As Michael Warner explains, "Space and time, in the Puritan ideology, did not sever print from the speaking body or its fingers—they bring it inexorably under metonymic discipline. Because New England culture structured print in this way, print discourse had not become the basis for the community's self-representation."[93] This analysis proves generally true for metropolitan English Protestants as well, even though their superior access to print allowed them more opportunities to contemplate what John Milton, in his refutation of the Licensing Order of 1643, called "such a universal thing as books are."[94] Yet what Shepard, specifically, failed to see is that his attempts to commit his texts to print in order to control their transmission, on the production side, could unintentionally enable creative uses by readers, on the consumption side. Instead, Shepard seems to have imagined that print, properly produced, safeguards authorial intentions against material corruptions. His naïveté about mediation, in other words, encourages Shepard in the otherwise vain hope that there is no real difference between ideas and their representation. In much the same ways that he and many other ministers imagined that a testimonial idiom was an effective measure of its own genuineness, Shepard presumes that good intentions track with godly actions. In so doing, he implicitly inverts the dilemma about representation in Augustine's *Confessions:* for Shepard, there need not be a real difference between experience and the representation of experience.

Shepard's implicit inversion of Augustine's account of representation may at first seem surprising, given the ways that much of Reformed theology draws on Augustine among its inspirations. But this inversion should not be entirely unexpected in light of what the foregoing genealogy of the confessional idiom has demonstrated—namely, that the fact of textual circulation promotes the mutation of forms, genres, and figures toward ends that their progenitors never imagined. Though the negative rhetorical figurations so prevalent in the Cambridge confessions speak in clear (if distant) echoes of Augustine's solution to a representational problem in the *Confessions,* it nevertheless remains the case that the idiom of the Cambridge confessions is best understood as a creative mutation of Augustine's rhetoric—not because its negative figures are that different, but because the use of these similar figures in testimony for church membership is not anything that Augustine (a Catholic and not a Protestant, and someone for whom confession and conversion

were not synonyms) could have expected. Ultimately, it is a perfectly ordinary aspect of the phenomenology of textual transmission that
Shepard, however unwittingly, could borrow rhetorically and theologically from some parts of Augustine's teachings while still inverting other
aspects of them. "In every respect," as Gilles Deleuze proposes, "repetition is a transgression."[95]

Additionally, some explanation for the ironies of the seventeenth-
century use of Augustine's model should fall on Augustine himself.
If the absence of a conception of *media* as communication in the
seventeenth-century gets snared in the Augustinian problem of experience being irreducible to the representation of experience, it remains the
case that, for anyone in the modern world to know this, we must rely on
the material mediation of Augustine's text. As Augustine cannot mediate
his teachings to us orally—as he is not, *pace* Bob Dylan, "alive as you or
me"—we rely on the written corpus he produced for others who also
could not be in his presence.[96] And Augustine was a cognizant producer.
Many of his works were published in his lifetime through the production
of manuscripts by copyists, which were then sold.[97] The circulation of
Augustine's manuscripts as well as his extant letters indicates that he
drew self-consciously on multiple networks for textual dissemination,
including those that related to the administrative functions of the late
Roman Empire, those developed by the Catholic Church, and those enjoyed by the learned men and intellectuals of late antiquity.[98] Augustine's
works were widely read among the literate, and late in his life he com-
mented on the appreciative reception of the *Confessions*, which "have
pleased and do please many of the brothers a great deal" [multis tamen
fratribus eos multum placuisse et placere scio].[99] In addition to these efforts to reach contemporaries, Augustine made notable efforts at textual
preservation. For example, he arranged for the library of Hippo to house
exemplars, or master copies, of all the texts and letters he composed
through dictation and all the sermons and disputations that had been
recorded by stenographers in shorthand *(notae tironianae)* and then
written out in longhand.[100] These served as the basis for the late antique
and medieval manuscript copies of Augustine's works. Suspicious as he
may have been toward representation, Augustine invested in textual
production. As Tzvetan Todorov once observed in a slightly different

context, Augustine's "interest in the problematics of semiotics . . . seems to be greater than he himself admits or even suspects."[101]

Yet this phenomenological tension between the ideas of the *Confessions* and their mediation might be excused if we recall that, however much care Augustine takes to make sure that the rhetorical form of his text does not naïvely embrace a form of representation of which he is suspicious, nevertheless that negative representation is far from the main point of the *Confessions*. Its point, rather, is to demonstrate something about the nature of experience. As Brian Stock explains, "What made life exemplary by ancient standards was not setting down events in a permanent form but living in an ethically informed manner."[102] Likewise, Pierre Hadot argues that ancient "philosophical discourse must be understood from the perspective of the way of life of which it is both the expression and the means."[103] Expression—including representation—is subordinate to experience. For Hadot, as for the later works of Foucault that he influenced, expression is aspirational. A range of classical virtues—truth, restraint, judgment—are not an authentic reflection of the character of the person who expresses them, so much as they are elements of a greater truth that the person has mastered in order to master themself. In Foucault's words, the goal of ancient philosophy "is to arm the subject with a truth it did not know." Moreover, "One can see that this control of representations is not aimed at uncovering, beneath appearances, a hidden truth that would be that of the subject itself; rather, it finds in these representations, as they present themselves, the occasion for recalling to mind a certain number of true principles."[104] But because the expression of a cultivated self was the goal of philosophy, that self came to matter much more than the technical and material apparatus that led to that cultivation. Augustine was a learned inheritor of this ancient tradition, and his suspicions of representation do everything to reinforce this ignorance of the media apparatus by which the representation of an exemplary life was transmitted.

Transmission, moreover, is never linear. Quite in spite of Augustine's probable intentions, the material transmission of his texts, which he encouraged, created the potential for mutations in their uptake. Unlike some antique texts, Augustine's were never lost, but neither were they consistently disseminated. For instance, based on reconstructions from extant manuscripts produced before 900, Michael M. Gorman observes that "the popularity of the *Confessiones* was . . . limited—roughly, to the area of the Loire Valley and to centres like Tours, Ferrières, and Auxerre."[105] While some of Augustine's writings enjoyed only limited popularity, the corpus itself grew through pseudonymous additions. Texts bearing Augustine's name were among the most widely circulated in the Carolingian Renaissance of the late eighth and ninth centuries, eventually necessitating the authority of those texts to be consolidated by the "complete works" created by Cistercian monks in the twelfth century, based on the comparison of multiple exemplars.[106] Only from this point, nearly eight hundred years after their creation, did Augustine's texts circulate as an established corpus. The transition of this corpus from manuscript to print, meanwhile, helped it to standardize. During the sixteenth century, almost five hundred editions were published in Augustine's name, including multivolume works published in Basil (1505–1506), Rotterdam (1528–1529), and Leuven (1576–1577), amounting, in Arnoud S. Q. Visser's estimation, to "probably more than fifteen thousand sets of these expensive and bulky books."[107] By the time of the first English translation of the *Confessions* in 1620, Augustine's name was well known by learned men across Europe.[108] Yet it was not just the ideas of these texts that were being transmitted; many readers, indeed, were studying Augustine's rhetorical form as well. His texts proved to be an especially popular guide, even compared to other early church fathers, during the late fifteenth century for students practicing their Latin prose style.[109] In this same period, the rhetorical and formal features of the *Confessions,* specifically, influenced emerging genres of biographical writing.[110] As I have argued throughout this chapter, the negative rhetorical forms of early seventeenth-century confessions were also Augustine's distant heirs. What remains to be seen, however, is the extent to which novels are as well.

⊰ 2 ⊱

The Character of Steady Sellers

C haracterological figures were in circulation well before the appearance of novels in the mid-eighteenth century. Rather than the liberal individuals who populate scholarly accounts of novelistic character, many antecedents instead figured character negatively, in terms of their vulnerability and weakness before more powerful forces. Such negative figures were being developed and refined through the seventeenth century in Protestant writings, including confessional narratives. As Chapter 1 demonstrates, these writings helped this negative characterological figure to achieve some conventionalization, and they did so, moreover, by means of circulation via manuscript mediation and scribal publication. Before there were characters in printed novels, there were characters in manuscript confessions.

This story is not a strictly progressive one, however. Through the seventeenth and especially into the eighteenth century, manuscript and print coexisted in the Anglophone world, and feedback loops across these different media forms were common.[1] For example, one Capt. Gookin, a member of Thomas Shepard's Cambridge congregation, recalled in his public confession in 1648:

> In my young years, [when I was] about 16 years, the Lord left not
> himself without some gracious witness to my soul, in letting me see
> the state of misery, and some arrows he shot in my heart, and espe-
> cially in the *Practice of Piety* showing the state of any unregenerate
> man. I saw my woeful estate, and living where I wanted public min-
> istry, I read Scripture and other books and so saw myself a wretched
> sinner.[2]

Gookin's self-figuration—describing himself in "the state of misery," as
"unregenerate," in "my woeful estate," and as "a wretched sinner"—
conforms to the pattern of negative figuration established in Chapter 1 as
typical for Reformed Protestant confessional narratives. Somewhat less
typical, however, is the source of Gookin's epiphany: rather than experience conversion in the presence of a pious man, he does so in the presence of a pious book. Gookin is provoked by reading Lewis Bayly's *The
Practice of Piety: Directing a Christian How to Walke That He May
Please God* (1610), a text belonging to a class of printed books now commonly called devotional steady sellers. These volumes were predominant among Anglophone books across the whole of the seventeenth
century, where readers of their pages came into contact with negative
figurations of character that in some cases were anticipated by the figurations found in manuscript confessional narratives discussed in Chapter 1,
and that in other cases, such as Gookin's, informed those figurations.

The present chapter considers devotional steady sellers as a print corollary to the manuscript mediations of Chapter 1. Moving from manuscript to print, this chapter trades some of the scarcest extant evidence of
Protestant devotional practice for some of the most abundant. Both
chapters aim to show that the kinds of characterological figures that
blossom in eighteenth-century novels had existed previously and had incubated in various genres of Reformed Protestant writings. While manuscript as well as print incubated these figures, and while both media
forms historically coexisted, the present chapter's turn more exclusively
toward print allows us to see some additional historical movements of
these figures. Specifically, this chapter continues the story of how negative characterological figures conventionalized and mutated, but it seeks
also to consider how readerly engagement with these figures changed

over time. By the end of the seventeenth century, negative figurations of character are well established, but the ways these figures are read has changed substantially. As we will see, this same figure, read in a different way, becomes central to the late seventeenth- and early eighteenth-century texts most widely recognized as clear antecedents to the Anglophone novels that appeared in the 1740s.

I

"Steady seller" is not a seventeenth-century term.[3] It belongs, rather, to the economic vocabulary of the twentieth century, where the regular and reliable, long-term sales of a steady seller needed to be distinguished from the short-term, high-volumes sales of a best seller.[4] In the absence of both this term and any comprehensive sales figures for seventeenth-century steady sellers, they have been retrospectively recognized by scholars through bibliographic data: steady sellers generally remained in print through multiple (often several dozen) reprintings and, in some cases, multiple editions.[5] These multiple reprintings indicate something about a book's durability in the market, and indeed many steady sellers remained in print for several decades, and some for as long as two hundred years.[6] The durability of these titles had to do with the fact that they were rarely topical or political in nature, and instead they tended to be associated with matters of perennial interest, such as Christian devotional practice. Indeed, a majority of their titles inventory pious aspirations: *The Plaine Mans Path-Way to Heaven, The Practice of Piety, The Sincere Convert.* Margaret Spufford calculates that "the trade lists of the specialist publishers show approximately a third of their output was made up of small godly books" by the 1680s.[7] Matthew P. Brown similarly proposes that steady sellers "are best understood through numbers of editions, and these numbers far outweigh editions of poetry or drama published in the period."[8]

Though the abundant numbers of editions of steady sellers have made these books particularly useful to scholars attempting to reconstruct the popular reading habits of everyday seventeenth-century readers, an equally important feature of steady sellers are their physical properties.

Usually printed in octavo, duodecimo, or sextodecimo sizes, with many hundreds of pages, these parallelepipeds resemble, in Stephen Foster's memorable phrase, "short, tubby bricks."[9] Though brick-like in shape, steady sellers were nevertheless lightweight (compared to works printed in folio or quarto) and could easily fit into a pocket, making them the kind of book that one could carry around and peruse in a spare moment. From a design standpoint, devotional steady sellers shared a distinct aesthetic as material texts.[10]

The significance of this distinct aesthetic, moreover, has to do with what it indicates about how the producers of steady sellers imagined their use. The physical design of a book makes it available for specific kinds of functionality, and, as Bradin Cormack and Carla Mazzio have explained, "When authors or printers deployed textual forms to make books more navigable or useful, they often reflected upon those technologies to emphasize the book's relation to specific fields of knowledge and specific forms of thinking."[11] The distinct aesthetic of steady sellers had utilitarian implications. One crucial such implication of the aesthetic and material properties of steady sellers—such as their size and their page layout, as these were replicated across many editions—was to encourage noncontinuous reading.

Steady sellers were often printed with a generous use of ornamental design features such as indentation, subheadings, type variations, numerical characters, and decorative flourishes. These design features indicate that steady sellers were not necessarily intended to hold a reader's attention through an extensive, cover-to-cover reading. Thomas Shepard's late work, *Theses Sabbaticae* (1649), for example, presents a string of several hundred pious postulates, broken into short single- or multi-paragraph sections. Though to read the *Theses Sabbaticae* from beginning to end would give account of a systematic theology such as had become fashionable among Reformed Protestants by the mid-seventeenth century, there is no necessary reason to read these theses in such an extensive fashion. The book's indented and italicized subheadings orient readers where to enter the text on nearly every page. Such a design readily facilitates (and even, potentially, encourages) the habits of a reader who might be inclined to open the book at random. With passages typographically broken into discrete bits, readers can engage the text without committing very much time, and, due to the ample use of numerical markers, readers (who may or may not have previously read the book cover to cover) can return to particular passages with relative ease. The physical design and page layout of devotional steady sellers created books that could be, as Ian Green puts it, "dipped into at need."[12] This point is further demonstrated if one compares *Theses Sabbaticae* with William Bradshaw's *A Discourse of the Sinne against the Holy Ghost.* The latter is a printed sermon, a work meant to represent a cohesive, start-to-finish narrative performance. Its text includes generous margins, where a thoughtful reader might make their own notes or indices, but opening at random this text as it is printed would not orient the reader as readily as would opening *Theses Sabbaticae.* And lest this distinction seem like the unmotivated difference between any two books, both were in fact printed in the same place (London), in the same year (1649), and by the same printer (John Rothwell). Differences in imagined use between these two works are reflected in the material properties of their printing.

II

The material properties of devotional steady sellers, then, indicate that their imagined use was the access and contemplation of bits of pious thought, rather than the delivery of a substantial narrative. The kinds of reading habits that derive from the use of books associated with this combination of devotional content, abundant reprinting, and portable size are best illustrated in the case of the greatest of the seventeenth century's sellers, Bibles.[13] Though the Bible printed in Mainz by Johannes Gutenberg in the mid-fifteenth century is widely mythologized as the West's first printed book, the layout of the earliest printed Bibles did not reflect many of the design conventions with which modern editions are associated. Design elements such as italicization, indentation, and variable type size, which emphasized random access (and which were later borrowed by devotional steady sellers), were indeed pioneered in the printing of Bibles, but only very gradually became conventionalized as generic aids to readers. The watershed came with French

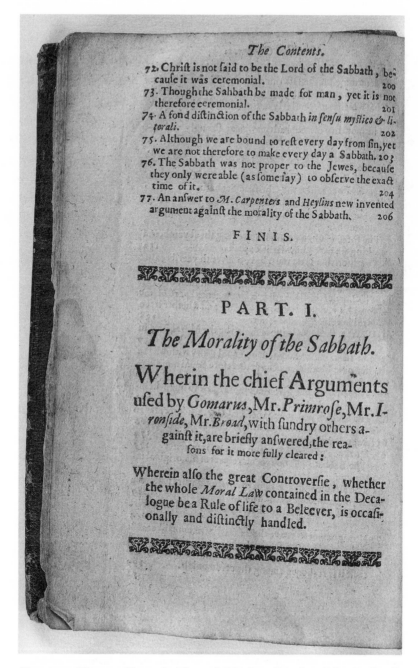

FINIS.

PART. I.

The Morality of the Sabbath.

Wherin the chief Arguments ufed by *Gomarus*, Mr. *Primrofe*, Mr. *Ironfide*, Mr. *Broad*, with fundry others againft it, are briefly anfwered, the reafons for it more fully cleared :

Wherein alfo the great Controverfie, whether the whole *Moral Law* contained in the Decalogue be a Rule of life to a Beleever, is occafionally and diftinctly handled.

Figure 2.1. Thomas Shepard, *Theses Sabbaticae* (London: John Rothwell, 1649). (American Antiquarian Society)

THE
MORALITY
OF THE
SABBATH.

Thesis 1.

Ime is one of the moſt precious bleſ-
ſings, which worthleſſe man in this
world enjoyes, a jewell of ineſti-
mable worth, a golden ſtream diſſol-
ving, and as it were, continually running downe by us, out of one eter-
nity into another; yet ſeldome taken
notice of untill it is quite paſſed a-
way from us; Man (ſaith *Solomon*) knowes not his time, *Ec-
cleſ. 9. 12.* It is therefore moſt juſt and meet, that he who
hath the diſpoſing of all other things leſſe precious and
momentous, ſhould alſo be the ſupreme Lord and diſpoſer of all our times.

Thesis 2.

He who is the diſpoſer of all our times, is the ſovereigne
Lord of our perſons alſo, and is therefore the utmoſt and laſt
end of both : for if our perſons and all our times be of him,
they are then to be improved for him, as he ſees moſt meet.

Thesis 3.

Now although all creatures in the world, are of God,
and for God, ſo that being of him, they receive their being
from him as their firſt efficient, and being for him, are
therefore * preſerved and governed by him, as their utmoſt
end; yet no other inferiour viſible creature is ſet ſo near to
God, and conſequently is not in that manner for God, as
man is.

Thesis 4.

For although all inferiour creatures are made *laſtly* for
B God,

* *Deus quâ
principium dat
eſſe qua finis
firmat & ſtabi-
lit eſſe dari uni
Gibbeuf. de li-
Dei & creat.*

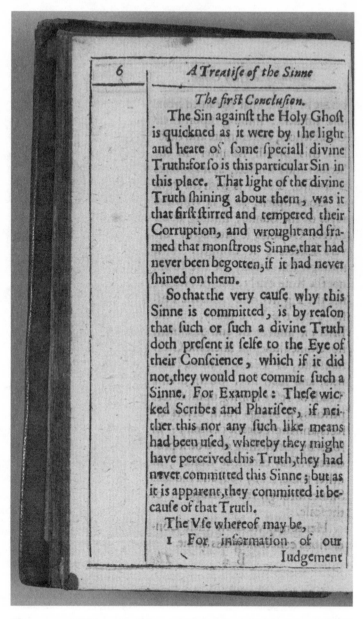

Figure 2.2. William Bradshaw, *A Treatise of the Sinne against the Holy Ghost* (London: John Rothwell, 1649). (Burke Library, Union Theological Seminary)

Iudgment concerning this Sin. We
fee many commit many ftrange
aud defperate Sinnes againft the
light of Gods Word, of Confci-
ence, yea of Nature it felfe; and that
alfo moft wilfully, and ftubbornly,
& obftinately ; yea, with this height
of defperate refolution, that though
they were fure they fhould goe to
hell for it, yet they would doe it.
Though fuch Sinnes be a fighting
againft the Truth, yet are they not
this unpardonable Sinne, except
the firft and principall motion of it
doe arife from that divine Truth, in
fuch a manner, that he would not
commit that Sinne, but for that divine Truths fake. For this is a Sin,
the very firft motions whereof,
are conceived by the fight of a divine Truth ; fo that it is a Sinne not
only committed in the light, and
againft the light ; but by means
of it, and even for the Truths fake.

2 Sith by reafon of the Cor-
ruption of Mans minde, the divine
Truth of God, the principall Or-
gan or Inftrument of all grace and
B 5   goodneffe

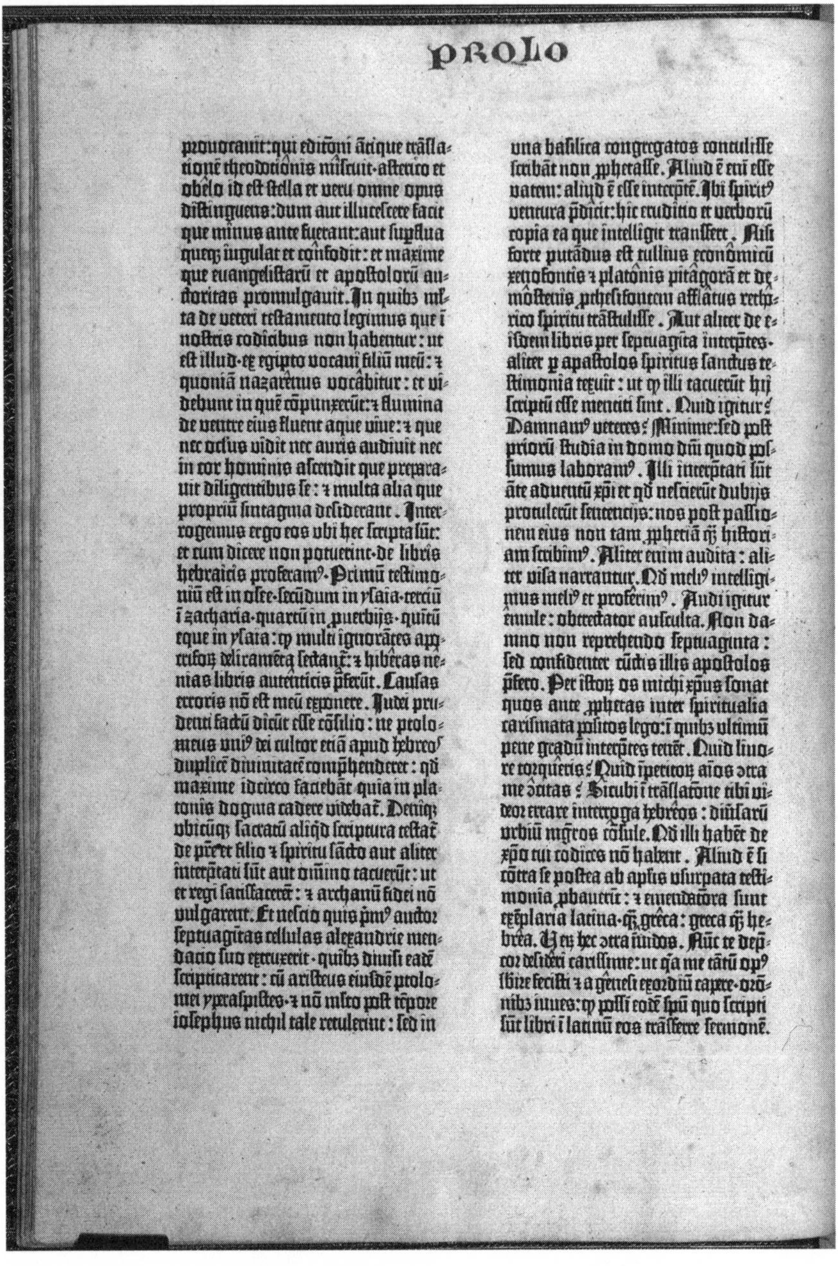

Figure 2.3. Gutenberg Bible (1454), printed in Latin. (British Library)

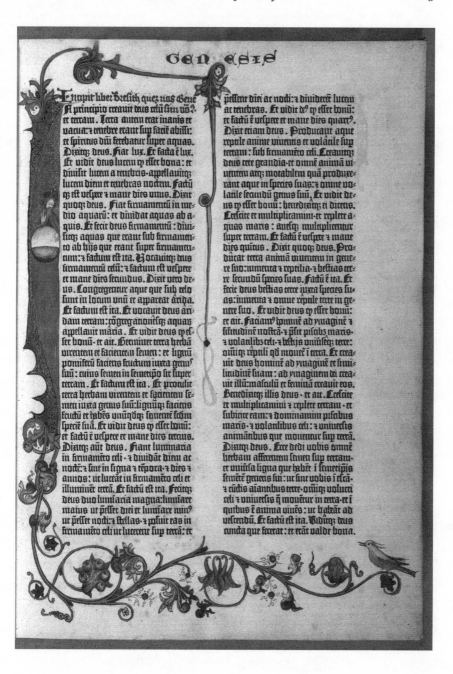

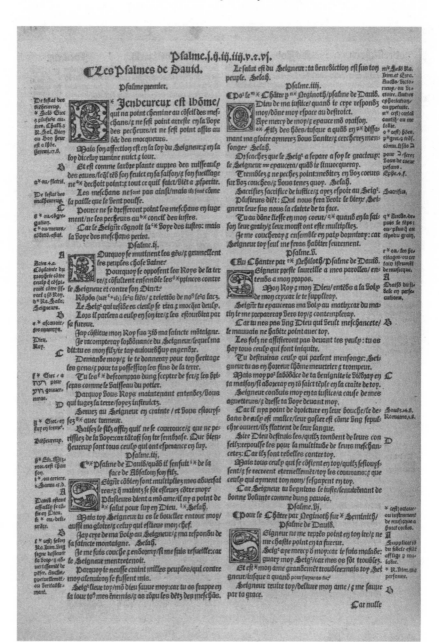

Figure 2.4. Olivétan Bible (1535), printed in French. (New York Public Library)

vernacular Bibles in the sixteenth century, which employed design features such as printed marginalia and chapter headings and which later editions adopted and gradually standardized.[14]

It is neither possible nor advisable to extrapolate any absolute connection between these developments in the design of Bibles or steady sellers and the uses to which they were put. The physical features of printed books can suggest things only about the kinds of uses that they would have facilitated, not those in which they were definitely employed. But with such caveats in mind, it is clear that the steady sellers, like the Bibles whose design features they borrowed, facilitated kinds of reading besides the continuous mode. And while cause and effect remain difficult to determine, it is the case that the emergence of Bibles printed to accommodate being "dipped into at need" coincides historically with one of early modern Protestantism's singular exegetical methods: typological reading.

Theologically speaking, "typology" is a method for deciphering a providential conception of history, in which the unfolding of events follows a divinely authored plan for redemption. Though this plan has not been revealed to humans, it has been both preordained by God and prefigured in scripture. Glimpses into the shape and meaning of the redemption to come could thereby be achieved through careful exegesis of biblical events. Single biblical events thus become "types," insofar as they may be seen to repeat or to indicate a general pattern of meaning in the progress of salvation. Herbert Palmer explained in the 1644 preface to one of his printed sermons that *"the Records of Holy Scripture . . . are not only* Stories *of things done in that Age, but* Prophecies *also of future events in succeeding Generations."*[15] Palmer's rhetorical equivocation among *"Records,"* "Stories," and "Prophecies" demonstrates some of the ways in which typological reading, as Erich Auerbach long ago observed, allows for certain kinds of abstractions.[16] The very work of typological exegesis was to determine which aspects of a biblical event were literal records and which were figurative stories. Much like novel reading centuries later (although with entirely different stakes), typological reading required discerning readers to delineate what was real, what was not, and what could be.

Typological reading fired the imaginations of many seventeenth-century Reformed preachers, allowing them to consider the Old Testament as a means of prefiguring their own fate as God's elect. We see, as William Guild wrote in a resonantly Pauline formulation in 1620, *"the eclipsed and dimme light of the Moone"* until *"the true* Phosphorus, *that glorious Sunne himself did arise in the Horizon of our humanitie."*[17] Guild's soft emphasis on *"our"* humanity underscores that attempts to interpret biblical precedents for one's own experiences tended to show that the prefigurative component of the Old Testament was enshrined in its events and outcomes, rather than its actors. What might have been considered the history of the Jewish people was instead understood to be the prefigurative history of the Puritans. Captivity, trial, and redemption were part of the literal truth of the Old Testament, while the Jews themselves were the metaphorical part. Such distinctions were often hard-won, requiring elaborate exposition and argument. "There was and is a *double use of Types* and parables," warned Samuel Mather in 1705. "If explained and understood, they do exceedingly enlighten and illuminate; but if not explained, they are like a Riddle, they call a dark mist and cloud upon the thing."[18]

Typological expositions often ran to hundreds of pages on a single biblical verse or to dozens of sermons in a single cycle. John Cotton's *A Brief Exposition of the Whole Book of Canticles* (1642) claims an expansive 236 duodecimo pages in its first edition, though it interprets a text occupying only five folio pages in the 1560 Geneva Bible.[19] Edward Taylor's uncompleted manuscript sermon cycle *Upon the Types of the Old Testament* (written between 1693 and 1706) runs over nine hundred pages in its closely printed modern edition.[20] The outsized length of these expositions points to the more elemental fact that typological reading requires digesting texts in small bits. These drawn out expositions are possible, in other words, because their authors did not presume that their job was to account for biblical truth as a composite whole. Rather, they could provide lengthy expositions precisely because their reading allowed them to "dip into" the Bible at need.

There are several obstacles to tracking a causal relationship between the coflourishing of ornamental biblical design and typology in the seventeenth century. For one thing, although typological reading was popular among Reformed theologians, and especially well-honed among those whose beliefs were inflected by Calvinism (such as the seventeenth-century New England elite), it was by no account the period's definitive style of exegesis. Early English biblical translators such as William Tyndale were suspicious of typology, and many influential Reformed theologians such as Martin Luther used it among many other exegetical methods.[21] What can be safely concluded, however, is that typological reading was very well accommodated by the design features of seventeenth-century English Bibles, which enhance the random textual access that the printing technology of the codex already makes possible.

Another challenge is the sheer variety of Bibles in circulation in this period. Through the late sixteenth and early seventeenth centuries, as printed Bibles adopted their generic design conventions, substantially more English readers were able to access them. Approximately ten times as many English Bibles were printed and marketed in the 1630s as had been produced in the 1570s, and conservative historical figures place that number at 250,000 Bibles for a population of about four and a half million people.[22] The Geneva Bible alone went through more than 140 editions between the 1560s and the 1640s, selling over half a million copies across Europe in just the sixteenth century, and making it, in William H. Sherman's estimation, "the most widely distributed book in the English Renaissance, and the one that played the most crucial role in changing the patterns of lay book ownership in the age of print."[23] Though records of actual sales are sparse, circumstantial economic evidence helps to put book ownership in perspective. Frances E. Dolan, for instance, reasons that "if women of the middling sort had the money to purchase poison, as accounts of domestic crime suggest they did, then they might also have been able to purchase cheap texts."[24] Further supporting such suppositions is the fact that the prices of books during the seventeenth century remained relatively stable, while wages increased and production costs decreased, leading Stephen Foster to conclude that books were "one item that in real terms became steadily more affordable."[25] Though Bibles, then as now, ranged in price, depending on the size, binding, or elaborateness of the edition, inexpensive Bibles were often less expensive than other kinds of religious books, such as psalters, which existed in fewer editions and were more consistently priced.[26]

Further evidence of Bibles' domestic significance in the period comes from the numerous probate records that use the phrase "a Bible and other books" to describe the bibliographic contents of an estate.[27] Thus recorded, Bibles appear not only commonly owned but also emblematic for books in general.

Though scholars cannot definitely track how Bibles were used, they tend to agree that Bible use was paradigmatic for Anglophone books in the period. The emblematic status of the Bible as *the* book is certainly something that devotional steady sellers implicitly acknowledged, and it was presumably out of some deference to the authoritative status of Bibles that steady sellers borrowed some of the former's increasingly conventionalized design features as their own. A consequence of the expanding access to book ownership in the seventeenth century, then, was the likelihood that a common reader would have been generally familiar with not only the contents of Bibles, but also with the increasingly standardized design conventions of Bibles. Such a reader would know how to use these books, and would presumably have some facility with the noncontinuous modes of reading to which these books lent themselves. As we will see, however, such general tendencies do not rule out the possibility that books can always be read in other ways.

III

Physically, steady sellers were designed like Bibles and could be read like Bibles; but at the level of cultural signification, steady sellers were not Bibles and were not presumed to contain precisely the same kind of revealed truth. Readers of steady sellers may have been able to take advantage of the noncontinuous reading practices toward which these books lent themselves, even as the goals of this reading may have been slightly different. To put the matter another way, we have seen that one consequence of seventeenth-century Bible design was its complicity with typological exegesis, but among books only the Bible required exegesis. If other books borrowed a design that allowed for the careful examination of distinct bits, rather than a consideration of the narrative whole, the payoff of that careful examination was necessarily different than in the case of Bibles. And indeed, for many seventeenth-century Protestant readers, that payoff was increasingly personal. Typological exegesis of the Bible, as we have seen, tended to interpret the events and outcomes of the Old Testament rather than its actors; but reading other books discontinuously bore no such requirements. Typology could be an exegetical method, but it could also be a devotional one.[28]

As a class of pious books that were not Bibles but which nonetheless could be read like Bibles (intensively, in discrete bits), devotional steady sellers conform with what Barbara Kiefer Lewalski identifies in the seventeenth century as "the new Protestant emphasis upon the application of Scripture to the self."[29] However, and as we saw in Chapter 1, "self" in this context does not signify in the more familiar, post-Enlightenment sense of the term. Lewalski, like many other scholars, understands this application to the self less as a progress of individualism and more as a progress of practical piety. According to William Haller, "the more actively" seventeenth-century Reformed Protestant preachers "responded to ever-increasing audiences the more they gave up abstractions in order to mirror the individual consciousness of spiritual stress, to convince the individual of sin in order to persuade him of grace, to make him feel worse in order to make him feel better, to inspire pity and fear in order to purge him of those passions."[30] Just as Auerbach identifies typological exegesis as a move toward abstraction—a parsing of literal and figurative contents with a single scriptural episode—many seventeenth-century preachers sensed that the process was reversible: if biblical events can portend episodes in human lives, so human lives might be comprehensible in terms of biblical events. This rhetorical move casually developed in practice, even though it was rarely theologically sanctioned before the eighteenth century.[31] With and without sanction, however, the idea that personal experience could apply to the Bible, rather than the other way around, was not necessarily understood in the seventeenth century to attribute any particular importance to the self. The sense of self that could be reflected in scripture was not the "possessive" individual whose self-interested pursuits flourished in later Enlightenment discourse, but a diminished and vulnerable figure.[32] As Janice Knight puts it, "The primary purpose of scriptural application was to pull down the individual will."[33]

The challenge of devotional reading, then, was to curb the freedom that readers have. "Reading," writes Roger Chartier, "is a creative practice, which invents singular meanings and significations that are not reducible to the intentions of authors of text or producers of books."[34] From this point of view, a textual feature like continuous narrative can be seen as a way of working against the random-access feature of the codex, encouraging readers to access information in a prescribed order. The consequences of this agential shift from readers to creators are various. Gérard Genette has enumerated the ways that narrative sequences works astride temporal sequences, granting narrators the power to re-present events (through recollection or foreshadowing, for example) in order to heighten certain effects on the reader.[35] Somewhat more pessimistically, D. A. Miller has shown how narrative ordering is linked to the ideological protocols of social order.[36] Continuous narrative represents one way to control how readers engage with books, and its absence among devotional steady sellers required that these works attempt to shape readerly experiences by other means.

At a formal level, the creators of devotional steady sellers tended to design their texts in ways that work against the potentially self-indulgent pleasures of reading. From a modern perspective, devotional steady sellers consistently lack the basic features of narrative that might effectively draw readers in: setting, plot, and character. A very few attempted some kind of narrative progression, and the most enduring of these is Arthur Dent's *The Plaine Mans Path-Way to Heaven* (1601), which reached twenty-five editions by 1640. Yet *The Plaine Mans Path-Way to Heaven* stages a dialogue between four allegorical figures, whose pedantic conversation rehearses Protestant platitudes about the dangers of worldly distractions and about the importance of moral cultivation; moreover, it does so in a manner that leaves little room for character development. That is to say, devotional steady sellers do not typically have characters, and even when they do, these characters do not in any clear way seem to be figured in terms of the psychological complexity that would anticipate the kinds of characters one finds in nineteenth-century novels. Absent any such characterological complexity, however, devotional steady sellers nevertheless expend considerable effort creating human figures, especially in order to describe how these books can and should be used.

Because the physical design of steady sellers overwhelmingly accommodated discontinuous reading, it was instead the formal properties of these texts that worked against the potential anarchy of readerly agency. The major way that steady sellers established this control was to figure ideal readers, readers whose use of these books complied with the author's pious intentions. The seventeenth-century's most reprinted devotional works—including Samuel Hieron's *A Helpe unto Devotion* (1608), Richard Rogers's *A Garden of Spiritual Flowers* (1609), Henry Scudder's *The Christian's Daily Walke in Holy Securitie and Peace* (1627), and, most popular of all, the above-mentioned *The Practice of Piety* by Lewis Bayly—all lack a continuous narrative, but these texts nevertheless do things to shape readers' experiences of them.[37] The formal design of these texts counters the significant power that readers have to construct meanings through use, by offering explicit instructions as to what pious reading practices might be.

The Practice of Piety, for example, includes a section called *"Briefe directions how to reade the Holy Scriptures, once every yeere over, with ease, profit and reuerence."*[38] The text of this section instructs its reader to "apply these things to thine owne hart, and reade not these Chapters, as matters of *Historicall* discourse: but as if they were so many *Letters* or *Epistles* sent downe from God out of *heauen* vnto thee."[39] The injunction to "apply" evokes a recurrent Protestant devotional concept—influentially formulated, for instance, as the third element of the three-part template for sermons found in William Perkins's preaching manual *The Arte of Prophecying* (1592).[40] To apply the scriptures that one reads to one's self bespeaks a method of shaping the self in a more pious direction. As Richard Bernard's 1607 preaching manual put the matter, "application works upon affection."[41] Such an imperative shapes how readers might read any devotional text, but does so by working with, rather than against, the agency that readers have to organize their experiences of a codex. Though the directions in *The Practice of Piety* place the reader on a yearly cycle of reading and rereading the Bible, there is in fact no instruction that this reading would necessarily take the text in sequential order. Rather than prescribe *which* biblical passages to read when, the text instead places emphasis on *how* any passage ought to be read: *as if* they were sent down from God to the reader. It matters less which passages one reads than that one reads in order to apply what one reads to one's self.

Arguably no devotional steady seller does more work to delimit the figure of the reader in this mode than Thomas Shepard's *The Sincere Convert* (1640), a text that bears the additional distinction of being the most widely reprinted book in London by a seventeenth-century New England colonist.[42] Thus, where *The Practice of Piety* instructs its reader to read the Bible *as if* these words were sent down from God "vnto thee," *The Sincere Convert* instead demands that its reader "mourne for thy secret neglect of holy duties, mourne for thy secret hypocrisie, whoredome, &c. and with shame in thy face come before this God for pardon and mercy."[43] Though both texts stress the necessity of careful reading and application, *The Sincere Convert* does so in a way that requires readers to see personal limitations, instead of emphasizing, as *The Practice of Piety* does, divine opportunity. While not all devotional steady sellers take as strongly a Calvinist line as does *The Sincere Convert,* this text shares with many others an insistence that application should not provide readers with any occasion for self-indulgence.[44] Instead, pious reading diminishes the self, emptying the self of sin and transforming it into a better receptacle for divine grace.

In all these examples, the pious reader of the steady seller is represented as a vulnerable figure. The kinds of figurations that Shepard employs are best understood as an extreme instance of what Margaret Spufford has called "the predominance of the negative" across Anglophone devotional chapbooks in this period.[45] For example, Hieron's *A Helpe unto Devotion* gives instructions on meditation by reminding its reader "That our owne vilenesse must bee remembered, it is evident, Ge. 32.10. I am lesse then the least of thy mercies."[46] And even Scudder's fairly gentle devotional work *The Christian's Daily Walke in Holy Securitie and Peace*, which announces in the preface that its aim is to promote happiness, notes that "through the grace of God," one will recognize one's sins and think that one is "so ill to requite him, so little to fear him, vile wretch that I am!"[47] These texts conform to the pattern I have been describing, where even in the absence of character and plot, they expend rhetorical energy figuring their readers, and, indeed, figuring those readers negatively, in terms of their vulnerability.

Based on the foregoing observations, steady sellers appear to be part of a media ecology that includes not only a codex format, an index-like layout, a discontinuous reading practice, and a nonnarrative form, but also a pious reader.[48] On their own terms, these books cannot be used properly without a reader who shares in the desire for pious cultivation that these books espouse. That reader supplies the books with the opportunity to perform the functions for which they are designed. At the same time, due to the functional opportunities and limitations of the book's design, readers stand to be transformed into pious Christians; not unlike the ways that cars turn travelers into drivers—that is, users whose particular engagement with technologies contributes to a particular nuance of identity. To understand this identity as specific to the media ecology I'm describing, however, requires recognizing that the particular styles of piety these texts promote are predicated on access to and use of books, rather than on theology as such.[49] The cultural power of printed books to transform readers has long been recognized, and indeed Stephen Greenblatt's influential 1980 study described books as "the primary sources of self-fashioning."[50] Drawing on this designation in his 2007 study of steady sellers, Matthew P. Brown called their project one of "Renaissance soul-fashioning."[51] And though he expressed himself in a different idiom, it is in precisely this ecology that Capt. Gookin, in his confessional narrative before Thomas Shepard's Cambridge congregation, used *The Practice of Piety,* as "some gracious witness to my soul, in letting me see the state of misery."[52]

The tendency toward personal application is less an alternative to biblical typology than a variation of it. Application functions in a slightly different ecosystem, where the books being read are not Bibles; where the interpreters of those books are not necessarily preachers, scholars, or trained theologians; and where the application may move from personal experience to biblical precedent rather than the other way around. Yet the boundaries between these ecosystems are porous. The reader who reads a devotional steady seller and applies it personally is not necessarily a different person than the reader who reads a Bible and applies it typologically. In practice, ordinary readers may have little appreciation for the variations in their reading habits, and that appreciation may be especially minimal when the readers in question have devotional piety among their motivations for reading in the first place. Nonetheless, that varieties of reading comfortably coexist makes room for the possibility of even more idiosyncratic or unorthodox uses of books. And as we shall see, such variations also allow for more substantial practical mutations over time.

IV

As the negative figuration of the vulnerable, pious reader becomes more refined through the seventeenth century, the material properties of steady sellers themselves remain fairly consistent: they continued to be produced as "short, tubby bricks," and they continued to have index-like layouts. Many titles were reprinted well into the eighteenth century: Dent's *The Plaine Mans Path-Way to Heaven* (first published in 1601) went through thirty-five editions in the seventeenth century and another seven before 1775; Shepard's *The Sincere Convert* (first published in 1640) went through thirty editions before 1695 and another four before 1742; Bayly's *The Practice of Piety* (first published in 1610) went through an impressive ninety-one editions before 1699 and another twenty-six before 1792. The cultural significance of these steady sellers through at least the end of the seventeenth century is indicated by the large number of places in which they turn up where other kinds of books do not—and Capt. Gookin's relation before Shepard's Cambridge congregation is only one example. Michael Wigglesworth, for instance, records in his diary sometime during 1654 that a man came to speak with him *"after God directed [the man] to that book called The Christian's Daily Walk of Mister Scudder."*[53] John Bunyan reported in his spiritual autobiography, *Grace Abounding* (1666), that he and his wife "came together as poor as poor might be, yet this she had for her part, *The Plain Mans Path-way to Heaven,* and *The Practice of Piety,* which her Father had left her when he died."[54] Back across the Atlantic, the value of these books is also is suggested by the fact that in both 1665 and the period between 1685 and

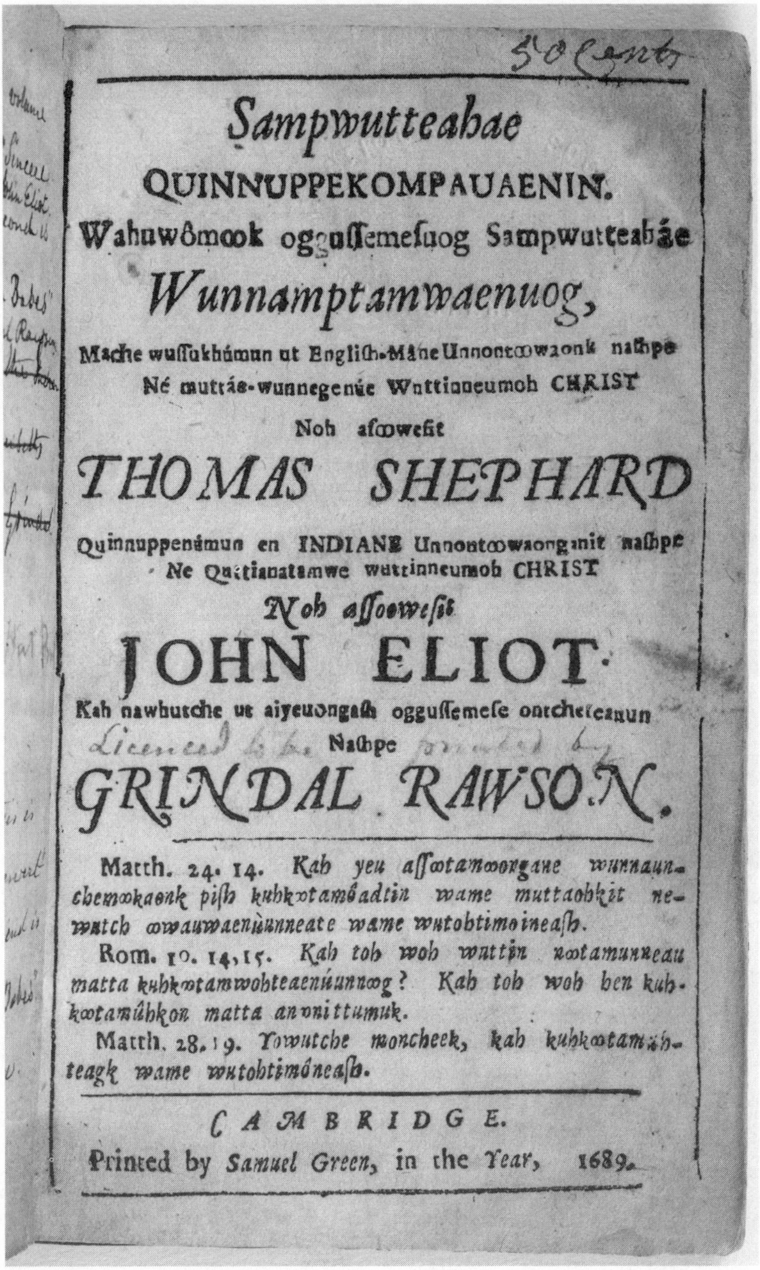
50 Cents

Sampwutteahae

QUINNUPPEKOMPAUAENIN.

Wahuwômook oggussemesuog Sampwutteahâe

Wunnamptamwaenuog,

Mache wussukhúmun ut English-Mâne Unnontoowaonk nashpe

Né muttáe-wunnegenúe Wuttinneumoh CHRIST

Noh asoowesit

THOMAS SHEPHARD

Quinnuppenúmun en INDIANE Unnontoowaonganit nashpe

Ne Quttianatamwe wuttinneumoh CHRIST

Noh assoowesit

JOHN ELIOT.

Kah nawhutche ut aiyeuongash oggussemese ontcheteanun

Licenced to be printed by

Nashpe

GRINDAL RAWSON.

Matth. 24. 14. *Kah yeu assootamoongane wunnaunchemookaonk pish kuhkootamóadtin wame muttaohkit newutch oowauwaenúunneate wame wutohtimoineash.*

Rom. 10. 14, 15. *Kah toh woh wuttin nootamunneau matta kuhkootamwohteaenúunnoog? Kah toh woh ben kuhkootamûhkon matta anoonittumuk.*

Matth. 28. 19. *Yowutche moncheek, kah kuhkootamúhteagk wame wutohtimôneash.*

CAMBRIDGE.

Printed by *Samuel Green*, in the *Year*, 1689.

Figure 2.5. Thomas Shepard, *Sampwutteahae Quinnuppekompauaenin* [Algonquin translation of *The Sincere Convert*] (Cambridge: Samuel Green, 1689). (American Antiquarian Society)

1689, *The Sincere Convert* and *The Practice of Piety* are two of the texts, along with the Bible, that are translated into Algonquin and printed in Cambridge and Boston, Massachusetts, as signs of the missionary progress among the local Native American tribes.[55]

And yet in spite of these relative consistencies in the material and formal properties of steady sellers, the ways that readers use these books unexpectedly mutates toward the end of the seventeenth century: Anglophone readers become increasingly inclined to read in continuous ways. Based on the evidence examined so far, it should be clear that the act of reading a book from cover to cover amounts to little more than a perversion of a long-standing Protestant engagement with codices. But while few seventeenth-century scriptural authorities advocated for continuous reading, their directives did not necessarily discourage Protestant readers from doing so. For example, though discontinuous reading remained a standard practice, readers nevertheless faced numerous injunctions, across a surprising array of English Reformation and Counter-Reformation texts, to read the Bible in terms what one annotator of a Geneva Bible described as "how it hangeth together."[56] Other Protestant biblical paratexts and commentaries enjoined readers to think about the Bible in terms of its *coherence,* which required that they apprehend something about the whole.[57] Or, as John Owen wrote in a 1677, responding to scholastic objections that biblical composition took place over many hundreds of years, "Yet there is upon the whole and all the parts of their writing, that *Gravity, Majesty,* and *Authority* . . . as must excite an Admiration in all that seriously consider them."[58] The whole, according to Owen, had a coherence that was more than the sum of its parts, and readers should therefore look at the parts in terms of the whole. This emphasis on coherence gave readers the responsibility of ratifying the unity of the Bible's many episodes.

As an instruction for how to read, finding coherence in the Bible was roughly congruent to finding application in steady sellers. In both cases, a simple but open-ended instruction took the considerable freedom that readers had to interact with texts and funneled it toward the ultimate goal of pious cultivation. Unlike application, however, the injunction to read for coherence meant this cultivation required a reader to know something about the entirety of what was between a book's covers. At minimum, reading for coherence required more than just a haphazard "dipping in." While the injunction to comprehend biblical coherence did not mandate continuous reading, neither did it entirely accommodate the more desultory versions of discontinuous reading. Reading for application and reading for coherence coexisted as modes of engaging texts, requiring slightly different efforts on the part of their practitioners, without appearing in any recognized way as alternatives. While some readers or some preachers may have preferred one over the other, I have found no evidence that any seventeenth-century readers saw these modes of reading as, in any strong sense, opposing. This lack of opposition is due to the fact that both modes of reading had salvation as their goal. Both were means of pious cultivation, and that cultivation was far more important than small differences in the way it was attained.

Nonetheless, a widespread ignorance of these subtle practical variations creates fertile ground for mutation. By the beginning of the eighteenth century, discontinuous reading was losing favor. As early as 1707, John Locke's *Essay for the Understanding of St. Paul's Epistles* complained of the practice of dividing scripture into chapters and verses "whereby they are so chopp'd and minc'd, and as they are now printed, stand so broken and divided, that not only the common People take the Verses usually for distinct Aphorisms, but even Men of more advanc'd Knowledge, in reading them, lose very much of the Strength and Force of the Coherence, and the Light that depends on it."[59] Locke's solution was continuous reading, and he makes the case by arguing against the index-like design features that characterize not only Bibles but, as we have seen, devotional steady sellers.[60] Though Locke did not win the argument and Bibles continued to be printed in chapters and verses with index-like layouts, his sensibility nonetheless appears to anticipate other publishing trends for the eighteenth century. For the absence of index-like design features and the mandate to read a narrative continuously are, of course, properties that would later be associated with novels.

Exactly what causes this shift to continuous reading is unclear, including whether it is more a cause or an effect of changes in European book production in the second half of the seventeenth century. The decades between 1640 and 1660 were highly transitional for the book market specifically, as Lucien Febvre and Henri-Jean Martin observe, in which book fairs begin to lose their importance as international trading posts, rates of piracy balloon, and "the great editions of religious works, which were such a feature of the Counter-Reformation and intended as much for export as for home consumption sold fewer copies, fewer works in Latin were published, scholarly works began increasingly to appear in the vernacular, imaginative and popular literature increased and the first newspapers were published."[61] These trends toward vernacular publications, focused more on current events and circulated more within national boundaries, at first blush point to changes in the kinds of books that were being printed rather than the kinds of ways those books were being read. Yet, as we have seen, book design indicates (even if it does not predict) the use to which readers may put books. And one genre of books encouraging more continuous reading does indeed become far more prevalent in the middle of the seventeenth century: the almanac.

The popularity of almanacs skyrockets in this period, nestling on shelves and tables alongside steady sellers and Bibles as some of the only printed books that common people would have owned.[62] Though not new (almanacs begin to be printed in England in 1545), almanacs become phenomenally common by the 1640s, with above four million almanacs printed in England in the seventeenth century. As Keith Thomas proposes, "Not even the Bible sold at this rate."[63] Like steady sellers, almanacs are designed to accommodate reading in discrete bits (typically month by month), yet unlike steady sellers, almanacs do encourage continuous reading, at least insofar as their chronological organization would seem to create the expectation that a reader could cover the whole text successively, in the prescribed order. As with the difference between reading for application and reading for coherence, the difference between the discontinuous reading of a steady seller and the discontinuous reading of an almanac was subtle and, for many readers, probably quite minimal. It is also the case that, as Stuart Sherman has argued, the almanacs "privileged occasion over continuum," placing emphasis on holidays, for example, rather than treating all time as an equivalent succession of days.[64] In this regard almanacs drew on earlier Protestant calendars, which, in turn, drew on earlier pre-Reformation calendrical systems, "retaining some traditional elements while repudiating others," in

Alison A. Chapman's words.[65] Compared to steady sellers, almanacs do encourage more continuous reading, though they cannot in any simple way be credited with heralding the "homogenous empty time" that Benedict Anderson (borrowing a turn of phrase from Walter Benjamin) attributes to the temporal structure of the nineteenth-century novel.[66]

The trend toward continuous reading by the eighteenth century is multiply caused, very gradual, and somewhat uneven. It happens alongside some changes in both the European and the Anglophone book markets, but it seems to spill across genres, such that readers have some increasing inclination to read continuously whether books are designed to accommodate that mode of reading (as are almanacs) or not (as are Bibles). Steady sellers, as we have seen, were for the most part designed to be read discontinuously, and, logically, the trend toward continuous reading should have rendered them unfashionable. Instead, something else happened. Steady sellers began to accommodate continuous reading, all the while retaining not only their material textual properties ("short, tubby bricks"), but, crucially, some of their formal ones as well. What the trend toward continuous reading does not seem to affect, in other words, are characters figured negatively in terms of their vulnerability.

V

No text more successfully exemplified both the durability of the steady seller's formal (as well as material) properties, on the one hand, and the emergent appeal of continuous narrative, on the other, than John Bunyan's *The Pilgrim's Progress*. First published in London in 1678, *The Pilgrim's Progress* went through at least fourteen editions before the close of the seventeenth century, was owned by people at all ends of the socioeconomic spectrum, spawned a sequel and imitations, and became one of the most widely translated books in the history of the world.[67] Though this number of editions alone qualifies *The Pilgrim's Progress* as a steady seller, the text differs from nearly all prior seventeenth-century steady sellers in that it presents a continuous narrative. This distinction seems much more like a formal innovation, however, than like some kind of polemical alternative (as, for example, Locke would offer in his commentary on St. Paul). Bunyan's very title promises a progressive story and thereby implies a casual linkage between narrative and soteriological progression that nearly all readers of the text have recognized.[68] Additionally and somewhat more subtly, however, the text further justifies itself as a continuous narrative by dilating on the media ecology of devotional books.

The Pilgrim's Progress famously opens with a dream in which our narrator *"saw a Man cloathed with Raggs, standing in a certain place, with his face from his own House, a Book in his hand, and a great burden upon his back."*[69] While Christian's rags and his burden are allegorical images for humankind's fallen condition, the book he holds is instead a literal image. The comparative literalism of the book stems from the widely held Protestant assumption that the Bible was the literal word of God and therefore not an allegory for anything.[70] At the same time, this passage extends this literalism from the biblical text to its media format, what Bunyan's narrator calls simply *"a Book."* This extension from text to format is due to a long-standing (in fact ancient) association of the biblical text with the codex format specifically. The designation of sacred Christian texts as codices dates to the second century CE, whereas pagan texts evince a preference for the codex somewhere between the late third and the fourth centuries, while Jewish texts seem prejudiced against the codex until the eight century.[71] This early privileging of the codex as the preferred format for sacred Christian texts meant, in Peter Stallybrass's words, that "for more than six centuries, the distinction of the book from the scroll materially differentiated Christianity from Judaism."[72] As we have seen, however, the Christian preference for books over scrolls accommodated the development of exegetical practices that allowed readers to take the Bible in discrete bits. Bunyan's Christian holds a book that he and his readers are to take for the literal word of God, but nothing about the history of reading that book specifically, nor anything about the technology of the codex generally, implies a progressive narrative or mandates continuous reading.

That mandate comes to Christian from a more ancient technology. Having learned from his Bible that he will die and come to judgment, Christian weeps because "I find that I am not willing to do the first, nor able to do the second."[73] His biblical reading is an act of application, but he starts on his journey only when another character, Evangelist, shows him "a *Parchment-Roll*."[74] Evangelist is an allegorical figure of John the Baptist, who comes chronologically before Christ and who therefore has at his disposal the Jewish scroll rather than the Christian book—the scroll remaining a feature of John the Baptist's iconography through the sixteenth century.[75] Yet it proves to be a significant justification for the narrative that follows that Christian is set on his journey by a residual technology.[76] Unlike the codex, which lends itself to random access, the scroll lends itself to continuous reading. Though a motivated reader can of course skip to any part of a scroll, scrolls are designed to be read progressively, and, as with the Jewish Torah, cyclically. Christian applies the biblical text to himself, and in so doing fits easily into the media ecology of the steady seller. His act of reading Evangelist's scroll reduplicates his earlier act of application (the entire text of the scroll is simply Matthew 3:7, *"Fly from the wrath to come"*), but here he mutates the ecology of the steady seller toward a slightly variant ecology. Christian's encounter with Evangelist offers a *mise en abyme* for that ecology, setting the stage for both Christian's and his reader's journey. That is, both Christian, as a character in a devotional narrative, and the reader, who engages that devotional narrative, from this moment are meant to follow their texts progressively, through acts of continuous reading.

Despite this narrative mutation of the ecology of the steady seller toward continuous reading, *The Pilgrim's Progress* conforms overwhelming to the formal features we have already seen to characterize this class of books. In particular, Christian is figured in terms of a vulnerability before God that has been established and refined in devotional steady sellers for a century before *The Pilgrim's Progress*. As early as the narrator's opening vision of Christian, we learn that "I looked, and saw him open the Book, and Read therein; and as he Read, he wept and trembled: and not being able longer to contain, he brake out with a lamentable cry; saying, *what shall I do?*"[77] *The Pilgrim's Progress* borrows its interest in application and the challenges of application from earlier devotional steady sellers. But the most significant point of continuity between *The Pilgrim's Progress* and earlier steady sellers has to do with the ways that all these texts imagine that reading for application—in other words, reading for the cultivation of a pious self—ought to leave readers very much in the state in which we find Christian in this scene: proper reading should create extreme humility before God, should enhance one's sense of weakness and sin, should, in a word, create vulnerability. Christian, weeping and trembling while reading his Bible, participates in what, by 1678, was a centuries-old means of figuring characters.

Arguably no part of the publication history of this book makes its appeal to conservative Protestant readers more evident than the fact that the second edition of *The Pilgrim's Progress,* published in 1681, was printed in Boston, Massachusetts. The edition has been noted by bibliographers as an exception to the trend of importing London books to the colonies (where, due to material and capital shortages, printing longer works was always more expensive).[78] But it has been less appreciated that this second edition of *The Pilgrim's Progress* was also the first book printed under a restructured printing regime. In the autumn of 1681, the Massachusetts General Court moved the official press across the Charles River from Cambridge (where it had been established in 1638) to Boston, where it came under the supervision of Samuel Sewall and under the operation of Samuel Green.[79] Between October 1681 and September 1684, when Sewall served as manager, the Boston press printed twenty-four books, pamphlets, and broadsides, of which *The Pilgrim's Progress* is chronologically the first.[80] The particular reasons for this printing are obscure, and Massachusetts legislative records only elliptically detail that Sewall undertook the management of the press "at the instance of some friends, wth respect to the accommodation of the publicke."[81] Though Sewall was a prolific diarist, his diaries are missing or unaccounted for this entire period, from July 1677 to February 1684/1685.[82] Circumstantial evidence suggests, however, that the 1681 Boston publication of *The Pilgrim's Progress* was a political choice. All fourteen of the seventeenth-century London editions of *The Pilgrim's Progress* were printed by Nathaniel Ponder, a Dissenter introduced to Bunyan by John Owen, a minister and friend (whose investments in typological reading we have previously discussed).[83] Owen, in turn, was a longtime correspondent of the prominent Boston minister Increase Mather, the two having jointly authored a short essay, *Some Important Truths about Con-*

version (1674); and Mather was almost certainly among the "friends" who insisted that Sewall oversee the management of the Boston press. In other words, Bunyan's London and Boston printers were indirectly connected through an informal but dense transatlantic network of Protestant ministers.[84] Yet it is not just these connections that suggest a political significance for the Boston edition of *The Pilgrim's Progress.* Indeed, similar connections were a common engine for the movement of books in the seventeenth century, and Mather's correspondence alone is full of examples of ministers and friends living in England, Scotland, or the Netherlands (as well as New England friends and relatives abroad) sending him books.[85] Given the large number of English books circulating in Boston in 1681, the choice to print an edition of *The Pilgrim's Progress,* apart from any others, suggests a ringing endorsement of this text.[86]

It's impossible to determine precisely which aspects of the text would have made it so important to endorse, and surely political alliance with Owen or Ponder (or perhaps Bunyan himself) may have been factors in the decision to publish an edition of *The Pilgrim's Progress* in Boston. A more suggestive possibility, however, can be found on the final page of the 1681 edition. This page is an advertisement for future publications from the Boston press, and it lists three works. Two are sermons, one each by Mather and by Samuel Willard "Shewing the Authors, Ends, & Effects of *Persecution*," and the third is the narrative of "the Captivity and Redemption of Mrs *Mary Rowlandson;* and of her Children. Being pathetically written, with her own Hand."[87] All three texts have in common the theme of persecution, and all comply with the diminutive figurations of self that we have already seen elsewhere in devotional steady sellers. Rowlandson's text, the only one of the twenty-four printed during Sewall's tenure to be authored by a woman, is exemplary in its powerful effacements of its author's own agency in surviving her captivity. In a now-famous passage marking her vulnerability before God's sovereignty, Rowlandson observes, "Some are ready to say, I speak it for my own credit; *But I speak it in the presence of God, and to His Glory.* Gods power is as great now, and as sufficient to save, as when he preserved Daniel in the Lions den; or the three *Children* in the fiery Furnace."[88] Rowlandson's passivity, like Christian's lament, rings clearly with the negative figurations of self that characterize steady sellers. One reason, then, that the overseers of the Boston press may have wanted to endorse *The Pilgrim's Progress* was that they valued its figuration of character in negative terms.

While it does not seem merely coincidental that all three texts advertised in the back of the Boston 1681 edition of *The Pilgrim's Progress* share with that text a practice of negative figuration, it is nonetheless doubtful that the motives for bringing these works into print were primarily aesthetic. Instead, as Teresa Toulouse has argued, the publication of this group of texts between 1681 and 1682, themed around persecution, came at a moment of heightened anxiety about the status of Reformed Protestantism in the late years of Charles II, when Popish Plots were rumored and the next in line for the throne, James, Duke of York, was a Catholic.[89] For New England colonials whose self-governance depended on royal charters, imperial succession was a source of great concern. This context indicates one probable reason that Bostonians like Sewall and Mather would have (consciously or not) identified with vulnerable characterological figures in *The Pilgrim's Progress*. However, and significantly for the present discussion, this context also means that their interest in those figures was not due to an enduring concern for topics of perennial interest, but an urgent political concern for affairs of the day. Indeed, in 1681 neither *The Pilgrim's Progress* nor any of the other three texts advertised at the back of its Boston edition were steady sellers. All were instead newly published works. All are also continuous narratives.[90] None was obviously printed to be "dipped into at need."

We have seen that devotional steady sellers refine a figurative practice that places emphasis on the vulnerability of characters. The fact that steady sellers were some of the most widely owned, read, and circulated books in the seventeenth century suggests that these books were likely an important point of dissemination for the figurative practices that represent characters negatively. Moreover, this negative figuration of vulnerability is a key feature of the media ecology of the steady sellers, which begins to account for how and why these figurations are so consistent there. Materially and formally, *The Pilgrim's Progress* draws on conventions established by devotional steady sellers; yet in spite of these material and formal continuities, *The Pilgrim's Progress* is also complicit

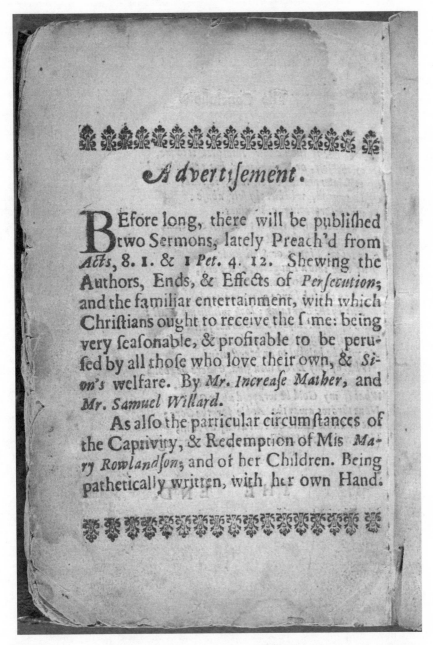

Advertisement.

BEfore long, there will be publiſhed two Sermons, lately Preach'd from *Acts*, 8. 1. & 1 *Pet.* 4. 12. Shewing the Authors, Ends, & Effects of *Perſecution*; and the familiar entertainment, with which Chriſtians ought to receive the ſame: being very ſeaſonable, & profitable to be peruſed by all thoſe who love their own, & *Sion's* welfare. By *Mr. Increaſe Mather*, and *Mr. Samuel Willard.*

As alſo the particular circumſtances of the Captivity, & Redemption of Mis *Mary Rowlandſon*, and of her Children. Being pathetically written, with her own Hand.

Figure 2.6. Advertisement page, from the second edition of John Bunyan, *The Pilgrim's Progress* (Boston: Samuel Green, 1681). (Huntington Library)

with a more diffuse and slow cultural transition toward continuous reading, which was notably absent from media ecology of devotional steady sellers. But the story of character neither begins nor ends with steady sellers, and as the slow transition to continuous reading begins to suggest, their media ecology exists in relationship to other ecologies.[91] Put differently, we might say that the trope of figural vulnerability endures, even after the media ecology of the steady seller is disrupted by alternative practices of reading, such as the slowly evolving, more continuous mode, which favors narrative and which in turn makes *The Pilgrim's Progress* into a steady seller in the eighteenth and nineteenth centuries.

VI

It is not steady sellers but novels that Gabriel Betteredge, manservant and narrator of Wilkie Collins's *The Moonstone* (1868), reads devotionally. The opening pages establish his unwavering devotion to *Robinson Crusoe*, and the joke recurs more than a dozen times through the novel. Part of that joke, however, has to do with Betteredge's manner of reading. The opening sentence of his narration directs his reader to a passage on "page one-hundred and twenty-nine," to which, "only yesterday, I opened my *Robinson Crusoe*."[92] This strategy of dipping into the text is paired with Betteredge's attempts to relate *Crusoe* to his own experience. About halfway through the narrative, unable to cheer up another character, Betteredge recalls, "It suddenly occurred to me that here was a case for the wholesome application of *Robinson Crusoe*. I hobbled out to my own room, and hobbled back with that immortal book," only to find, in the comic pathos of the scene, "nobody in the library!"[93] Betteredge reads novels in the wrong ways—dipping in, applying—and part of the success of these jokes has to do with the fact that their readers encounter them dozens of pages into a novel published in 1868. That is, readers encounter these jokes at a moment when their own investments in continuous narrative should be fairly well established.

Yet another part of the joke here also depends on the assumption that *Crusoe* is undeniably a novel. Like *The Pilgrim's Progress*, *Crusoe* exemplifies the emergent type of prose narrative at the turn of the eighteenth century, which is a continuous narrative, anchored around a character, where "character" is figured negatively. Part of the drama of *Crusoe,* of course, is his gradual coming to figure himself in negative terms. As he recalls shortly before he begins to read the Bible,

> I had, alas! no divine Knowledge; what I had received by the good Instruction of my Father was then worn out by an uninterrupted Series, for 8 Years, of Seafaring Wickedness, and a constant Conversation with nothing but such as were like my self, wicked and pro-phane to the last Degree: I do not remember that I had in all that Time one Thought that so much as tended either to looking up-wards towards God, or inwards towards a Reflection upon my own Ways: But a certain Stupidity of Soul, without Desire of Good, or Conscience of Evil, had entirely overwhelm'd me, and I was all that the most hardened, unthinking, wicked Creature among our common Sailors, can be supposed to be; not having the least Sense, either of the Fear of God in Danger, or of Thankfulness to God in Deliverance.[94]

This passage strings words like "not" and "nothing" along with the de-tails of Crusoe's wickedness and stupidity and what he did not know and failed to do, indicting not only Crusoe himself but the entire class to which he had belonged (though of which he was "the most" offensive). Such a negative figuration of self rhymes clearly with the kinds of figura-tion we have seen in devotional steady sellers, as well as in the earlier seventeenth-century confessional narratives discussed in Chapter 1. Thus, if *Crusoe* is the novel that Betteredge (and, it would seem, Collins) supposes it to be, it is nonetheless also part of the same mutation of the devotional steady seller that *The Pilgrim's Progress* represents.

Many of the most well-known interpretations of *Crusoe* acknowl-edge its debts to Protestant soteriological writings, but they also tend to diminish this aspect of the text in favor of its nascent vision of liberal-capitalist individualism. Influential discussions by Jean-Jacques Rousseau in *Émile* (1762) and by Karl Marx in the first volume of *Capital* (1867) helped to cement this understanding of Crusoe's po-tent individualism.[95] Among twentieth-century critics, Ian Watt did the most to shape the consensus that the English novel is a story of individualism and that Crusoe is its paradigm figure, though by 1957 the point had long been made, and, as Watt's own discussion noted, "That Robinson Crusoe . . . is the embodiment of economic individualism hardly needs demonstration."[96] What did seem to require demonstration in the decades following, however, was the possibility that there was something other than a strictly individualist interpretation of the English novel. A number of scholars after Watt connected *Crusoe*'s economic representations with its religious argument, just as, a generation later, other scholars have connected the text's economic representations to colonialism and to the nonhuman aspects of Crusoe's world.[97] The evolving consensus seems to be that novels are indeed the stories of liberal individuals, though such individuals have far more nuance than any early twentieth-century account of *homo economicus* would suggest.[98]

My own view, as elaborated in this chapter, is that *Crusoe* bears significant formal continuities with negative figurations of character, that such negative figurations of character had a long and significant gestation as part of some of Christianity's complex theories of representation, and that the class of books now recognized by bibliographers as devotional steady sellers were an important point of dissemination for those negative figures among common readers in the generations leading up to the publication of *Crusoe*. The negative characterological figures in *Crusoe* do anticipate those that will populate Anglophone novels later in the eighteenth century and beyond, as does the continuous narrative structure by which readers are encouraged to engage *Crusoe*. In both of these formal senses, *Crusoe* unmistakably anticipates later novels. Nevertheless, from the perspective of *Crusoe*'s initial readers, these concerns about the status of future novels would be far from inevitable. It is the text's ties to antecedent narrative and figural forms and reading habits—it is, in other words, its participation in an existing media ecology—that would have made *Crusoe* legible to its first readers; whereas, it is the text's mutation of that ecology that makes it a progenitor of the nineteenth-century novel (which, as the case of *The Moonstone* already suggests, happily claimed *Crusoe* among its own). My contention, then, is that *Crusoe* and the world that created it exist in an ironic relation, and the tensions such irony brings should be understood as a key to *Crusoe*'s significance.

Part of the power of any popular text is its ability to absorb and organize ideational and cultural contradictions.[99] If one agrees that culture is vectored by history unfolding in unpredictable ways, then all texts stand to become what Fredric Jameson designates as "transitional," texts in which "individual passions and values" are part of history's "unwitting instruments for the construction of a new institutional space in which they fail to recognize themselves or their actions and from which they can only, either slowly or violently, be effaced."[100] The story I have been telling—from changes in Bible layout to the discontinuous reading of devotional steady sellers to more continuous reading practices of these same kinds of books at the end of the seventeenth century—puts emphasis not only on the slowness of that effacement, but also on its incompleteness. Even at a historical moment such as the early twenty-first century, when novels feel neither like emergent nor residual literary forms—when, for example, they deliberately and unequivocally are called and marketed and read as novels, with separate sales figures and bestseller lists for fiction and nonfiction, or with generic subtitles like *Beloved: A Novel*—they nonetheless continue to draw, however distantly and unwittingly, on a practice of figuring characters that, historically speaking, found formal refinement and amplified circulation in texts that absolutely did not and could not (and probably, had such things been possible, would not) have been called and marketed and read as novels.[101] To put the matter more succinctly, contemporary novels, self-conscious of their novelism, of the novel's supposedly distinct generic history, and of the novel's particular contemporary market share, nevertheless bear indirect traces of the antecedent forms from which they transitioned centuries ago. In much the same way that a computer's "desktop" remediates the expanse of wood or fiberglass on which we might conduct our nondigital labors, any text's formal features are difficult to imagine in radically new terms. The distinctions between different kinds of texts do matter and should be preserved. They should not, however, be accepted too readily, nor without historical qualification. Calling *Crusoe* and *The Pilgrim's Progress* "transitional" texts is my attempt to bring such qualification into relief.

If representations internal to *Crusoe* tie it to earlier printed books in what are now recognized to be other genres, the material text itself none-theless bears some important distinctions from those other books. *Crusoe* was first published on April 25, 1719, and went through six print-ings that year, an unusually large number.[102] The quantity of copies in each printing, however, was around one thousand, a typical number for a prose narrative published in London at the time, leading one bibliogra-pher to the conclusion that publishers were "disinclined to risk unusu-ally large edition numbers for works that might go out of fashion."[103] This disinclination locates *Crusoe* as an artifact of a series of volatile changes in the Anglophone print market, including changes in licensing laws and the effective end of prepublication censorship, the expansion of literacy to nonelite sectors of the population, and a significant expansion of the number of texts in print.[104] But it also makes *Crusoe* something of an exception to those changes, as, ultimately, it never did fall out of fashion. Indeed, the most important detail for understanding the mate-rial history of *Crusoe* (no less than of *The Pilgrim's Progress*) is that the text became a steady seller. It was a book whose sales were sizeable but, more to the point, enduring.

The ways that *Crusoe* became a steady seller, however, did not en-tirely conform to the pattern of devotional steady sellers in the seven-teenth century. This ecology too had mutated by the 1720s. Devotional steady sellers were more or less faithfully reprinted in multiple numbers of editions, and though *Crusoe* was too, its afterlife assumed additional material forms. Within a year of its initial publication *Crusoe* spawned a sequel, *The Farther Adventures of Robinson Crusoe* (1719), with a second sequel, *Serious Reflections during the Life and Surprizing Adventures of Robinson Crusoe* (1720), a year later. These sequels were often appended to the original text and sold as a single work in multiple parts.[105] Addi-tionally, *Crusoe* was serialized in whole and excerpt, though, in distinc-tion from the conventions that would emerge in Victorian London and the post–Civil War United States, serialization followed (rather than an-ticipated) book publication.[106] Selections of *Crusoe* were anthologized; parts of its three volumes were translated into more than twenty lan-guages; it was frequently illustrated; and bowdlerized editions, such as those marketed to juvenile readers, appeared, according to the fashions of the day, well into the nineteenth century.[107] These multiple material forms of the text overlap, expand, and proliferate its plot and its characters under the uniform sign of "Robinson Crusoe." And, as the next chapter will show, it is these multiple material forms—rather than specifically any formal innovation—that make a text look like it belongs to the history of the novel.

⤞ 3 ⤝

The Rise of the Text-Network

Through the whole of the seventeenth century, steady sellers enjoyed durable popularity, nonspecialized readership, and modest but consistent sales, over multiple printings and for generations following their initial publication. By contrast, the rise of the novel within the marketplace of print traded the reliable returns of the steady seller for short-term, high-volume sales.[1] Novels did not render steady sellers entirely extinct, and some novels (including *Robinson Crusoe*) later became steady sellers in their own right. But the real novelty of the novel was in the volume of its sales, and the means by which that volume was achieved is key to the emergence and eventual recognition of the novel as a genre.

If a high sales volume distinguished novels from other kinds of books, however, that volume nonetheless cannot simply be explained by texts printed in single editions. The first edition of *Crusoe*, for example, was printed in 1719 as an octavo volume with 182 leaves (about 364 pages), but as early as that same year and lasting for over two hundred more, the size of this text would continually expand through sequels, serializations, illustrations, translations, and other remediations.[2] It was through these expansion processes that a text like *Crusoe*, which borrowed much formally from the ecology of the devotional steady seller, came to be recognized as one of the canonical pillars of the English novel. Such textual expansions became gradually more common in the eighteenth and nineteenth centuries, providing a central episode in the media history of the novel as a genre. This chapter details two interrelated historical developments behind these expansions.

First, the material advance standing behind the novel's commercial success was a phenomenon that can be called "the text-network." Drawn from the study of classical antiquity, "text-network" refers to texts that exist in a multiplicity of different versions, retailored to fit a host of different contexts, sometimes without a definite original source.[3] This phenomenon of textual multiplicity is recognized by other names in a late capitalist marketplace, where its mutations have led to studies of "supertexts," whose various reiteration "articulates an array of distinct and often conflicting desires," and "media paratexts," distinguished by "textual proliferation at the level of hype, synergy, promos, and peripherals."[4] Text-networks enable multiple points of contact with texts that belong to the same franchise—as, for example, when one sees a *Hunger Games* movie without having read the novel on which it was based, or when one reposts a *Game of Thrones* meme without having watched the show. These multiple points of contact with texts sometimes grant readers (or potential readers) a kind of ambient awareness of proprietary texts, characters, scenes, or details that they may not themselves have encountered by way of an ur-text, thereby amplifying the ur-text's fame without requiring any act of reading it—without, in some cases, requiring that one be able to read at all. Such multiple ways of coming into contact with texts were not an invention of the eighteenth century, but the middle of that century witnessed a particular takeoff of this phenomenon, and two text-networks in particular, those surrounding Samuel Richardson's *Pamela; Or, Virtue Rewarded* (1741) and Jonathan Edwards's edition of *The Life of David Brainerd* (1749), serve as exemplary cases.

By nearly all accounts *Pamela* is among the earliest English texts that can be classified unproblematically as a novel; by many of the same accounts, *Brainerd* is not. Thus, while the rise of text-networks in the eighteenth century Anglophone marketplace marks a major historical development behind the novel's ascendency, it did not immediately occasion a recognizable formal innovation in the kinds of figures that novels represented. The second historical development behind the ascendancy of novels as a genre in the mid-eighteenth century is, paradoxically, the fact that their contents continued to seem relatively similar to the devotional texts that dominated the Anglophone print market in the century prior. In ways that we will become clear, the parallel mid-eighteenth-century text-networks around *Pamela* and *Brainerd* clarify that the material infrastructure for the novel was in place historically before its generic features crystallized. Specifically, while the proliferation of editions and remediations in a text-network helped maintain the high-volume, short-term sales that gradually distinguished novels from other kinds of prose narratives by the *end* of the eighteenth century, pairing *Pamela* and *Brainerd*—two prose narratives that now quite clearly belong to different genres—demonstrates that Anglophone novels, at the moment of their emergence in the *middle* of the eighteenth century, shared significantly similar formal and material features with the religious genres from which they later most pointedly differentiated themselves. Here, as we saw in Chapters 1 and 2, character—the figural representation of persons—provides the connective tissue that links all these prose writings.

I

Anyone in London in 1741 would not have had to read *Pamela* to know all about it. The story of the *Pamela* text-network begins with the first edition of *Pamela,* printed in November 1740 in two octavo volumes (postdated 1741). This edition was reprinted in Dublin in January 1741, just before a second London edition in February and a third in March. When Richardson issued a fourth edition in May 1741, tongue-in-cheek parodies like *An Apology for the Life of Mrs. Shamela Andrews* and *Pamela Censured* had already appeared. An unauthorized, anonymous sequel, *Pamela's Conduct in High Life* (since attributed to John Kelly), was published in London at the end of May and in Dublin by the end of June. James Parry's *The True Anti-Pamela* likewise followed in June, and the two parts of George Bennet's *Pamela Versified* appeared sequentially in June and July. By October 1741—a mere eleven months after *Pamela*'s initial appearance—*Pamela's Conduct in High Life* had a second volume and a reissue of the first, *The True Anti-Pamela* was in its second edition, and a fifth edition of the original two-volume *Pamela* had appeared, as had the authorized (but anonymous) French translation, *Pamela ou la vertu recompensée*. November saw the appearance and multiple piracies of *Pamela: A Comedy* and the first printing of Charles Povey's *Virgin in Eden*. The first edition of Richardson's sequel, volumes 3 and 4 of *Pamela*, appeared in December (again postdated 1742), by which point *Shamela* and *Virgin in Eden* were being reprinted in London, the first volumes of *Pamela* and *The True Anti-Pamela* were being pirated in Dublin, and new responses, such as the anonymous *The Life of Pamela*, were still appearing. *Pamela* was in a sixth edition in 1742, as further responses (including Henry Fielding's *Joseph Andrews*) continued to appear in London, and meanwhile all these texts were reprinted in Dublin and imported to the continent, where they were subject to further reprintings, unauthorized translations, and multimedia (visual and theatrical) adaptations.[5] In the North American colonies, London (and possibly Dublin) imprints of *Pamela* were for sale in bookshops from Boston to Charleston in the 1740s, and the diarist Doctor Alexander Hamilton recorded that at a Boston auction in 1744, Richardson's *Pamela* and Eliza Haywood's *Anti-Pamela* were among the most common titles.[6] The colonial vogue for the book was so great that Kevin J. Hayes calculates that "every copy sent to America was read by about half a dozen people."[7] Such vogue, perhaps, is what motivated Benjamin Franklin to print a single-volume edition in Philadelphia in 1744, but its sizeable production costs meant that imported editions would retail for about half the price.[8] Forty-four copies of *Pamela* remained in the inventory Franklin turned over to his successor in business, David Hall, in 1748, and some of these appear to be still unsold in a state-of-account document between Franklin and Hall as late as 1766.[9] Having learned this costly lesson, in 1751, Franklin and Hall advertised *Clarissa* in an imported London edition.

Like that of *Pamela*, the *Brainerd* text-network consisted of authorized and unauthorized reprintings, multiple adaptations, multiple authors, editors, and translators, and multiple publishing locations. In June 1746, the Presbyterian Society in Scotland for Promoting Christian Knowledge (SSPCK) voted in Edinburgh to print part of Brainerd's missionary journals in the newspaper if, after reviewing it, "they find the same proper."[10] It was not until March 1747 that the SSPCK learned that Brainerd's journals "had caused to be printed" the previous year in Philadelphia, overseen by Brainerd himself, and published in two installments with continuous pagination under the titles *Mirabilia Dei inter Indicos* and *Divine Grace Display'd*. The SSPCK missionary committee reported at the same meeting that "it is proposed by his friends at London, that the Journals be reprinted, [and] The Committee are of the mind that an Abridgment of the same will be sufficient to be reprinted, as there are in many parts thereof, only Repetitions of the same thing."[11] That abridgment was published in London in 1748, with a preface by Philip Doddridge, as *An Abridgement of Mr. David Brainerd's Journal among the Indians*.[12] Subsequent to these two editions was *An Account of the Life of the Late Reverend Mr. David Brainerd,* edited by Jonathan Edwards and published in Boston in 1749.[13] The Edwards edition was reprinted in Edinburgh in 1765, but not before it had been translated into Dutch and printed in Utrecht in 1754. John Wesley's abridgment, based on the Edwards edition, was published in Bristol in 1768, where it was reissued in a second edition in 1771 and again as part of Wesley's *Works* in 1772. A third edition appeared in London in 1793, to be reprinted in Worcester, Massachusetts, the same year. This third edition was reprinted several more times in London and Edinburgh, before a fourth edition appeared in 1812. Meanwhile, another abridgment, this time by John Styles, was printed in London in 1808 under the title *The Life of David Brainerd, Missionary to the Indians, with an Abridgment of His Diary and Journal. From President Edwards*. The Styles edition was reprinted in Newark, New Jersey, in 1811, in Boston in 1812, and went into a "second edition" in London in 1820, followed by a Boston reprinting in 1821. Meanwhile, the Edwards and Wesley editions continued to be reprinted in London, Edinburgh, Glasgow, and Boston, among other places, through the 1810s and 1820s, until the American Tract Society in New York began regularly reprinting a "somewhat abridged" version of Edwards's abridgment, generating "some 68,000 or

70,000 copies" in the scant sixty years between 1833 and 1892.[14] Other notable nineteenth-century editions include a French translation (Lausanne, 1838) a German translation (Zurich, 1851) and a Swedish translation (Stockholm, 1862). An 1856 German translation was also published in New York by the American Tract Society.

Even these brief narrative bibliographies should make a similarity between the two text-networks quite clear: both were aggressively international in scope, with *Pamela* moving from London to the continent and the colonies, and *Brainerd* moving from colonial peripheries and English provinces eventually to London. This inversion in the transatlantic direction of each network begins to explain why the *Pamela* network explodes immediately, while the *Brainerd* network is ultimately broader, producing more copies in more editions but gathering momentum more slowly. Through the whole of the eighteenth century, London was the printing center of the Anglophone world, whose print production far outstripped other printing centers.[15] The immediacy of the *Pamela* network's explosion in the 1740s, then, is in part a consequence of its London debut, which afforded that text kinds of exposure that *Brainerd*, initially published in smaller print centers (Philadelphia, Boston, Edinburgh, Bristol), could not achieve nearly as fast.[16]

The *Pamela* network's London provenance further accounts for the text's subjection to the twin processes of anthologization (extraction) and abridgment (compression), which Leah Price has shown to be a central strategy for marketing novels to readers in the eighteenth and nineteenth centuries.[17] In the case of anthologization, Richardson himself was an agent in this story, reserving the eighth volume of *Clarissa* for *A Collection of Such of the Moral and Instructive Sentiments* as found in the novel, which he also sold separately as early as 1751. He later gutted his other two novels of their plots and recycled the remaining "sentiments" and bons mots into *A Collection of the Moral and Instructive Sentiments, Maxims, Cautions, and Reflexions, Contained in the Histories of Pamela, Clarissa, and Sir Charles Grandison* (1755)—with page numbers corresponding only to the authorized octavo and duodecimo editions of the novels.[18] In the case of abridgment, Richardson's three novels were compressed by 80 or 90 percent into nonepistolary narratives, first published in London in 1756 as *The Paths of Virtue Delineated; or, The History in Miniature of the Celebrated Pamela, Clarissa Harlowe and Sir Charles Grandison, Familiarized and Adapted to the Capacities of Youth.* This text was reprinted in London in 1764 and, subsequent to Franklin's failed 1744 edition of *Pamela*, was the first *Pamela* to be printed in the United States, in Philadelphia in 1791 and again in Cooperstown in 1795.[19] The text was also recycled into a "new edition" in London in 1813, as *Beauties of Richardson.*[20]

While the kinds of multiplatform textual re-presentations that one finds in the case of *Pamela*'s anthologization and abridgment result partly from the text's London origin, this geography proves ultimately to be more of a necessary condition than does genre. While Price has argued that abridgment and anthologization were reserved for the novel by the nineteenth century, their early application to *Brainerd* suggests that this text was not treated any differently in the mid-eighteenth century than a contemporary novel. What is different, however, is the scale of their application. In the case of anthologies, *Brainerd* was never distilled into a collection of sentiments, though several of his words appear in disparate collections. For example, five pages of the Edwards edition were excerpted into *Historical Collections relating to Remarkable Periods of the Success of the Gospel and Eminent Instruments Employed in Promoting It,* published in Glasgow in 1754. Ten more pages of Brainerd's letters appear in several editions of *A Collection of Religious Tracts,* the collective title page for an assortment of separately issued pamphlets bound and sold together, mostly in Philadelphia, marketed to the religious instruction of African Americans, beginning in 1767 and appearing as late as 1784.[21] Six of these ten pages of Brainerd's letters are affixed to the end of a Philadelphia edition of *An Extract of Miss Mary Gilbert's Journal.*[22] Meanwhile, we have already seen that *Brainerd*'s multiple editions include many more abridgments than *Pamela*'s. It is not advisable, however, to attribute *Brainerd*'s corollary contraction to its designation as a religious narrative (as opposed to a novel), for in this respect *Brainerd* was treated like many other generically diverse texts handled by clergymen, such as Wesley, with substantial editing credits.[23] Indeed, within the material form of the text-network, the multiple editions of *Brainerd* are the variations on the text that should be interpreted as the corollary to the multiple responses to *Pamela*.

In both the cases of *Pamela* and *Brainerd,* their textual proliferations often traverse the ur-text's language, form, and medium; however, the reason they can all be recognized to be part of the same text-network is due to the fact that they share a common figure, whose characteristics and story may vary but whose proper name organizes the network. Character became an anchoring feature of text-networks, regardless of whether the name was Pamela or Brainerd, or later, Julie, Charlotte Temple, Werther, or, more distantly, Harry Potter. Comparing eighteenth-century Pamela to twentieth-century Superman, Terry Eagleton identifies each character as "the name for a diverse set of social practices, an emblem encountered at every turn, a domestic talking-point and public declaration of faith."[24] Insofar as the figures at the center of the eighteenth-century's emergent text-networks were multi-sourced commodities whose currency in the marketplace depended on the name affixed to the commodity more than on its form or format, these figures can indeed be seen to be the predecessors of twentieth-century capitalism's trademarks and twenty-first-century capitalism's brands.[25] What does distinguish text-networks from trademarks and brands, however, is that the latter are considered intellectual property, the expression of a corporation's identity. (Furthermore, a corporation dislodges the otherwise tight fit between person and character: Pamela indexes *Pamela,* but Superman indexes DC Comics.) Such a proprietary relation to a character or figure was unknown in the eighteenth century, enabling what James Granthan Turner has described as "a mass of small entrepreneurs [who] exploited the fact that, whatever their individual sensibilities, authors and publishers could *not* own characters and ideas."[26] The figure at the center of the eighteenth-century text-network could be distributed to multiple, nonidentical commodity objects, whose market value was increased through contact with the figure, just as the value of the figure was shored up by the proliferation of commodities bearing its name.

Materially speaking, a text like *Brainerd,* which by nearly no classification could be a novel, could anchor a text-network just as successfully as a text like *Pamela,* now widely recognized as a novel. Genre, in this sense, proves largely irrelevant to the explosion of a text-network in the mid-eighteenth century. However, it would be inaccurate to say that just any text could anchor a text-network. The *Pamela* and *Brainerd* text-networks are each organized around characters, and due to the ways that plot, setting, theme, and even medium become subject to revision among the many texts in a text-network, it is character that comes to matter significantly for the readers who engage with these texts. (It is not an accident, for example, that it is the proper names Pamela and Brainerd that appear or are alluded to in a majority of the titles in their respective text-networks subsequent to their ur-texts.) It should not be surprising, then, that the means of figuring characters in a text-network often relies on the long-refined practices of figuration already detailed in Chapters 1 and 2. Drawing on these established practices, both *Pamela* and *Brainerd* figure their principal characters negatively—that is, in the Augustinian sense, both texts figure their principal characters in terms of their vulnerability.

II

While David Brainerd achieved some fame into the nineteenth century for being the man who allegedly observed that Chauncey Whittelsey "had no more grace than a chair," his truly significant accomplishment was to have died young.[27] His early death followed five years of work as an Indian missionary, beginning in 1742, when Yale expelled the Connecticut native on charges of disrespecting his tutor, and especially following March 1743, from which point Brainerd's missionary work was supported by the SSPCK. The latter position was established through mutual convenience, as Brainerd needed work and Daniel Williams, a Presbyterian minister in England, had recently donated a large sum to the SSPCK, earmarking funds for "three missionary qualified Ministers to abide in infidel Countries."[28] The SSPCK previously had no such programs, and so corresponded with "his Excellency the Governour of *New-England* in *America,* and diverse Ministers and Gentlemen there, in Order to the finding out and employing fit Persons for instructing the native *Indians,*" with Brainerd and Azariah Horton eventually receiving appointments.[29] As a condition of its patronage, the SSPCK stipulated that Brainerd send his missionary diaries to its headquarters in Edinburgh twice annually, and this same organization sponsored the publication of an edited and printed edition of these diaries in 1746 as *Mirabilia Dei inter Indicos; or The Rise and Progress of a Remarkable Work of Grace amongst a Number of the Indians in the Provinces of New-Jersey and Pennsylvania.*[30] Brainerd's death from consumption in October 1747, at the age of twenty-nine and in the Northampton, Massachusetts, home of Jonathan Edwards, occurred as Brainerd was editing a second edition of his missionary diaries for publication, a task that Edwards then assumed and completed two years later.[31] The Edwards edition, *An Account of the Life of the Late Reverend Mr. David Brainerd,* was published in Boston by Daniel Henchman; subvented by subscriptions; and, making only passing acknowledgment of the prior edition, was advertised instead as "chiefly taken from his Diary and his other private Writings, written for his own Use."[32] Brainerd's death, then, enabled him to come forward as a character in his published text and to recede as its principal author, to such an extent that both the immediate and enduring international notoriety occasioned by the Edwards edition has principally reflected on Edwards (in whose complete *Works,* for example, the authoritative scholarly edition of *Brainerd* was published in 1985). *Brainerd*'s significance to intellectual history in the twentieth century was almost entirely, in Joseph Conforti's words, as "Jonathan Edwards's most popular work."[33]

For obvious reasons of chronology, however, the interest taken by the SSPCK in publishing a version of Brainerd's diaries cannot be attributed to Edwards's involvement. And if this prestigious provenance could not plausibly be a motive for the SSPCK, neither entirely could the efficacy of Brainerd's mission, as the printed text does not demonstrate particularly efficient conversion of even a single Native American to Christianity.[34] Instead, the reason the SSPCK invested the time and money required to publish the mission activities of this otherwise unknown soldier of faith—and to have them "delivered at London among Donors and other Charitably disposed Persons"—lies with the remarkable extent to which Brainerd's self-representation in the diaries exemplified certain ideal aspects of Christian figuration.[35] The protagonist of *Brainerd* is an extraordinarily pious young man.

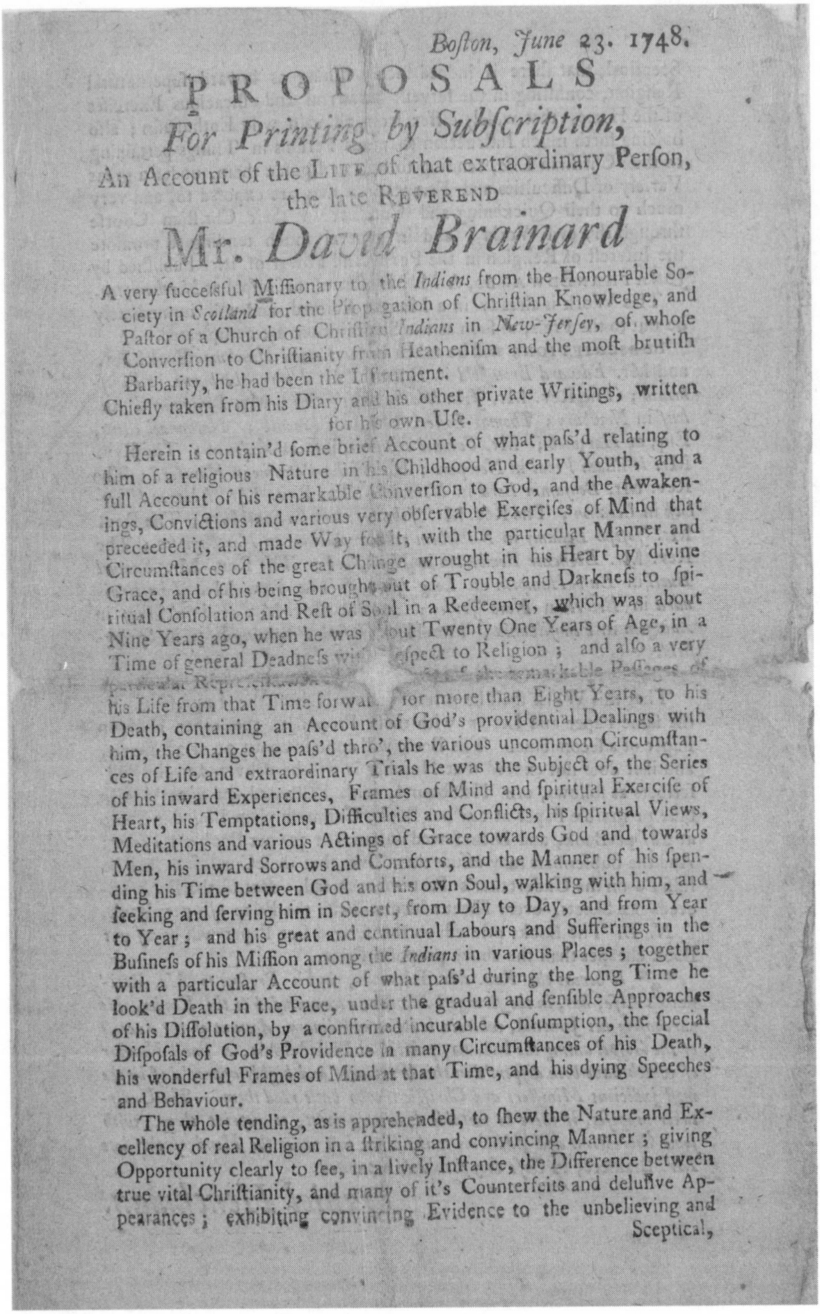

Boston, June 23. 1748.

PROPOSALS

For Printing by Subscription,

An Account of the LIFE of that extraordinary Person, the late REVEREND

Mr. David Brainard

A very fuccefsful Miffionary to the *Indians* from the Honourable Society in *Scotland* for the Propagation of Chriftian Knowledge, and Paftor of a Church of Chriftian *Indians* in *New-Jerfey*, of whofe Converfion to Chriftianity from Heathenifm and the moft brutifh Barbarity, he had been the Inftrument.

Chiefly taken from his Diary and his other private Writings, written for his own Ufe.

Herein is contain'd fome brief Account of what pafs'd relating to him of a religious Nature in his Childhood and early Youth, and a full Account of his remarkable Converfion to God, and the Awakenings, Convictions and various very obfervable Exercifes of Mind that preceeded it, and made Way for it, with the particular Manner and Circumftances of the great Change wrought in his Heart by divine Grace, and of his being brought out of Trouble and Darknefs to fpiritual Confolation and Reft of Soul in a Redeemer, which was about Nine Years ago, when he was but Twenty One Years of Age, in a Time of general Deadnefs with refpect to Religion ; and alfo a very particular Reprefentation of the remarkable Paffages of his Life from that Time forward for more than Eight Years, to his Death, containing an Account of God's providential Dealings with him, the Changes he pafs'd thro', the various uncommon Circumftances of Life and extraordinary Trials he was the Subject of, the Series of his inward Experiences, Frames of Mind and fpiritual Exercife of Heart, his Temptations, Difficulties and Conflicts, his fpiritual Views, Meditations and various Actings of Grace towards God and towards Men, his inward Sorrows and Comforts, and the Manner of his fpending his Time between God and his own Soul, walking with him, and feeking and ferving him in Secret, from Day to Day, and from Year to Year ; and his great and continual Labours and Sufferings in the Bufinefs of his Miffion among the *Indians* in various Places ; together with a particular Account of what pafs'd during the long Time he look'd Death in the Face, under the gradual and fenfible Approaches of his Diffolution, by a confirmed incurable Confumption, the fpecial Difpofals of God's Providence in many Circumftances of his Death, his wonderful Frames of Mind at that Time, and his dying Speeches and Behaviour.

The whole tending, as is apprehended, to fhew the Nature and Excellency of real Religion in a ftriking and convincing Manner ; giving Opportunity clearly to fee, in a lively Inftance, the Difference between true vital Chriftianity, and many of it's Counterfeits and delufive Appearances ; exhibiting convincing Evidence to the unbelieving and Sceptical,

Figure 3.1. Boston, June 23. 1748. Proposals for Printing by Subscription, an Account of the Life of That Extraordinary Person, the Late Reverend Mr. Brainard (Boston: Daniel Henchman, 1748). (American Antiquarian Society)

Other scholars have noted the ways that Brainerd's narrative draws on prior rhetorical models. Such models included biblical sources, which Sandra Gustafson and Laura Stevens have identified, respectively, in terms of Brainerd's self-ascription as a "stranger and pilgrim" (a refrain drawn from Hebrews), and his self-exhaustion to the point of *kenois* (an emptying of self exemplified in 2 Corinthians 12:15).[36] Brainerd's models also included nonbiblical soteriological writings, such as John Grigg has observed in the narrative structure of Brainerd's conversion episode, which conforms to that outlined by Samuel Stoddard (whose *A Guide to Christ* [1714] Brainerd elsewhere identified as "the happy means of my conversion"), and in the day-by-day structure of the whole, which draws on the revival narrative popularized in a 1743 letter by Boston minister Thomas Prince (which was in turn based on Edwards's *Faithful Narrative* [1737]).[37] *Brainerd* citing these sources is not surprising, but their collective presence in the text nevertheless indicates two of its most significant (and underappreciated) aspects. First, the presence of these sources quietly suggests the importance of reading and genre in the construction of narrative self-presentation, even in the case of nonfictional narrative and personal history.[38] Second, and by corollary, the canny means by which *Brainerd* grounds personal history in generic precedent also has the effect of enabling the generic to appear genuine.[39] The text's success, in other words, depends on a self-consciousness about genre that is nevertheless unselfconsciously rendered, so that a reader of the published text would hardly recognize it as a literary construction.

Nevertheless, *Brainerd*'s ability to parlay generic citations into genuine truths meant that the text was always taken to be representative of something. At the manifest level of content, that something was consistently (and clearly) the spiritual struggles of a morally upright young man. Though *Brainerd* offers many pious claims about the power of God, the narrative even more potently delivers an account of its protagonist's reflection of his own deep depravity. The vulnerability of Brainerd's self is often figured as vileness, such that he reports: "I saw so much of my hellish vileness that I appeared worse to myself than any devil"; "felt so vile and unworthy that I scarce knew how to converse with human creatures"; "had still a sense of my great vileness"; "had an afflicting sense of my vileness and meanness"; "still much depressed in spirit under a sense of my vileness and unfitness for any public service"; "saw myself so vile and unworthy that I could not look people in the face when I came to preach."[40] (The trope becomes so frequent than even Edwards condenses wearily: "The three next days he continued in this frame, in a great sense of his own vileness, with an evident mixture of melancholy, in so small degree."[41]) The figurations at the expense of his own goodness work in tandem with observations made about God's greatness, which the text imagines can alone save souls. Such language, for example, characterizes Brainerd's conversion episode, wherein "the more I did in prayer or any other duty, the more I saw I was indebted to God for allowing me to ask for mercy, for I saw it was self-interest had led me to it, and that I had never once prayed for the glory of God."[42] Brainerd here represents the principle according to which self-interest is the opposite of virtue, and, conversely, by which a properly vulnerable self is a disinterested self.

Figuring himself as vulnerable before God, Brainerd both claims and demonstrates his own disinterest; yet, as a model of self-disinterest, his narrative ironically serves the interest of the politically various Christian organizations who publish it. Indeed, different editions of *Brainerd* often calibrated the narrative to different uses. For example, the title of *Mirabilia Dei inter Indicos* announces *"a remarkable work of grace . . . justly represented in a journal,"* while Edwards's preface to the 1749 text asserts instead that the narrative offers an "instance and example" for "representing and recommending true religion and virtue to the world."[43] What had in the first instance been valuable as a representation of grace shifts in the second instance to be valuable as an occasion for provoking grace. These uses differ in emphasis rather than kind. And, indeed, this slippage from record to example does not register as a discrepancy across these two texts because both uses of *Brainerd* are presented as expatiations of the text's manifest figuration of Brainerd's vulnerability before God. They simply expatiate toward slightly different ends, as would subsequent editions of the text. Such different emphases regarding the same vulnerable figure mutated the text to serve multiple, competing but nonexclusive interests over the next hundred years, as the text was printed by Presbyterian, Methodist, and ecumenical societies and in editions often targeted to specific readerships (such as donors, children, or missionaries).

The text's adaptability to these different interests and audiences was reinforced by paratextual commentary (usually prefaces) designed to guide the ways one was supposed to read disinterestedly. The preface to *Mirabilia Dei inter Indicos,* written by SSPCK officials overseeing the publication of the text, argues that "nothing certainly can be more agreeable to a benevolent and religious Mind, then to see those that were sunk in the most degenerate State of human Nature, at once, not only renounce those barbarous Customs, that they had been inured to from their Infancy, but surprisingly transformed into the Character of real and devout Christians."[44] The passage primes the reader's response by describing both the text and a proper reaction to it. Running parallel to this preface's exaltation of Christian character at the expense of Native American custom is the implication that the Christian reader of this text should necessarily take pleasure or delight in this same priority of character over custom. The passage figures a correct or ideal reader response and primes any particular reader to measure their response against it. If that particular reader is not delighted or fails to find the narrative agreeable, the text makes clear that there is something wrong with the way they are reading the text, and not with the text itself. This preface gestures toward conditions of certainty or inevitability as the origin of the same reader response that the text in fact trains the reader to have. Just as *Brainerd*'s generic elements made the text's representations seem genuine, so its paratextual instructions make the reader's response appear deeply felt.

A starker example of such instruction appears in the 1748 London abridgment of *Brainerd* by Philip Doddridge, wherein the editor

> could not hope it might, under the divine Blessing, excite in the Breasts of others that agreeable Mixture of Admiration and Joy, which I had felt in the Perusal of it ; and might engage them likewise to glorify God for the Appearance of his Power and Grace in these wonderful Displays of the mighty Energy of his Gospel ; that I hoped it might also animate the Prayers of many in favour of those who are employed in propagating it, and awaken my Brethren in the

> Ministry to bear their Testimony with greater Zeal and Affection, to those glorious Truths which have been the Power of God to the Salvation of those happy Creatures, who tho' so lately in the darkest and most wretched State, and now *Light in the Lord.*[45]

As before, this preface posits a readership that is conscripted into particular kinds of affective responses to the text (excitement, agreeableness, wonder, animation). To a much greater degree than the preface to *Mirabilia Dei inter Indicos,* however, this preface lays bare its conscripted affective response as a near-tautology: Christian writings will lead back to Christ, readers will glory God in the face of God's glory, salvation will come to the saved. But, as we have seen in Chapters 1 and 2, such tautological reasoning rarely generates problems for readers concerned with pious ends, and, in any case, future paratexts would continue to treat *Brainerd*'s textual figuration as exemplary evidence of piety itself. "Suppose that David Brainerd was not, in fact, the instrument of the saving conversion of a single aboriginal native," proposed a letter to the American *Theological Magazine* a half century later, "was it nothing, however, to the Church of God at large, and considering its endless duration, that he spread among them the knowledge of Christ, and exemplified the power of divine grace, in such illustrious virtue?"[46] Reprising the spirit of the earlier prefaces, this letter estimates exemplification in terms of its self-evidence.

Such estimations, moreover, appear to be consistent with Brainerd's own. Shortly before he died, Brainerd himself wrote an anonymous preface to the 1747 Boston reissue of Thomas Shepard's *Three Valuable Pieces,* in which

> *whoever reads attentively, I'm perswaded must own that he finds a greater Appearance of* true Humility, Self-Emptiness, Self-Loathing; Sense of great Unfruitfulness, Selfishness, exceeding Vileness of Heart, Smallness of Attainments in Grace; *I say he must needs own that he finds more Expressions of deep unfeigned* Self-Abasement *in these Experiences of Mr.* Shepard's *that some are willing to admit of.*[47]

In a manner reminiscent of his own self-figuration, Brainerd enjoins readers to espy in Shepard's journals a deep sense of vileness and vulnerability before God. As with the paratexts affixed to his own publications,

Brainerd's preface avowedly describes another man's inward state and tacitly ignores that the point of such description is both to figure Shepard as disinterested and to solicit his reader's interest. As Brainerd has it, Shepard's virtue simply stands on its own, and the preface's rhetoric describes this virtue without considering whether it also shapes the reader's conception of it.

All these paratexts promise that interested readers could become disinterested selves. Moreover, when Brainerd asks Shepard's reader to "*consider whether there be any Manner of Agreement between* his [experience], *and* theirs" or when Edwards asks Brainerd's reader to consider the latter as an example, these recommendations steer readers toward such disinterest by way of acts of identification with the characters who star in these spiritual narratives.[48] These prefaces don't imagine that acts of identification would conflict with the cultivation of disinterest, and, consistent with the styles of pious reading we have seen in Chapters 1 and 2, these acts of identification vary in at least two ways from the kinds of self-indulgence with which, increasingly frequently, novel readers will be charged through the remaining decades of the eighteenth century. First, identification in these paratexts is not an act of absolute absorption or involuntary mimesis. The reader of Brainerd or Shepard who identifies with these men's experiences is figured as already a Christian, seeking to cultivate his piety. Second, identification in these paratexts requires identifying with weakness, vulnerability, and personal limitations. The extreme vileness displayed in a saint's life is meant to humble the reader, suggesting that reading for identification is not in any simple sense synonymous with reading for pleasure.

Paratexts that solicited readerly identification with Brainerd repeatedly appealed to the self-evident exemplarity of this character. By the 1760s and 1770s, the text-network had become so large due to the main character having become so self-evidently exemplary, that subsequent editions of *Brainerd* trafficked in Brainerd's (and possibly Edwards's) name and fame without needing any further explanation. As the text's various editions circulated more, guidance for the reader (via paratext) could be less. For example, John Wesley encountered the Edwards edition in 1749, and nearly twenty years later, in 1768, reissued his own abridgment as a vehicle by which to promote Methodism in both England

and the American colonies.[49] The Wesley edition includes much of
Edwards's editorial commentary but omits the preface and neglects to
add one of its own, containing only an advertisement assuring that the
following text includes Edwards *"for the most part sumarily [sic] representing the chief things contained in* Mr. Brainerd's *diary: the rest is the
account he gives of himself in his private writings, in his own words."*[50]
This most mediated form of *Brainerd* to date (being an edited abridgment of Edwards's edited abridgement of Brainerd's edited text and
manuscript sources) was advertised as private writing and otherwise
captioned minimally. The consequence of Wesley's transaction in Brainerd's name, however, was not only to proliferate an exemplary text, but
to give readers generous license in determining what about it might be
exemplary. Wesley's edition was thus complicit with what Theodor W.
Adorno, in another context, has diagnosed as the pitfall of didactic art,
that "for the sake of political commitment, political reality is trivialized,
which then reduces the political effect."[51] The irony of the Wesley edition is its assumption that Brainerd's self-evident exemplarity is that
his narrative does not require articulated criteria, and the lack of such
criteria, *pace* Adorno, ultimately entails some creative redefinitions of
exemplarity.

Creative identifications with Brainerd become most evident in the
missionary context.[52] By the middle of the nineteenth century, missionaries had brought various editions of *Brainerd* to six continents, and
many had brought themselves there by his example. Henry Martyn, an
Anglican missionary to India and Persia, read *Brainerd* often, coming to
a sense of clarity in his role as a minister "in the morning after reading
Brainerd" and once recording in his diary "Read Brainerd. I feel my
heart knit to this dear man, and really rejoice to think of meeting him in
heaven."[53] William Carey, a English Baptist missionary to India, who in
youth avoided novels and plays "as much as I did books of religion, and
perhaps from the same motive," later read *Brainerd* with great enthusiasm.[54] Carey's widow Eustace compared him to Brainerd in her edition
of his *Memoir* (though not without noting sardonically that the comparison was overdetermined, Brainerd having been "imitated to the extreme by Mr. Martyn; though the copy is a great improvement upon the
original, it being far less tedious, and in a measure freed from its irreliev-

able gloom").[55] Samuel Marsden, an English Methodist missionary to New Zealand, recalled in his diary "the success of Mr. Brainerd among the Indians" and announced that "this gives me encouragement under my present difficult undertaking."[56] And Robert Morrison, a Scottish missionary to China (and later an accomplished grammarian), reminded himself that "Jesus saves from hell; is now interceding for us, can make us more than sufficient for our mission; and if we be faithful unto death, he will give us a crown of life, and a place, if not with Paul, with Brainerd, or [John] Elliot [*sic*], his faithful missionaries."[57] These missionaries identified with Brainerd, drawing strength and inspiration from the parallels between their service to God and his; accordingly, however, their readings of his narrative were clearly not disinterested.

In short, if David Brainerd was an unlikely candidate to anchor one of the eighteenth century's broadest text-networks, the foregoing analysis should suggest that his self-proclaimed unsuitability is hardly the only irony at work in this history. While the unpredicted reach of the *Brainerd* text-network undoubtedly depended on historically specific conditions of market expansion and transatlantic religious networks, it also depended on the centrality of Brainerd's character within the narrative. More specifically, the success of the *Brainerd* text-network depended on Brainerd's exemplification of piety, in a most Augustinian vein. The narrative's drama is psychodrama, circling around the question of whether Brainerd will realize himself by denying himself. *Brainerd* gave this question its overdetermined answer and in so doing did not fail to appeal to a readership whose commitment to the text (and its characters) had nothing to do with finding out how it ended. Thus, as a character valued for his exemplification of a type, Brainerd could very easily appear in text after text, edition after edition, and continue to attract both printers unfettered by the legal constraints attached to someone else's intellectual property, and readers who, in David Brewer's pithy phrase, "did not seem to worry much about the inauthenticity of a given manifestation."[58] Nevertheless, if a character like Brainerd anchored a text-network, he did so in some tension with the pious aims by which his exemplarity was being figured. Such exemplarity, while routinely held as an ideal by the paratexts that advance *Brainerd*'s earlier editions, was clearly read in variant ways, and while ministers may encourage readers to be disinterested like Brainerd, his readers sometimes seemed all too interested in following suit.

III

Like many missionaries who came after him, Gideon Hawley modeled his career on the example of Brainerd.[59] Nine years younger and still a student at Yale when Brainerd died in 1747, Hawley's most intimate acquaintance with Brainerd's story derives from the Edwards edition, which he carried into the wilderness on a mission to Stockbridge, Massachusetts, in 1755. When Hawley visited Jonathan Edwards's home the next year, however, his attention turned from the minister's edition of *Brainerd* to the minister's copy of *Pamela*.[60] Recorded in Edwards's extant catalog of books as a four-volume edition (and thus a London or Dublin import, based on the revised edition of 1742), this copy of *Pamela* must have been particularly well thumbed, as Edwards lent it to others at least five times between 1754 and 1756, including once to Samuel Hopkins in the same armload as Thomas Prince's *Christian History* (1743) (which popularized the revival narrative on which Brainerd would base his own).[61] Edwards's daughter Esther would borrow it after reading her father's eight-volume *Clarissa,* balking at first that Richardson "has degraded our sex most horridly, to go and represent such virtue as Pamela, falling in love with Mr. B in the midst of such foul and abominable actions," but later writing to Sarah Prince (Thomas's daughter) that there are "some excelent [*sic*] observations on the duties of the Married State in *Pamela.* I shant repent my pains I guss [*sic*]."[62] She was by no means the first to be won over to *Pamela* on pious grounds. Mere months after the book's appearance in London, Rev. Benjamin Slocock recommended *Pamela* from the pulpit of St. Savior's Church, Southwark.[63] Viewing this endorsement skeptically, Brian Downs nearly a century ago proposed that it resulted from a bribe, and this view is corroborated by a contemporary denunciation of Richardson's text in *The Life of Pamela* (1741) "even tho' a Parson should have ten Guineas to recommend it from the Pulpit."[64] Such skepticism about the motives for Slocock's endorsement should not, however, encourage the idea that novels generally, nor *Pamela* particularly, sat awkwardly on a minister's bookshelf in the mid-eighteenth century. Indeed, Edwards was not exceptional in owning many works now regarded as literary but which he esteemed equivalently with works now regarded as religious. A note in Edwards's book catalog characterizes James Hervey's proto-Gothic epistolary tales *Meditations among the Tombs* (1746) and *Reflections on a Flower Garden* (1746) as "the most polite of any that has been written in an evangelical strain" in England.[65] This characterization suggests that Edwards valued these (and presumably other) works for their pious ends, without supposing (as detractors of the novel later would) that genre determined whether those ends were likely to be achieved. Neither ministers like Edwards or Slocock, nor writers like Hervey or Richardson, nor readers like Hawley or Esther Edwards appear invested in the distinctions of genre that would by the nineteenth century partition literary texts from religious ones.

One reason for this generic indistinction may be that, much like *Brainerd*, *Pamela* aims to make an example. Richardson's anonymous "editor's" preface clearly announces that the text's aim is to "Divert *and* Entertain, *and at the same time to* Instruct, *and* Improve *the Minds of the* YOUTH *of* both Sexes," though in what domain, exactly, the text would instruct youth proves somewhat less clear.[66] A subsequent preface by Jean Baptiste de Freval proposes that "this little Book will infallibly be looked upon as the hitherto much-wanted Standard or Pattern for this Kind of Writing," and this view of *Pamela* as an epistolary guide is echoed in an anonymous preface (possibly written by the Rev. William Webster) identifying the book as an "edifying and instructive little Piece" and "a fine, and glorious Original, for the Fair to copy out and imitate."[67] While imitation in this last endorsement could refer to writing lessons as much as moral instruction, it is the latter kind of imitation that preoccupies Pamela herself at several points of her captivity. When Mr. B. attempts to disparage the heroine's reputation in a letter to a farmer on his Lincolnshire estate, Pamela records blearily in her journal that the farmer "made me the Subject of a Lesson for his Daughter's Improvement."[68] Later, contemplating her demise, Pamela writes to her parents with the hope that other youths will not make her "the Subject of their Ballads and Elegies; but that my Memory, for the sake of my dear

Father and Mother, may quickly slide into Oblivion!"[69] While the para-texts figure Pamela as exemplary for her writings as much as (if not more than) for her conduct, Pamela herself can only imagine being judged for her conduct. And, moreover, her interest in being an example is, in these passages, clearly limited to being a good example. The idea of exemplarity in *Pamela* is thereby in tension with the paratexts' promotion of Pamela's exemplary conduct (which conforms with the project of a text like *Brainerd*) and Pamela's self-conscious desire to avoid being a bad example (which does not).

The presence of this tension has everything to do with the fact that exemplarity in *Pamela*, no less than in *Brainerd*, requires citation. *Pamela* frequently alludes to biblical sources, especially Proverbs, as well as to classical ones (Richardson's prefatory comment, for example, references Horace's dictum of "teach and delight"). Dramatic structures and elements of amatory fiction would also appear to be among *Pamela*'s models.[70] While Richardson implicitly denied such citationality in a 1741 letter to Aaron Hill, where he famously claimed that his design was to "introduce a new species of writing," this denial proves far less plausible than his explanation, in the same letter, that *Pamela* was based on actual persons and events.[71] As Morris Golden has demonstrated, London newspapers throughout the 1730s carried stories of Pamela-esque trysts, marriages, and occasionally captivities taking place between men and their maids.[72] Dovetailing with these scandals, an anonymous tale, "Constant and Fidelia; or, Virtue Rewarded," appeared in three installments of the London *Weekly Register* in September and October 1731, though this title may itself be a citation to the anonymous London edition of *Vertue Rewarded; or, The Irish Princess* (1693), a long prose narrative now thought to be an "Anglo-Irish novel" and, perhaps, an indirect influence on *Pamela*.[73] Richardson's heroine's name, meanwhile, was a neologism coined by Philip Sydney in the *Arcadia* (c. 1580).[74] On the whole, a London reader encountering *Pamela* in 1741 might be less struck by its "new species of writing" than by its familiar field of citation.

Similarly unoriginal is *Pamela*'s figuration of virtue. Resonant with the Protestant confessional narratives recorded in Thomas Shepard's Cambridge congregation, with Christian's dilemma in *The Pilgrim's*

Progress, or with Brainerd's journals, *Pamela* relies on a negatively figured character, vulnerable before a more powerful divine force. At the
least, *Pamela's* most famous scene takes pains to register that Pamela's
actions were not her own. Reporting how she fainted as Mr. B. attempted
to rape her, she writes her parents, "Your poor *Pamela* cannot answer
for the Liberties taken with her in her deplorable State of Death. And
when I saw [Mr. B. and Mrs. Jewkes] there, I sat up in my Bed, without
any Regard to what Appearance I made, and nothing about my Neck."[75]
Further, Pamela has "Reason to bless God, who, by disabling me in my
Faculties, enabled me to preserve my Innocence; and when all my Strength
would have signified nothing, magnify'd himself in my Weakness!"[76]
This flurry of negatives ("cannot," "without," "nothing," "disabling,"
"nothing") preserves Pamela's virtue by figuring her deliverance as a
kind of rhetorical negation of harm: Pamela is not unsafe.

While *Pamela's* negative figuration not identical to *Brainerd's* language of "vileness," its rhetorical valuation of the self figured in negative
terms is nevertheless of a piece with that vileness. To be clear, the claim
here is not that *Pamela* or Richardson accepted the theological arguments of Brainerd or Edwards or any earlier writers.[77] Rather, the claim
is that by 1741, a negative figuration of character was rhetorically well
honed, distributed widely in the period's print media, and entirely natu-
ralized as the terms by which Pamela's deliverance would logically be
represented. Drawing on this negative figuration, however, the text also
mutates it, reproducing it with a difference and repurposing it under
conditions that are far more dramatic and far less meditative than those
in which it tended formerly to appear. This difference begins to account
for the questions that many readers raised with regard to the morality of
Pamela, for though the text names the stakes of this potential violation
as Pamela's vulnerability before God, it also dramatizes that violation as
her vulnerability before another man.

If *Pamela,* no less than *Brainerd,* aims to instruct its reader on matters
of moral conduct, *Pamela's* execution of this aim has, broadly speaking,
struck many readers as insufficiently abstract. Defending his nonideal-
ized representations in *Pamela,* Richardson wrote to George Cheyne in
August, 1741 that "in my Scheme I have generally taken Human Nature
as it is; for it is to no purpose to suppose it Angelic, or to endeavour to

make it so."[78] Richardson's stated determination not to represent human nature any better than it is implies that he imagines the objections to *Pamela* are focused on its villain. The tone of this defense, then, reads somewhat prickly, pointing indirectly to the fact that Mr. B. is the one character who, unlike the comparatively angelic heroine, experiences a conversion in the course of the narrative. Mr. B. does so, moreover, in the same manner that Bunyan, Brainerd, and much of Brainerd's audience did: by *reading*—in this case, by reading Pamela's letters. These implications may clarify Richardson's aims, but they also suggest that he was a bit tone-deaf to the actual objections to his narrative, which overwhelmingly scrutinize not its villain but its heroine. Henry Fielding's *Joseph Andrews* (1742), for example, targets the gendered specificity of Pamela, boorishly demonstrating that a male protagonist would not customarily be vulnerable to the same kinds of violations: "How ought Man to rejoice, that his Chastity is always in his own power, that if he hath sufficient Strength of Mind, he hath always a competent Strength of Body to defend himself: and cannot, like a poor weak Woman, be ravished against his Will."[79]

Like Fielding, a majority of *Pamela*'s more expressive readers do not seem to have been persuaded by to the text's aim at exemplarity. While colonial and international responses to *Pamela* were, on the whole, far more laudatory than London responses, the text met with two immediate concerns, both of which shaped the *Pamela* text-network in determinant ways. The lesser of the two objections was to the raciness of the story. Pamela, sitting up in bed "without any Regard to what Appearance I made, and nothing about my Neck" encouraged more delight than instruction in many readers who found, as James Grantham Turner suggests, that "dramatic immediacy operates directly to arouse the spectator, male or female."[80] Or, as the contemporary *Pamela Censured* worried with mock hand-wringing, "In the narrative Part of her Letters, you have interpreted too many Scenes that directly tend to inflame the Minds of Youth."[81] *Pamela*'s raciness proved to be a lesser objection, then, not because many readers missed it, but because many readers didn't ultimately object, and *Pamela* served as a model for pornographic fiction from John Cleland's *Memoirs of a Woman of Pleasure* (1759) to the Marquis de Sade's *Justine ou les malheures de la vertu* (1790).[82] Even Joseph

Highmore's 1742 graphic remediation, *Twelve Prints of Pamela,* frames the story's virtue around an image of "Pamela undressing herself."[83]

In the *Pamela*-inspired pornography, the heroine's alleged virtue succumbed to concupiscent vice, but in the anti-*Pamela* writings more generally, the term opposed to "virtue" was not "vice," but "interest." Thus the second, more serious objection was about Pamela's motives, which for many readers accomplished too much in the way of self-interest to be plausibly virtuous. As Parson Oliver states flatly in Fielding's satire *An Apology for the Life of Mrs. Shamela Andrews* (1741), "I was in hopes that young Woman would have contented herself with the Good-fortune she hath attained, and rather suffered her little Arts to have been forgotten than have revived their Remembrance, and endeavoured by perverting and misrepresenting Facts to be thought to deserve what she now enjoys."[84] Or, in Bernard Kreissman's much later and rather (one hopes, deliberately) droll formulation, "As a simple little serving maid she is unbelievable, but as the sly-puss drawing B. on to marriage, she is only too real."[85] Pamela failed to appear adequately disinterested to many readers because she benefits too splendidly from her acts of virtue. Her negative figurations ultimately turn into positive rewards.

Objections to Pamela's self-interest tapped into an eighteenth-century intellectual problem. The idea of interest began to appear in accounts of human motivation by the late sixteenth century, in what Albert Hirschman long ago described as a "hybrid form of human action" between destructive passions and ineffectual reasoning, "the passion of self-love upgraded and contained by reason."[86] As a name for the copresence of passion and reason, "interest" properly describes the motives for action and not the means. Any action could be an interested one, depending on its cause rather than its effects. Thus, as Nancy Glazner has more recently argued, the rhetorical conflation between "interest" and "motive" enables "interest-thinking to invade domains beyond its original purview," and one could accordingly suspect self-interest behind nearly any action.[87] The expansiveness of this conflation was operative by at least the mid-eighteenth century. For example, Eliza Haywood's *Anti-Pamela* (1741) plays this conflated sense of *interest* for dark comedy, as Syrena Tricksy's mother enjoins her daughter to "let your own Interest be your only Aim," but later, when Syrena becomes so angry with

Figure 3.2. Joseph Highmore, "Pamela Undressing Herself," plate 7 of *Twelve Prints of Pamela: Representing the Principle Actions of Her Life* (London: Carington Bowles, 1774). (Rare Book Collection, Kislak Center for Special Collections, University of Pennsylvania)

...le Mr B. disguised in the Maids clothes with the Apron thrown
...e execution of his Plot. ————
St Pauls Church Yard, LONDON. Published 25 June 1774.

a suitor that she strikes him, "he, who neither loved nor regarded her, but for Self-Interest, return'd with Interest."[88] Haywood's pun on "interest" implies that the right response to a world dominated by a conflation of interest and motive is cynicism.

Within the decade after *Pamela*'s initial publication, Richardson not only began to recognize this objection but also found a way to address it. He started assuming credit for his (initially anonymous) publications, making recourse to a concept of novelistic authorship in an attempt to defend himself and his work from what William Warner has called "the torrent of critique, defense, sequels, and rip-offs unleashed by *Pamela*"— that is, from the *Pamela* text-network.[89] The consequence of this move was to make Richardson's subsequent novels into the authoritative components of the *Pamela* text-network. His next major work, *Clarissa; or, The History of a Young Lady* (1748), accordingly peppers its first volume with the word "interest," but attaches the word overwhelmingly to the eponymous heroine's greedy and ambitious brother, James Harlowe. As early as letter 8 (of the 537 through which readers will wade), Clarissa reports to her confidante Anna Howe that her parents "have not the *interest* in compelling me [i.e., to marriage], as my brother and sister have." Again, in letter 14, she writes, "My brother's interest, without hers [i.e., their sister's], is strong enough, for he has found means to confederate all the family against me."[90] Correcting for something that *Pamela* ignores, *Clarissa* clarifies that interest may indeed align with motive, but that it does not in this heroine's case.[91] Clarissa's actions contribute to her destruction, but her actions are also overdetermined by other people's motives; ultimately, rather than gain economically for her virtue, Clarissa loses fatally. The text's structural displacement of interest from its heroine to other characters renders *Clarissa* Richardson's own, authoritative anti-*Pamela*. The revision of motive in *Clarissa* attempts to scrub the *Pamela* text-network of the taint of interest-thinking. Richardson's determination to make this revision, however, does not suggest that he changed his mind, so much as he changed tactics, representing what he imagined was more or less the same conception of interest in a much less objectionable way.

For all of the foregoing reasons, *Pamela* and *Brainerd,* as objects and phenomena in the literary market of the early 1740s, were ultimately more similar than different. They are similar insofar as both texts draw on the kinds of figurative practices that emerged out of the steady seller and belong to the history of the mediation of characters traced in Chapters 1 and 2. Formally, both texts are modeled on the kinds of devotional literature in which practices of negative characterological figuration were refined, and each are named for characters figured in terms of their vulnerability before God. *Pamela* and *Brainerd* each likewise anchor a text-network that, despite serving multiple interests, ultimately encourages readerly identification with the vulnerability of their respective protagonists. However, the chief formal difference between these two texts is that *Brainerd,* as we have seen, pursues an exemplarity that anchors the humility of its protagonist in his character—that is, in an interior depth illustrated by psychological struggle and doubt. *Pamela,* on the other hand, pursues an exemplarity defined by constancy in the face of dramatic circumstances, such that Pamela's characterological depths appear subordinate to her circumstances. If, as Samuel Johnson reportedly quipped, one does not read Richardson for plot, it nevertheless remains the case that *Pamela* has a plot, a narrative logic that *Brainerd* lacks in the same degree.[92] With respect to their material format, rhetorical form, and moral instruction, the proto-novel differed from the consummate personal narrative only in its execution of their shared aims.

IV

There is an additional way that *Pamela* and *Brainerd* would have appeared similar in the 1740s—and that's simply that they were printed, sold, and read by the same networks of people. Though Richardson was himself an accomplished printer by 1740, he did not publish the first edition of *Pamela*. Instead, in a retrospective letter to Aaron Hill, in late January or early February 1741, Richardson recounts that printers Charles Rivington and John Osborne "had long been urging me to give them a little book (which, they said, they were often asked after) of familiar letters on the useful concerns in common life," and that, as he was assembling this collection of letters, "I thought of giving one or two as cautions to young folks circumstanced as Pamela was."[93] Whether this story is true or apocryphal, it remains the case that Rivington made a habit of soliciting authors, and he did so without any apparent regard for what we would now think of as the market niches they might occupy. Thus, four years before *Pamela,* in May of 1736, Rivington solicited a young and as-yet-unordained George Whitefield for sermons to publish, at the recommendation of an SSPCK official named Thomas Broughton.[94] Rivington was thereby responsible for Whitefield's first printed sermon, *The Nature and Necessity of a New Birth in Christ* (1737), but this success failed to secure him exclusivity with Whitefield, who before the decade was out had published with a number of prominent London printers including James Hutton, John Syms, and, after 1739, William Strahan.

In addition to transacting with the same printers, writers of both "religious" and "literary" texts were subject to the same publishing economics. Strahan's career clarifies that Rivington's simultaneous dealings with the novelist Richardson and the minister Whitefield were not anomalous, though Strahan was yet more economically involved with the successes of the various writers he printed. In the case of Whitefield, Strahan not only printed and published Whitefield's works—that is, both producing the copies and assuming the financial risks—he also played banker, extending Whitefield significant amounts of credit. According to Frank Lambert, "Printing costs constituted Whitefield's single greatest expense, and Strahan enabled the revivalist to flood the Atlantic world with print even when he had insufficient cash."[95] It is not clear one way or the other that Strahan ever recovered Whitefield's debts.[96] But even if Strahan sustained some financial losses, it is important not to misrecognize these, or Strahan's impulse to extend credit to the preacher, as acts of pious charity. Strahan may indeed have had what one contemporary estimation described as a "sympathetic heart" that "beat time to the joy or sorrow of his friends," but nonetheless Strahan's professional interest in Whitefield was as a *celebrity preacher,* as much (and probably more) than as a preacher.[97] Such a conclusion, at least, follows from the fact that Strahan's practice of extending credit to the religious author Whitefield was also his practice with literary authors, such as Samuel Johnson.[98] When Strahan and fellow London-based Scottish printer Andrew Millar brought out Johnson's reputation-making *A Dictionary of the English Language* in 1755, Johnson repaid the compliment in suitably economic terms: according to James Boswell, Johnson's signaled his respect for Millar's literary judgments with the apothegm that "he has raised the price of literature."[99] However, these means were the same by which these men had already, so to speak, raised the price of religion.

What might now be called the "religious" and the "literary" markets for books were relatively unified during the mid-eighteenth century, in London as well as in the North American colonies. The congruence between these markets is generally a consequence of the colonial dependence (before the Revolution) on importation (rather than in-house printing) as a source for books, and more particularly a consequence of the prominent place that Benjamin Franklin assumed among Strahan's clients. Franklin began buying and importing books from Strahan in 1743, writing the next year that he had "long wanted a friend in London whose judgment I would depend on, to send me from time to time such new pamphlets as are worth reading on any subject (religious controversy excepted), for there is no depending on titles and advertisements."[100] Such pamphlets probably had two purposes: they would have allowed Franklin to keep abreast of learned developments in London, and they would have provided him with new materials of a finite length—shorter and therefore less financially risky to print than the *Pamela*-length books he imported—that he could reprint and sell for a profit (effectively, that he could pirate). Franklin's objection to pamphlets on "religious controversy" should be read as a hesitation only to import such materials and not as a hesitation to read or to sell them. Indeed, numbered among the titles Franklin was printing during the same period as his letter to Strahan are Ralph Erskine's *Gospel Sonnets* (1740), Isaac Watts's *Psalms* (1740) and *Hymns and Spiritual Songs* (1741), Joseph Alleine's *Alarm to the Unconverted Sinners* (1741), and *The New England Psalter* (1744).[101] Moreover, an extant bookseller's catalog from 1744 lists among Franklin's inventory Jonathan Edwards's *Some Thoughts concerning the Revival of Religion in New England,* almost certainly the 1742 Boston edition, suggesting that Franklin would not have needed to write to any place as far as London in order to import "religious controversy."[102] If anything, then, the objection to pamphlets on "religious controversy" has to do with their abundance in the colonial book market.

As Michael Warner has concluded, "Eighteenth-century evangelical practices came into being through many of the same media and norms of discourse" as those associated with the Enlightenment.[103]

This copresence, at the production end of the eighteenth-century Anglophone print market, of what are now recognized as distinctly religious and distinctly literary genres, is also reflected at the consumption end. Booksellers' advertisements from Enlightenment London often directed their customers to shops in the vicinity of St. Paul's Churchyard, while in Quaker Philadelphia and Puritan Boston advertisements instead directed potential customers to bookshops adjacent to London-style coffeehouses.[104] This geographical chiasmus in the organization of these key Atlantic commercial ports suggests a grand irony for any literary historian invested in segregating the works of George Whitefield from those of Samuel Johnson. But insofar as these men and their works traveled those market routes together, it perhaps makes more interpretive sense to accept their copresence as evidence of the relative meaninglessness of the categories "religious" and "secular" to describe significant social and economic aspects of daily life in these mid-eighteenth-century cities.[105] From the local inventory of the bookshop to the abstract configurations of "the market," there is little evidence that the presence of unequivocally religious materials (such as sermons or Bibles) alongside comparatively literary works (such as poetry or dictionaries) registered as a significant difference for the vast majority of mid-eighteenth-century readers any more than for writers, printers, or publishers.

Moreover, what does register within the historical record are gentle conflations of these now-discrete markets, often at the level of generic comparisons. For example, Franklin's *Pennsylvania Gazette* reported in 1744 that "no Books are in Request but those of Piety and Devotion; and instead of Songs and Ballads, the People are every where entertaining themselves with Psalms, Hymns and Spiritual Songs."[106] Here, song and spirit are presented as equivalent market commodities. But if this instance of equivalence seems too easy—hymns, after all, are religious songs—a more abstracted rendition of the same comparison registers in Franklin's observations about Whitefield's preaching, such that "without being interested in the Subject, one could not help being pleas'd with the

Discourse, a Pleasure much of the same kind with that receiv'd from an excellent Piece of Musick."[107] In both instances, religious content is compared favorably to music and song, and this poetic (or, by latter-day standards, literary) attribute of religiously themed texts is presented as though it were a desirable asset and not a generic aberration.

While the perceived musical quality of any sermon (and especially of Whitefield's sermons) has to do with the aural aspects of its delivery and the embodied performance of the preacher himself, it's also worth noticing that the printed page's inability to capture such sensory qualities did apparently little to hinder sales. Whitefield famously remediated his enacted performances into printed commodities with unprecedented success. As reported in his prolific *Journal*, he arrived in New York in late 1739 and was told that a local printer had taken two hundred subscriptions for his *Sermons* and *Journals*, while another printer claimed "he might have sold a thousand *Sermons*, if he had them."[108] While the numbers of this self-report may well be exaggerated, the phenomenon herein described, like the craze for devotional literature reported by the *Pennsylvania Gazette*, only confirms Walter Benjamin's sense that the acquisition of books bespeaks "a relationship to objects which does not emphasize their functional, utilitarian value."[109] Accordingly, a rigid partition between the uses of devotion and the uses of pleasure, or between the corollary genres of the sermon and the song, promotes misrecognition of the ways and means that printed books were encountered in the first half of the eighteenth century.

Even after the rise of the text-network changes the economics of printing, encouraging texts anchored around characters to go through all kinds of expansions and remediations, no real difference obtains between literary and religious works. At their appearance in the 1740s and 1750s, texts now recognized unobjectionably to be novels weren't understood as formally innovative, and certainly didn't seem to stand apart (in terms of their contents, their figurations, or their audiences) from other kinds of works that that are now unobjectionably recognized not to be novels. Nevertheless, if a text like *Pamela* is now often aligned with Johnson's *Dictionary* as literary, while a text like *Brainerd* is instead aligned with Whitefield's *Sermons* as religious, this is so as an indirect consequence of a later mutation in the intergeneric economic organization of the mid-eighteenth-century Anglophone print market that produced all these texts initially. Yet, as Chapter 4 will show, when that differentiation between the literary and the religious does begin in the last quarter of the eighteenth century, it has less to do with changes in novels themselves in this period than with the rapidly transforming fate of religious publishing.

❧ 4 ❧

Printers, Libraries, and Lyrics

In their formal and material manifestations, Anglophone novels were not significantly different than many other kinds of printed prose narratives in the mid-eighteenth century. Formally, novels drew on rhetorical devices honed previously in Protestant soteriological writings. Materially, all these books were generally available in the same bookshops and libraries, on the same tables and shelves, printed in equivalent size formats with similar lengths, and sold for comparable prices. As well, all these books were subject to processes of textual remediation (including anthologization, abridgement, adaptation, translation, serialization, and illustration) that expanded their notoriety by means of text-networks. A minister like John Wesley, for example, could abridge an edition of *The Pilgrim's Progress* in 1743 without concern for any significant distinctions between piety and plot, between ministers and creative writers, or between texts designated as novels and texts designated religious. Wesley's small duodecimo edition of just over fifty pages strips Bunyan's story to its pious pith. Doing so, however, implies no objections to character-driven narrative generally, nor to Bunyan's narrative specifically—other than to its length. Readers seemed generally satisfied with Wesley's editorial judgment, and his *The Pilgrim's*

Progress went through six editions in his lifetime, with a seventh before the century was out.

Little if anything in 1743 would have encouraged Wesley to distinguish between pious and literary texts—not printers, not readers, and, for the most part, not texts themselves. While Richard D. Altick is basically correct to argue that Wesley's aim was "to provide a course in polite literature that would relieve the cultural narrowness of Methodist readers at no cost to their piety or morality," the present chapter will demonstrate these categorical distinctions between literary and pious reading are anachronisms, projected back onto the 1740s from the vantage of a period after the 1790s.[1] Altick rightly sees that Wesley's *The Pilgrim's Progress* blurred what now look like generic lines, but he fails to appreciate that such lines were not in place in 1743. Indeed, as late as 1771, Benjamin Franklin, writing in the first part of his *Autobiography,* would matter-of-factly describe *Pamela* as an imitation of *The Pilgrim's Progress,* the latter being "the first that I know of who mix'd Narration & Dialogue, a Method of Writing very engaging to the Reader, who in the most interesting Parts finds himself as it were brought into the Company, & present at the Discourse."[2] Through much of the eighteenth century, polite literature cost nearly all its readers nothing in the way of piety or morality, for polite and pious works were not understood as categorically distinct.

By the end of the century, however, these similarities between Anglophone novels and Protestant narratives definitively break down, and the present chapter surveys multiple causes for that breakdown. In overview, the story goes like this: if texts we now recognize as novels and those, for the sake of this argument, I shall anachronistically call "books of piety," were both printed under the same material circumstances through the 1740s, that proved gradually less true in the second half of the century. Due to economic exigencies and changes in the capitalization of London printing, books of piety began to be printed under auspices other than just those of the commercial London print market, so that they could more readily be circulated for free by religious organizations. This subtraction of books of piety from the marketplace of print created room for the gradual expansion of novel reading, especially through an increase in circulating libraries, many of which, in the

1770s and after, were maintained by booksellers. These bifurcated material conditions under which novels and books of piety were printed initially had little impact on the habits of readers, in part because an expanding eighteenth-century commercial culture altered the social value of books as well as the motives and means by which readers access them. These last changes colluded with changes in publishing, without being clearly caused by them. When the social and market distinctions between novels and books of piety found belated recognition in the 1790s, each kind of book for the first time began to be seen as the other's competitor, giving rise to a polemical (and confused) antinovel discourse nearly fifty years after novels first began to appear in the Anglophone world. What we now thereby recognize as two different kinds of books were not, however, the only competitors in the literary field. In the wake of debates about the moral value of novel reading, the new species of Romantic poetry that emerged around 1800 vied as well for the categorical laurel of "literature," but which, like the books of piety with which novels were also competing, proved economically unsustainable by comparison.

Although novel reading eventually became a respectable middle-class habit in the nineteenth century, and though members of the late eighteenth-century bourgeoisie did increasingly read for identification with characters—becoming, in Jürgen Habermas's phrase, *"sujets de fiction* for themselves and others"—there was no inevitability to these circumstances.[3] Indeed, for most of the second half of the eighteenth century, many readers, ironically, may not have found either novels or novel reading especially *new*. As innumerable scholarly studies have demonstrated, novels were providing readers with points of identification—with characterological depths, in which readers were finding and creating aspects of themselves—but such characters were also found in theater, and Chapters 1–3 have detailed some of the ways that Protestant soteriological writings provided another long-developing set of rhetorical devices for characterological figuration. If by the late eighteenth century novels were beginning to be both a respectable pursuit and a catalyst for bourgeois self-identity, it is neither obvious nor prudent to pin these changes on novels themselves. Novels and novel reading are better understood as symptomatic of a series of broader changes in both printing and reading books, which novels did not themselves precisely cause.

More than the previous chapters, the present one concentrates on a series of historical developments and publishing practices. Its aim is to relate a sequence of roughly coincident changes in the economics of book publishing and in the social value of books as commodities. Most of this chapter's evidence moves away from that of readers, who prove unreliable because, as the middle of this chapter discusses in greater detail, they remain largely unaware of changes in late eighteenth-century book production until those changes are for the most part in place. My argument thereby expatiates on the thesis that the history of the novel as a genre cannot be considered independently of the material conditions under which those same novels are printed and read. Furthermore, it develops that thesis by demonstrating that "the rise of the novel" in the Anglophone world in the second half of the eighteenth century may have far less to do with the independent success of this genre than with the economic failure of its competitors.

I

In 1742 Parson Adams, wandering through the satirical London of *Joseph Andrews,* could be discouraged by a bookseller from printing his sermons on the grounds that "the Trade is so vastly stocked with them, that really unless they come out with the Name of *Whitfield* or *Westley,* or some other such great Man, as a Bishop, or those sort of People, I don't care to touch."[4] This exchange turns on a visual pun. Its humor comes with the misspelling of the names of the great men whom the bookseller seeks to print—suggesting both that he is sloppy in his trade and inattentive in his faith. This orthographic blunder is only legible to the reader of the printed book, but appearing there it tells a joke about the entire industry of printing sermons in midcentury London: that an author's greatness in life was tautologically bound with his appearance in print, sales making for fame and fame making for sales in equal and inseparable measure. If *Joseph Andrews* accordingly displays some cynicism toward the explosion of text-networks around figures like Whitefield and Wesley (to say nothing of Pamela), that cynicism is due in part to the relatively unprecedented conditions of the London print market during the first decades of the eighteenth century.

Among the more well-known of those conditions is the lapse of the Licensing of the Press Act of 1662, sometimes retroactively identified as the Copyright Act of 1710 (and alternately known to historians as the Statute of Anne), whose consequence was to end the publishing monopoly of the Stationers' Company of the prior century and a half, which indirectly enabled greater access to printing by effectively granting copyrights to individual authors.[5] The first decades of the eighteenth century accordingly saw the rise and invention in England of the role of author, though in complex ways this figure remained bound (economically and sometimes legally) to printers and publishers.[6] Would-be authors could not, after all, appear in print without printers to supply the technological means and publishers to risk the capital. Though more kinds of works by more kinds of people could potentially be printed after 1710, printing still entailed financial risks, and an increase in the number of potential printed works in itself did little to guarantee publishers reliable returns. The financial risks of printing were often finessed in midcentury London by partnerships between authors, printers, and publishers (of the sort discussed in Chapter 3 in the case of William Strahan) or by authorial claims to celebrity (of the sort *Joseph Andrews* mocks). Thus, while readers of *Joseph Andrews* are discouraged from assuming that Parson Adams's sermons deserve to be printed, the text nevertheless recognizes Adams's ambitions for print as typical and his inability to realize those ambitions as systemic.[7]

This system, which was in place by the 1740s, restructured significantly by the beginning of the nineteenth century. One factor in this restructuring was the infusion of capital into the printing business by third parties and corporate bodies. The precedent for such capital came in the form of job printing, a long-standing practice in the print trade by which a printer did not himself assume the financial risks of a particular print job but effectively did it on commission, with the customer paying for the whole edition and distributing it how he (or, more rarely, she) pleased. Job printing represented pickup work for printers, and, as we will see, through the eighteenth century, a particular form of job printing became economically important in London. Outside London, however, job printing was especially crucial to provincial and colonial printing economies.

To understand the significance of job printing for the business of early eighteenth-century printing more generally, the colonies—the "laboratories of modernity"—offer a useful example.[8] While nearly all eighteenth-century printers suffered from routine undercapitalization, this circumstance became exaggerated further from London, where supplies like paper and type were more scarce and more expensive, and where steady printing jobs were often less in demand. Even in larger colonial cities like Philadelphia, no successful printer could have sold only what he printed, and many colonial printers traded wares across regions in order to diversify their inventories.[9] As the most successful colonial printer of his time, Benjamin Franklin found additional ways to avoid the financial risks associated with his undercapitalized trade. Between 1728 and his retirement from active involvement in the printing business in 1748, Franklin printed a total of about 310 books and pamphlets, but 80 of these were government commissions, and about 110 (more than a third of the total) can be shown by his records to have been subsidized by third parties.[10] These subsidies came from several sources, one of which was corporate, and here Franklin's business practices were not unique. In New England between the 1740s and the 1780s, the printing costs of many election sermons, for example, were underwritten not only by their authors or, in the case of a deceased author, by his relatives and friends, but by assemblies, congregations, or other corporate bodies, many of which came together specifically for the purpose of bringing a text into print, organized by a church collection or even by the social opportunity to be part of a printer's subscription list.[11] Other subsidies came from wealthy individuals. Among the pamphlets Franklin printed were those paid for by Count Nicolaus Ludwig von Zinzendorf, on behalf of the United Brethren, an ecumenical organization affiliated with the Moravian Church, evangelizing among the German-speaking population of the mid-Atlantic.[12] Zinzendorf commissioned Franklin to print more than a dozen pamphlets in 1742 alone.[13] Likewise, Selina Hastings, countess of Huntington, as an extension of her commitments to the Methodist cause, sponsored several of the earliest London publications

B. LUDEWIGS

WAHRER

BERICHT

De dato *Germantown* den 20^{ften} Febr. 174$\frac{1}{2}$.

An feine liebe TEUTSCHE,

Und

Wem es fonft nûtzlich zu wiffen ift,

Wegen Sein und feiner BRÛDER

ZUSAMMENHANGES

Mit PENNSYLVANIA,

Zu Prûfung der Zeit und Umftánde *ausgefertiget*;

Nebft einem P. S. de dato *Philadelphia* den 5ten Martii;

Und einigen

Unfre LEHRE ûberhaupt und diefes SCHRIFTGEN infonderheit

Erláuternden BEYLAGEN.

PHILADELPHIA,
Gedruckt bey BENJAMIN FRANKLIN.

Figure 4.1. *B. Ludewigs wahrer Bericht de dato Germantown den 20sten Febr. 1741/2* (Philadelphia: Benjamin Franklin, 1742). (Historical Society of Pennsylvania)

by black British and African American authors, including Phillis Wheat-
ley's *Poems on Various Subjects, Religion and Moral* (1773) and *A Narrative of the Lord's Wonderful Dealings with John Marrant, a Black*
(1785).[14]

Huntington's example makes clear that it was not only in the colonies
that the undercapitalization of the print trade created entrepreneurial
opportunities. Both Zinzendorf's patronage of the United Brethren and
Huntington's of the Methodists were part of a larger trend through the
eighteenth century by which individuals would direct wealth, not to
churches or parishes or congregations, but to an emergent type of religious philanthropy. Known to historians as voluntary associations,
these philanthropic religious groups were sometimes aligned with de-
nominations but were typically staffed by laity and acted independently
of church authority. Many such societies had existed before the 1740s:
the Society for Promoting Christian Knowledge (SPCK) was founded in
1698; the Society for the Propagation of the Gospel in Foreign Parts
(SPG) in 1701; the Presbyterian Society in Scotland for Promoting Christian Knowledge (SSPCK) in 1709. However, in the early mid-eighteenth
century, voluntary associations began to take as part of their mission the
collection and supply of capital in order to finance the printing of large
numbers of pious texts. While voluntary associations had often relied,
like the United Brethren and the Huntington Connexion, on generous
donors, by the 1740s they began instead to grow subscription lists in
order to fund their publishing ventures. Between 1745 and 1765, for
example, the SPCK's subscription list nearly tripled in size (from 167
subscribers to 425), and the number more than doubled again by 1785
(to 939 subscribers).[15]

These subscription lists (along with other forms of charitable contribution) collected capital to finance printing that, significantly, was not
done in-house, but instead by job printers. Eighteenth-century voluntary
associations commissioned and printed works, but, unlike nineteenth-
century organizations such as the British and Foreign Bible Society
(founded in 1804) and the American Tract Society (founded in 1825),
eighteenth-century voluntary associations generally did not run their
own presses.[16] Their print jobs were more often commissioned and executed within the London market. After 1765, for instance, the SPCK's

printer was John Rivington. As we saw in Chapter 3, his established London firm had been responsible, according to Samuel Richardson, for requesting the volume of polite letters that became *Pamela*.[17] The progress of religious publishing in the second half of the eighteenth century can be roughly charted as a shift from job printing to tract printing, but, as we will see, the progress of this shift involved a large number of gradual and uneven developments.

Even the particular titles that voluntary associations sought to publish were subject to alterations over time. For much of the eighteenth century, the SPCK aimed to give away Bibles and volumes of the New Testament. These were, however, costly to produce, and between 1750 and 1790, the SPCK gave away somewhere just above 3,000 Bibles per year, and about 5,000 per year in the century's final decade. On the other hand, in the 1790s alone, they distributed more than thirteen times as many pamphlets of moral instruction (an average of 68,348 per year).[18] The SPCK's interest in publishing a variety of pious texts was typical of other voluntary associations. A 1741 catalog of the "Missionary's Library" from the SPG, for example, lists "ENGLISH Bible in Folio, of the last Edition, with the Bishops of *Worcester* and *Peterborough*'s Chronology. Common Prayer Books with 39 Articles, and Ordinals. Book of Homilies. Bp. *Sparrow*'s Collection of Canons. Archbishop's Book of Orders, Injunctions, &c. to be read in Churches. *Cambridge* Concordance best Edition."[19] A complete collection of such books did not come cheap, and more often than simply distributing texts like these for free, voluntary associations would sell them (sometimes directly through the text's printer, acting as bookseller) at a discounted price to members of the association, who were instructed to distribute them for free.[20] The Society for Promoting Religious Knowledge among the Poor (SPRKP), founded in London in 1750, took precisely this tactic, with one member in 1769 recalling two rules for distributing books: "The first was to give to the religious poor who appeared to be very serious, and earnestly longing after such helps to forward them in the divine life . . . The second was to give to such as seemed very ignorant, having little or no sense of religion, but appeared to be sober-minded, of good morals, and willing to receive religious instructions."[21] These rules applied to the distribution of both costly Bibles and inexpensive seventeenth-century pamphlet reprints, including works like Richard Baxter's *Call to the Un-converted* (1658) and Joseph Alleine's *An Alarme to Unconverted Sinners* (1672).[22]

While voluntary associations made a number of attempts to keep printing costs down, profit never seems to have been their aim. Their various subscriptions, donations, discounts, and printing subventions rarely if ever guaranteed profits, though they certainly guaranteed the amplified circulation of the contents of their printed works. Voluntary associations thereby offer an example, contra the historical presumption by which capitalist economics are seen as the footing of the print trade, in which circulation, rather than profit, is upheld as an end goal for printing.[23] In 1748, for instance, members of the SSPCK "directed Mr [Adam] Anderson [secretary to the correspondents at London] to purchase One hundred copies [of Brainerd's memoir] to be sent hither for the use of Members of this Society, and authorised him to purchase as many more copies as shall be found proper to be distributed among the correspondent members and other charitably disposed persons at London."[24] Purchasing books the printing of which your organization had already subsidized offers no recipe for keeping the SSPCK's ledger in the black. But it does suggest the possibility that texts printed under the auspices of religious organizations were positioned to drum up enough subscribers, and perhaps enough capital, so that their publishers—the voluntary associations—could move many more copies of these commissioned pious texts than of whatever other texts the same printers were publishing at their own expense.[25]

At least two different sets of motives were at work, then, in the publishing of religious texts by voluntary associations. From the economic perspective of printers, job printing for voluntary associations became a relatively reliable aspect of the London print trade after the middle of the eighteenth century. From the more pious perspective of voluntary associations, however, job printing was an expense—a necessary one if societies wanted to send printed works into circulation, but also one whose costs were always an obstacle to even greater circulation. While the proliferation of voluntary associations was important to the midcentury economics of the London print trade, the voluntary associations themselves were ever attempting to maximize circulation and minimize cost.

Consequently, voluntary associations began slowly to pull out of the jobbing economy of the London trade, which had expanded around them. Such attempts at subtraction from the jobbing economy are particularly clear in the case of John Wesley's printing practices. Beginning in the 1740s, Wesley supplied the Methodist Societies under his control with an eclectic range of books and pamphlets, and these were printed by various job printers—his 1743 edition of *The Pilgrim's Progress* was printed in Newcastle upon Tyne, and his 1768 edition of *Brainerd* was printed in Bristol, with other works also coming out of London and Dublin. In 1778, however, Wesley moved his Book Room to the new City Road Chapel in London and established a printing press, where he employed his own printer, John Paramore.[26] Apparently never interested in printing Bibles, Wesley's prolific media production focused mostly on short works, which can fairly be considered the forerunners of nineteenth-century tracts. These reprised the logic of the seventeenth-century steady sellers, insofar as they were reprints of familiar, well-loved, and unproblematically pious texts, inexpensively produced and easy to promote, for their targeted reader would already have heard of these titles, authors, and characters.[27] The in-house production of these titles, furthermore, lowered expenses, and Wesley and his Methodist organizations found it economically feasible to give these books away at little cost.

While not all voluntary associations hired their own printers, as did Wesley, many in the last quarter of the eighteenth century began to move away from the established version of job printing and toward partnerships with single printers. After 1720, Charles Ackers, printer of the *London Magazine,* did a few jobs for the SPCK and some of its prominent members, and in 1722, the SPCK commissioned Ackers to cut a fount of English Arabic type for a projected Arabic edition of the Psalter and New Testaments, which Ackers borrowed back in 1728 to print two biblical commentaries for the SPCK.[28] The SPCK was, at about the same time, working with Joseph Dowling and, after his death in 1734, with his widow (whose name I have not been able to recover), who perpetuated the business. In 1745, she was succeeded by Benjamin Dodd, though the SPCK continued in this period to employ others, including John Oliver, to print books and maintain warehouses. By 1765, however, the SPCK was working exclusively with the Rivingtons, a relation that continued through successive decades.[29] Likewise, the SPRKP worked with John Ward before 1763, and with Thomas Field between 1763 and 1788, and then with Thomas Wiche or Wyche, who joined the SPRKP in 1794.[30]

Printing for voluntary associations provided these printers with relatively reliable income, but a sizeable portion of their labor was directed toward the production of books and pamphlets that they could not catalog among their other titles for sale at market prices. Some printers nonetheless found related opportunities to the side of job printing and pursued "pious publishing ventures of their own," according to Scott Mandelbrote, in order to take advantage of "the captive market."[31] But these opportunities often required a lot of finesse. For example, Rivington printed Hannah More's anonymous tract in reply to Thomas Paine's *The Rights of Man* (1791), *Village Politics. Addressed to All the Mechanics, Journeymen, and Day Labourers, in Great Britain. By Will Chip* (1792), after she sought him out precisely because was he the SPCK printer, imagining that such a move would distance herself from suspicions about the pamphlet's authorship.[32] But her working relationship with Rivington counted for little when, three years later, More and Henry Thornton, inspired by Wesley's pious pamphlets for the poor, began to circulate their series of Cheap Repository Tracts, which were instead printed by the London firm Evans and Hatchard, as well as by a Bath printer, Samuel Hazard. It was only following on the enormous success of the Cheap Repository Tracts—which achieved, according to one historian's jaw-dropping estimate, nearly two million copies in their first year—that Rivington revived the relationship with More, producing in partnership with Evans, Hatchard, and Hazard a three-volume, uniform edition of the tracts, designed for a middle- and upper-class market, for which he was able to secure the copyright from Thornton.[33] Such a lucrative deal for the printer was noteworthy, in part because it was unusual.

Though all these examples confirm that London printers were printing books of piety through the end of the eighteenth century, the same printers were, generally speaking, not publishing them—that is, not risking the capital, not controlling the inventories, and not determining the contents of books of piety. Usually only when voluntary associations asked for their involvement did printers act as booksellers for one or another society, and in these cases they typically were selling quantities of books of piety at discounts to society members in order that these books could later be distributed for free. Additionally, books of piety themselves were circulating in record numbers by the 1790s, often in the form of pamphlets or tracts, many of which bypassed the need for a bookseller as they were sold directly to the poor, often for less than a penny. Whereas London printers had been regularly conscripted into job printing for religious societies in the early eighteenth century, by that century's close, tract printing was beginning to leave them behind. One exception who proves this rule is Joseph Johnson, who after 1790 would publish most major authors of British Romanticism, many of whom were Dissenters—including Mary Wollstonecraft, William Godwin, Joseph Priestly, William Wordsworth, Charlotte Smith, and Samuel Taylor Coleridge—but who also, since its comparably late inception in 1783, served as the exclusive printer for the Society for Promoting the Knowledge of Scriptures (SPKS). However, Johnson's printing for the SPKS and his more prestigious publications with these prominent authors can be seen as continuous, at least insofar as the SPKS was commissioning him to print relatively substantial and erudite works—objects physically as well as intellectually upmarket from many of the available books of piety—in accordance with its founding mission to combat injudicious enthusiasms disseminated by other societies through short religious tracts.[34] At the end of the eighteenth century, cheap, profit-neutral short books of piety were rapidly becoming synonymous with religious print. By 1814, the *Belfast Monthly Magazine* could report a meeting of the newly organized Cheap Book Society, explaining that "Societies exist in this country, for circulating Bibles and religious tracts, but none, the sole object of which, is, to provide good books not of religious description, for the use of the poor."[35]

What the London print trade witnessed at the end of the eighteenth century, then, was a focused subtraction of books of piety from the broader commercial production and consumption patterns—a subtraction by means of which books of piety continued to be printed, but as inexpensive, in-house productions with high-volume, profit-neutral, widely canvassed circulations. In the long run, I am suggesting, such changes in the production of these books is one reason we now regard them as generically distinct from many of the books that remain in the market, such as novels.

The same can be said of the examples considered in Chapter 3. In the twenty-first century, inexpensive copies of *Brainerd* are published by a purveyor of Christian books like Baker Publishing, while inexpensive copies of *Pamela* are published for a competitive textbook market by major firms such as Penguin and Oxford University Press. This distinction in the publishing of these texts had already obtained by the early nineteenth century, however, as *Brainerd* was kept in print by tract societies, and *Pamela* by commercial London publishers, a bifurcation that can in turn be traced back further to the above-narrated changes to the book market in the late eighteenth century. And while there are other complications along the way (for example, both *Pamela* and *Brainerd* also now exist in scholarly editions, marketed to libraries, as well as cheap, out-of-copyright reprints designed to undercut the textbook market), my point is that the enduring economic circumstances, which sent these two texts on trajectories toward homes with different kinds of publishers, simply did not exist in the 1740s, when each of these texts first appeared. They were not a feature of the London through which Parson Adams first walked, hocking his sermons, though they would almost certainly have been when, in the last years of his life, William Strahan reintroduced Parson Adams in a twelve-volume duodecimo edition of *The Works of Henry Fielding, Esq: With the Life of the Author* (1783).[36]

The preceding discussion has focused on the infusion of capital into, and its subsequent subtraction from, the London print market by voluntary associations assuming the financial risks for an increased number of printed books with pious themes. It has not talked specifically about novels, on the view that the significance of novels to the English book trade has a lot to do with the books from which they came to be distinguished. This view is not frequently stated, though it is implied by existing scholarship. To be sure, no sensible historian thinks that the London book trade failed to undergo significant transformations in the eighteenth century. William St Clair has detailed shifts in reading habits; James Raven has explored changes in job printing; David

McKitterick had documented a growth in the number of master printers at the end of the century (nearly doubling from 124 in 1785 to 216 in 1808).[37] These and other historians also display general agreement that over the course of the century the quality of printing technology gradually improved and the volume of printed items increased, as did the numbers of readers, authors, and book buyers. However, the event called "the rise of the novel" factors little into these developments. The generic distinctions between books—the niche publication markets that differentiate a novel and a sermon, for example—were not understood to be, and cannot easily be retroactively classified as, a significant aspect of the trade in this period. After the 1740s novels did attract the attention of printers and publishers interested in the potential payoff that comes with high-volume, short-term sales. But as a genre, novels spark no boom in the Anglophone publishing industry.[38] In fact the market economics of London printing displayed no significant growth between 1750 and 1800, during which period eighteenth-century novels were in ascendancy.[39]

None of this is to say that novels *aren't* significant. Rather, as we will see, the cultural significance of novels begins to be established through readers' interest and through the modalities of text-networks that familiarize potential readers (and, moreover, may reward those readers with cultural capital garnered by their familiarity) with characters in books they may or may not have read. Novels begin to matter in the eighteenth century for social reasons, having less to do with genre and more to do with the changing status of books among other commodities and the changing ways that readers access them.

II

The last quarter of the eighteenth century witnessed a bifurcation of the conditions under which novels and books of piety were being printed. Yet those differences did not have an immediate impact on readers. For the whole of the eighteenth century, various kinds of prose narratives cohabited the shelves of book owners of diverse social positions. As we saw in Chapter 3, Jonathan Edwards's library, for example, included copies of both Richardson's *Pamela* and *Clarissa.*[40] While a New England minister's library consisted largely of theological writings (especially through the seventeenth century), the relatively extravagant size of its holdings would signify even to nonspecialist readers what Michael Warner has called "the relation between bibliotechnical capital and professional authority."[41] Among ministers, however, Edwards was a particularly avid book buyer, and his collecting tended in some eclectic directions.[42] This eclecticism was consequential for Edwards's associates. The many people who (as we have seen) borrowed Edwards's copy of *Pamela* demonstrates that a minister's library was a significant point of dissemination for books in the colonies during especially the first half of the eighteenth century, particularly for those individuals (like his daughter Esther Edwards) without access to college libraries. Similar patterns emerge in the English provinces. In Wales, Eleanor Butler and Sarah Ponsonby, the "Ladies of Llangollen" who eloped together in 1778, entertained aristocrats and writers in their impressive approximation of a gentleman's library, despite the fact that their household was not headed by any gentleman.[43] One thinks as well of the Anglican rector George Austen, whose daughter Jane would hone her early literary skills in her father's library and among her bookish siblings in rural north Hampshire.[44]

While the contents of a minister's library tended to reflect the intellectual orientation of his vocation, the contents of a lay person's library would tend much more to reflect her or his individual tastes. The selections of Lady Mary Wortley Montague's library that surfaced for sale at Sotheby's in 1928, for instance, contained a particularly large amount of prose fiction for an eighteenth-century library—including Richardson's *Clarissa* and *Sir Charles Grandison,* but also Eliza Haywood's *History of Miss Betsy Thoughtless, Anti-Pamela,* and a large number of French romances.[45] Owning such books, however, did not indicate any unqualified endorsement of them, and the first volume of Montague's copy of *Clarissa* bears her scribbled note, "miserable stuff."[46] Moreover, nothing prevented these (or indeed any) readers from occasionally acquiring books that strayed into genres outside their dominant preferences. Samuel Johnson's comparatively omnivorous library included, at the time of his death in 1784, five volumes of Richard Baxter's church writings in seventeenth-century editions (and evidence of his intention to purchase a sixth volume shortly before his death), as well as twelve volumes of Richardson's *Clarissa* (in both English and a Dutch translation).[47] And this despite the fact that one rarely compares Jonathan Edwards's taste favorably to Samuel Johnson's.

Though they otherwise had little in common, Edwards and Johnson both lived through a period in the middle of the eighteenth century when access to printed books was changing. Any Anglophone reader with the means to purchase books in, say, 1750 would find a substantially larger number of relatively inexpensive titles from which to choose than would a common reader in 1650, who could have reliably accessed printed books but who might only have been able to find or to afford a Bible, an almanac, or a devotional steady seller. Looking back on his career from the vantage of the early 1790s, London bookseller James Lackington claimed that "the sale of books in general has increased prodigiously within the last twenty years" and went on to observe that

> more than four times the number of books are sold now than were sold twenty years since. The poorer sort of farmers, and even the poor country people in general, who before that period spent their winter evenings in relating stories of witches, ghosts, hobgoblins, &c. now shorten the winter nights by hearing their sons and daughters read tales, romances, &c. and on entering their houses, you may see Tom Jones, Roderick Random, and other entertaining books stuck up on their bacon racks, &c. If *John* goes to town with a load of hay, he is charged to be sure not to forget to bring home "Peregrine Pickle's adventures;" and when *Dolly* is sent to market to sell her eggs, she is commissioned to purchase "The history of Pamela Andrews." In short all ranks and degrees now READ.[48]

Lackington here emphasizes not just an expanded number of books in print at the end of the eighteenth century, but an expanded number of readers, across class and regional lines.

The celebratory tone of Lackington's memoirs suggests some probability of overstatement, though Richard D. Altick perhaps goes too far in dismissing Lackington's assessment of patterns of ownership among country people as "sheer fantasy."[49] Other evidence suggests that the value of books in the last quarter of the eighteenth century comes with owning them as much as reading them. Contemporary commentators frequently spoke of the perceived expanse of reading by invoking evidence of commercial sales. It is well known, for example, that in 1781 Samuel Johnson called England "a nation of readers," but it is less often appreciated that his judgment was based on sales figures for one of Jonathan Swift's printed pamphlets.[50] For Johnson and Lackington, as for many Anglophone readers, books had assumed an indispensability among other kinds of commodities, as simply the kinds of things one possesses. Any fine distinctions between readers and owners of books were not well appreciated.

The expanding commercial culture of the late eighteenth century demoted book collections from a rarefied pursuit for the likes of ministers and noblewomen to one far more available to the middle classes. As John Brewer observes, "The book had ceased to be merely a text and had become an icon and object which conveyed a sense of its owner. In genteel portraits books—and a book was almost as common a prop as a spouse, a house or an animal—no longer merely associated the sitter with a profession or vocation."[51] Historians tend to imagine that book ownership teaches us something about books, but, at least in the late eighteenth century, it equally teaches us something about ownership. As material objects, books increasingly assumed the immaterial quality that, in various registers, Karl Marx labeled "fetishism," Walter Benjamin called "aura," and Peter Stallybrass described as "the possibility that history, memory, and desire might be materialized in objects that are touched and loved and worn."[52] Books had certainly been endowed with some of the totemic powers of the commodity well before the late eighteenth century.[53] But in this later period their association with other commodities would be far more inescapable to anyone walking into a shop to buy them.

It is here that Lackington's description of *Pamela* alongside a load of hay or a basket of eggs makes an important kind of sense. Typical of London booksellers in the 1770s, the first John Murray sold books alongside stationery, quills, ink, sealing wafers, calling cards, account books, and diaries. He was also, according to his modern biographer, "happy to provide his customers with beer and wine, fever powders, Irish linen, lecture tickets, lottery tickets, even woodcocks and partridges."[54] A similar diversity of wares would have also stocked the shelves of bookshops in the English provinces, including stationery, patent medicines, groceries, tea, coffee, and sugar.[55] Colonial bookshops likewise boasted varied inventories, in part because they sometimes accepted payment in the form of trade, including imported goods. Andrew Bradford's Philadelphia print shop, for example, advertised "molasses by the barrel, whalebone, live goose feathers, and 'Barbadoes Rum'; corks, chocolate, the 'pure nut'; 'English pease'; and Spanish snuff, in half- and quarter-pound canisters; Jesuit's bark, Bohea tea, 'very good Pickled Sturgeon,' and beaver hats, as well as a variety of patent medicines with names such as 'Squires Grand Elixir,'" all in addition to books and other printed matter.[56] Such advertisements abound, though it is much more difficult to know what customers actually purchased, and in what combinations. A rare but definite exception appears in the register of the Bath Municipal Library, where, for reasons unknown, George Pitt somehow inserted all of his acquisitions on December 25, 1799, composed of "Fielding's Amelia Quire Best Writing Paper—& a few good Pens—Cheltenham Aperient Salts from Bond Street—."[57] It is impossible to say, though tantalizing to speculate, how often books like *Amelia* simply numbered among other commodities.

In the last decades of the eighteenth century, the intellectual or creative desire to read books competed prominently with the far more social desire to be the kind of fashionable person in proximity to such objects. Books—and, more specifically, books apart from Bibles—had of course carried social currency for some time prior. The rise of coffeehouses in late seventeenth-century London established public venues where pamphlets could be distributed, read, and debated, and coffeehouses maintained an intimate relationship with the book trade through the middle of the eighteenth century in London and through the Revolutionary period in the North American colonies.[58] Contemporaneous with the rise of coffeehouses, the lapse of the Licensing of the Press Act in 1695 created opportunities for more periodical publication, at the same time that it expanded competition among authors and therefore generated a greater need to advertise books in newspapers.[59] One of the long-term consequences of these developments is that books gradually became not just objects to be purchased but objects to be known. Printed texts increasingly existed in the kinds of feedback loops—including, as we saw in Chapter 3, text-networks—that characterize media circulation in a mass cultural context.[60]

While all of these phenomena suggest that book ownership carried social currency, some readers took the matter further and actually co-owned books with their fellows. Without making recourse to individual, private book ownership, three types of social institutions increased access to books in the eighteenth century. The first were book clubs, in which a group of individuals privately pooled resources to buy books, which were often resold after they had been circulated among members; the second were subscription libraries, in which individuals purchased memberships or "shares" and acted as part of the governing collective making decisions about inventory; and the third were circulating libraries, typically run by booksellers, in which individuals could purchase short-term memberships, effectively renting access to a collection of new books for a few weeks or more. All three kinds of institutions turned the acquisition of books into a social activity. "By thus clubbing our Books to a common Library," recalled Benjamin Franklin in his *Autobiography,* "we should, while we lik'd to keep them together, have each of us the Advantage of using the Books of all the other Members, which would be nearly as beneficial as if each owned the whole."[61] Though Franklin emphasizes the access he gained from his book club (which eventually transformed into a subscription library called the Library Company of Philadelphia), the social value of clubbing itself may have exerted a pull. David Allan has proposed that the period's mania for joining societies, or "associationalism," was often as much a factor in the patronizing of libraries as was the desire for reading.[62]

Of the three social institutions that expanded access to books beyond individual ownership in the eighteenth century, circulating libraries were chronologically the latest development, appearing in Edinburgh by 1725, in Bath and Bristol by 1728, in London by 1740, and in Philadelphia by 1767.[63] They flourished throughout the Anglophone world after the 1740s and became absolutely commonplace by the 1770s. Circulating libraries tended to appear in commercial centers, both because these were places where books were printed, and also because these were places full of consumers with ready money. By the final quarter of the century they had largely superseded coffeehouses as the kinds of public places where print was reliably accessed and discussed. Circulating libraries, however, extended the kind of sociability of the coffeehouse to women as well as to men, and they uniformly offered access to works more substantial than pamphlets (which, observes Paul Kaufman, only the "higher level" coffeehouses carried).[64] They also consistently housed large collections of novels.

To be sure, many circulating libraries also stocked other kinds of books, and they were not specifically designed to promote novel reading. As K. A. Manley concludes, "Circulating libraries turned reading into a commercial proposition, even though their proprietors may have had mixed motives."[65] What does seem generalizable, however, is that circulating libraries were a means by which booksellers tried (often successfully) to expand their consumer base. Indeed, one of the interesting features of circulating libraries is that while their inexpensive fees made them important points of access for working- and lower-class readers, they were widely patronized by members of varying social classes. The interest in novels, apparently shared by circulating library patrons across class lines, offers a challenge to the widespread scholarly presumption that ties novel reading to middle-class leisure, a presumption that, in Allan's phrase, "drives an overly schematic coach and horses through the subtleties of the available evidence."[66]

In the case of circulating libraries, available evidence for what patrons actually charged from the collections is quite scarce, though some conclusions can be inferred from the ways that a late eighteenth-century interest in novels extends, from circulating libraries in the 1750s and 1760s to subscription libraries in the 1770s and after. To take one example, a modern tabulation of the records of the Bristol Library Society (whose borrowers include Robert Southey and Samuel Taylor Coleridge) in the eleven-year period between August 1773 and December 1784, finds 900 titles and 13,497 borrowings. The most frequently borrowed titles are of travel narratives and belletristic works (including *Tristram Shandy* and Fielding's *Works*), despite the library's sizeable collection of theology and ecclesiastical history.[67] Similarly, to take a second example, the sixty members of the Library Company of Burlington, New Jersey, had access,

Figure 4.2. Beauty in Search of Knowledge (London: Sayer and Bennett, 1782). (British Library)

according to a 1758 catalog, to 346 titles, a majority of which were books of divinity (sermons, expositions on church doctrine, religious prayers, and hymns) and, depending on how one classifies works, about five of which were novels.[68] The library collection's relative strength in nonfiction does not command a clear majority of its charges, however, and through the 1760s and 1770s, a sizeable portion of the books borrowed are those few novels and other literary works (volumes of poems, tales, and letters) that Samuel Pepys, in reference to his own library, called "diversion" but that might more accurately be called not-nonfiction.[69] Finally, for a third example, no circulation records exist for Franklin's book club, but the earliest surviving catalog for the Library Company of Philadelphia from 1741, listing approximately 375 titles, leans toward history, philosophy, natural science, and reference books (such as dictionaries in multiple languages, epistolary guides, and Bible commentaries). The collection does include a number of literary works, for instance by Congreve, Swift, and Horace, as well as a selection of poetry. The only novel is Cervantes's *Don Quixote* both in Spanish (a 1719 edition) and in English translation (a 1733 London edition).[70] The next surviving catalog from 1757 shows a collection swollen to 850 titles, with considerable growth in travel writing and belles lettres. However, not all of these new acquisitions were new books. The library's 1749 *History of Tom Jones, a Foundling* was a first edition, but between 1741 and 1757, the library also acquired a 1742 London edition of *Gulliver's Travels* (originally published in 1726) and a 1749 London edition of James Hervey's *Meditation among the Tombs* (originally 1746).[71] Both the fact of these later acquisitions and their appearance in later editions suggest that readerly taste was moving toward imaginative literature and prose fiction.

Because circulating libraries were often run by booksellers, the subtraction of religious publishing from the London market would likely be evident in their inventories, especially toward the end of the century. But attempts to determine precisely why, by the 1770s in London, circulating library collections became synonymous with novel reading quickly get lost in a chicken-or-egg game. On the one hand, as I have said, because circulating libraries were often run by printers and booksellers, the inventory of a circulating library closely reflected the inventory of a print shop. On the other hand, library patrons were presented with larger numbers of books than they could read, and circumstantial evidence suggests that in the aggregate they selected and possibly preferred novels. Confronted with the interpretive question of whether the availability of books dictates current fashions or whether current fashions dictate the availability of books, the most correct answer is: both. The fact that subscription libraries, such as those in Bristol, Burlington, or Philadelphia, which were not beholden to the same inventory constraints, also gradually expanded their holdings of novels and literary works further points to the likelihood that economic exigencies and readerly taste came together as tandem causes of a broader cultural shift toward reading prose fiction, of which novels were becoming an increasingly favored kind.

What seems like much less of a causal agent in this story is, again, novels themselves. The relative abundance of novels on the shelves of circulating libraries should, logically, reflect something about the printing trade of the booksellers who ran those libraries. But while the influx of customers generated by the opportunity to rent books for a sixpence may indeed have mattered to the long-term health of the trade, and while novels may have been a consumer draw to the same libraries, neither circulating libraries nor novels are easily isolated as agents of the change that made what John Feather calls the "pre-industrial activity" of printing in 1750 into the "modern commercial enterprise" of 1850.[72] Neither an upswing in the production and consumption of novelistic fiction, nor the proliferation of libraries where novels might be encountered, were *causes* of this transformation in the book industry. At best they were mutually informing *developments*, unrelated in origin but contingently related in practice, each appearing (very gradually) to foment the other.

III

There is no doubt that Anglophone readers in the last quarter of the eighteenth century were developing a taste for novels, and, in any case, had greater access to them than ever before. But, as we have seen, this increase in readership has less specifically to do with developments in the novel as a genre than it does with more socially and economically macroscopic aspects of book collecting and circulation, as well as the increasing social value that books as commodities assume in this period for people of various social stations. The circumstances, detailed above, by which books were being printed under increasingly bifurcated conditions—with novels and books of piety economically distinguishable on the production end of the print market—did not prevent people from nonetheless consuming them together. Instead, eighteenth-century consumers avidly accumulated books among many other different kinds of things, and they used commodity acquisition as a basis for expansive forms of sociability, such as libraries, societies, and clubs. Under these circumstances, as we have seen, books were increasingly numbered as commodities and among other kinds of commodities. While the people making and selling books were working under transforming conditions, the people buying and reading books were largely oblivious of those changes.

Readers became increasingly aware of the economic stratifications in late eighteenth-century printing only after these conditions were already well in place. As such, unable to see gradual transitions in the supply or production chains, they tended to attribute the resulting changes in the material aspects of printing economics to the immaterial contents of books themselves. That is to say, readers were eventually able to attribute different social values to novels versus books of piety, ironically, because by the 1790s, the changes in book production from the decades prior had crystallized into place, and the changes themselves had slowed down. The 1790s were not a decade of media shift.[73] As physical objects, books appear to have changed quite little in the 1790s, and for this reason, the belated recognition of the bifurcation between novels and other texts circulating in the commercial print market, and books of piety, tracts, and other texts circulating to the side of that market, did not register as a difference in material textuality, but as a difference in content.

One measure of the belated recognition of these changes was a significant upswing, in the last decade of the eighteenth century, of the use of the term "novel." To be sure, "novel" was hardly new by the time it caught on. The word came to English in the middle of the sixteenth century (probably from the Italian *novella*), and was first used to designate a fictitious narrative, especially one of a collection (so that, for example, each of the stories in *The Decameron* was called a novel, while the whole work might be a romance).[74] By the 1690s, the word appeared in the subtitles of multiple London-printed prose narratives, usually as a way of indicating that the work is based on, or translated from, a putative French original. But Anglophone narratives published after 1740 and now recognized to be novels rarely referred to themselves with this generic designation, and, indeed, used nearly anything else.

The anonymous *Essay on the New Species of Writing Founded by Mister Fielding* (1751) credits its titular subject as a generic innovator, "the Founder of this new Biography."[75] Yet biography is one of the few generic terms that Fielding left out of the opening of *The History of Tom Jones, a Foundling* (1749), whose first chapter declares the work a "comic epic-poem in prose," and whose prefatory letter to George Lyttleton calls the narrative both a "history" and a "picture."[76] Johnson's *A Dictionary of the English Language* (1755) contains no entries for "novel" (nor either "fiction" or "literature") but offers its first definition of "history" as "a narration of events and facts delivered with dignity," and supports this rather formalist usage not with any historian's statement but with a couplet from Alexander Pope's *First Satire of the Second Book of Horace* (1733).[77] "History" was, meanwhile, just one of the synonyms in use during the second half of the eighteenth century for works we would now call by the name "novel." Others included "memoir" (as in John Cleland's *Memoirs of a Woman of Pleasure* [1749]), "epistle" (as in Eliza Haywood's *Epistles for Ladies* [1776]), "tale," (as in Susanna Rowson's *Charlotte, A Tale of Truth* [1791]), "romance," (as in Ann Radcliffe's *The Mysteries of Udolpho, A Romance; Interspersed with Some Pieces of Poetry* [1794]), and indeed "poetry" (in the case of Anna Seward's versified narrative, *Louisa: A Poetical Novel, in Four Epistles* [1792]). Through to the end of the eighteenth century, "novel" was an utterly confused category.

What does begin to distinguish novels from other genres, and from history in particular, is its embrace of fictionality.[78] Early eighteenth-century fictional prose narratives generally attempted to disguise or downplay their status as fiction. The preface to first edition of *Robinson*

Crusoe (1719) could describe a "private Man's Adventures in the World" made "Publick," with its author assuming the role of editor, just as one fictional Richard Sympson, signing the preface to *Gulliver's Travels* (1726), claims that the work would have been longer "if I had not made bold to strike out innumerable Passages relating to the Winds and Tides."[79] Samuel Richardson, likewise, looks back to this longer tradition of disguising fictional authorship as editorial work, in the preface to *Pamela* and again in *Sir Charles Grandison* (1753). (This subgenre of prefatory claim arguably reaches its apotheosis with *Julie, ou la nouvelle Héloïse* [1761], which anticipates objections to Jean-Jacques Rousseau's self-identification as editor, asking "Ai-je fait le tout, & la correspondance entiere est-elle une fiction? Gens du monde, que vous importe? C'est surement une fiction pour vous" [Did I make it up and is the whole correspondence but a fiction? People of the world, what do you care? It is surely a fiction to you].[80]

By the 1790s, however, the tenor of novel prefaces has changed, requiring writers to recognize and justify their fictions. Rowson calls *Charlotte* a "novel" over whose true events she, the "novel writer," has thrown "a slight veil of fiction."[81] Similarly, the title page of Hannah Webster Foster's *The Coquette* (1797) announces the work as "A Novel: Founded on Fact."[82] The original preface to William Godwin's *Caleb Williams* (1794) owns that this work is an "invention," but justifies itself with the aim of expanding the audience for Godwin's political critique.[83] Maria Edgeworth's *Belinda* (1801) claims instead to be "a Moral Tale—the author not wishing to acknowledge a Novel" for "so much folly, errour, and vice are disseminated in books classed under this denomination, that it is hoped the wish to assume another title will be attributed to feelings that are laudable, and not fastidious."[84] Though they come to different conclusions, all these examples acknowledge (as the likes of Defoe, Swift, and Richardson do not) that "novel" is a category that describes their works, and, moreover, is a category to be reckoned along the border of fact and fiction.

If one measure of the bifurcation of pious print from the London market is the belated recognition of the category "novel" within that latter market, the moral backlash against novels is another. Recall that in 1741, months after the book's appearance in London, Rev. Benjamin Slocock recommended *Pamela* from the pulpit of St. Savior's Church.[85] Four decades later, another Anglican minister, Vicesimus Knox, warned that "in vain is youth secluded from the corruptions of the living world. Books are commonly allowed without restriction, as innocent amusements; yet these often pollute the heart in the recesses of the closet, inflame the passions at a distance from temptation, and teach all the malignity of vice in solitude."[86] Knox's account praises the talents of Richardson, Fielding, and Smollett, worrying not that novels are themselves amoral, but that their readers cannot be trusted. Similar sentiments escalate through the 1790s. Mary Wollstonecraft's *Vindication of the Rights of Woman* (1792) abjures novel reading as sufficient for a young woman's education, in contrast "with those works which exercise the understanding and regulate the imagination."[87] The anonymous author of "Novel Reading, a Cause of Female Depravity" (1797) went deeper, arguing that "those who first made *novel-reading* an indispensible branch in forming the minds of young women, have a great deal to answer for," as it is from novels that the young female reader "imbibes erroneous principles, and from thence pursues a flagrantly vicious line of conduct; it is there she is told that love is involuntary, and that attachments of the heart are decreed by fate."[88] Worthy of a sentimental narrator as such rhetoric may seem, that essay's concerns were attractive enough to warrant multiple reprintings across the Atlantic, entirely in the *New England Quarterly Magazine* in 1802 and in the *Atheneum* in 1817, and partially in the *Monthly Anthology* in 1804.[89] It was tellingly with the same gendered rhetoric that Benjamin Rush disparaged novels as the diversions of "young ladies, who weep away a whole forenoon, over the criminal sorrows of a fictitious Charlotte or Werter."[90]

The consistency by which these accounts figure novel readers as female is only partly explained as male misogyny or a desire for men to regulate women's conduct. Rather, the gender of this figured reader indicates a broader social concern about the ways that expanding access to books makes them available to an unsupervised *anyone,* apart from the more regulated schools, colleges, ministries, and private libraries that had in decades prior restricted access to books. Only when such access becomes more common—through circulating libraries, book clubs, and a proliferation of books as commodities—do concerns belatedly register about who might be reading what.

These objections to the social conditions of novel reading were new in the 1790s, even though objections to novels were not.[91] Novels had in fact been denounced since their appearance in the 1740s, though in those earlier cases the tone of denunciation had tended to be more satirical than vitriolic. The tongue-in-cheek pamphlet *The Enormous Abomination of the Hoop-Petticoat* (1745), for example, imagined the greater ease of London life "if Reading of the BIBLE and other Books of Religion took up *at least half as much* of their Time as the Reading of *Plays, Pamelas, Novels, Romances;* nay *Tatlers* and SPECTATORS themselves."[92] The same year, James Miller's comedy *The Picture: Or, The Cuckold in Conceit* (1745) had its character Mr. Per-Cent upbraid his daughter Celia on the grounds that "these confounded Romances have been the Ruin of thee; I warrant thou canst say more of *Pamela* or *Joseph Andrews* than thy catechism."[93] Similar as these objections from the 1740s may be to the ones that come later, they are, crucially, not identical.

The difference in these objections—to novels in the 1740s and novel reading by the 1790s—reflects, however subtly, a change in the relationship between novels and the marketplace of print. By the end of the eighteenth century, novels were no longer recommended in sermons (as Slocock had done when he endorsed *Pamela* from the pulpit), nor were they so unobjectionably collected into ministers' libraries (as they had been for the likes of Jonathan Edwards). Readers were accordingly not coming into contact with novels through these clerically sponsored channels, which indeed were drying up in favor of endorsements for books of piety; instead, readers were discovering novels through things like social gossip and circulating library membership. The changing conditions by which readers access print—afforded by a growing market for commercial books and, by corollary, the more focused aims and particular circulation paths of books of piety—meant that novels, which had once been under the purview of moral authorities, were no longer so. Changes in the material production and circulation of books entailed changes not only in access, but consequently in the social authority by which books were governed. These changes were legible for satire as early as 1775, when Sir Anthony Absolute in Richard Sheridan's *The Rivals* caustically declares that "a circulating library in a town is, as an evergreen tree, of diabolical knowledge!"—though by the end of the play he marries his son to the play's chief novel reader, Miss Lydia Languish.[94] By the 1790s, however, the stakes seem higher, and the satire drops away.

Later objections to novel reading coded themselves as moral, yet they stop short of finding any wrongness or sin in the activity.[95] Beneath this moral lament are a set of varied objections to particular reading habits: a lack of supervision, a frivolity, an availability to all kinds of people (including young women) who do not have access to other forms of education. Accordingly, these objections are not really moral, at least not in the religious sense of the term; rather, they share a concern about the expanded access to print without a curatorial authority to guide that access. This concern about authority is highlighted by the fact that what remains almost incidental among all these objections to novel reading is, curiously, novels. Knox condemns novel reading, but not before reminding his reader that some novels are well written and some novelists are true artistic masters. Wollstonecraft decried the sufficiency of novels for female education in her *Vindication,* yet then began translating these same ideas into a novel of her own, *Maria: or, The Wrongs of Woman* (1798). Likewise, Hannah More's *Strictures on the Modern System of Female Education* (1799) could object that "novels and romances have been made the vehicles of vice and infidelity," yet also insist (in a denunciation of romantic love, no less) that "the novel of Cervantes is incomparable."[96] None of these objections to novel reading unequivocally condemn novels.

If the 1790s accordingly see novel reading in conflict with some imaginary sanctioned, authorized, and moral kind of reading, there is no evidence that this conflict is about the novel as a *genre*. Rather, the sign "novel" seems to hold the place of a kind of popular reading, easily accessed and injudiciously consumed (in, perhaps, a similarly imprecise fashion as when twenty-first-century readers glibly describe their divertissements as "reading the internet"). This sense of novels—as synonymous with demotic reading—is less a reflection of qualities inherent in the novel itself than it is a reflection of the conditions under which, by the 1790s, novels are being printed, circulated, sold, borrowed, and, relatedly, read. Recognizing something about these conditions, the detractors of novel reading repeatedly position that activity in opposition to some imaginary kind of moral reading, and the fact that they can do so suggests that they equally recognize something about the conditions—largely distinct from the ways that novels move through the London market—by which books of piety are printed, circulated, given away, and read.

Though I have argued that through the last quarter of the eighteenth century books of piety were losing substantial ground against novels on both the production and consumption ends of the commercial London print market, and though I have described this loss as a gradual subtraction of books of piety from the economics of the London print trade, it would substantially overstate the historical record to say that books of piety disappeared from the London market. Just as readers, authors, and critics belatedly registered these material changes with defenses and objections to the category "novel" in the 1790s, so printers in this decade redoubled efforts to turn a profit on religious books. Many London printers (including Charles Rivington) began in the 1790s to publish religious magazines, according to Isabel Rivers, "with clearly defined audiences and intellectual levels."[97] Other printers attempt to reverse the trend lowering the production costs of books of piety, and instead start to offer more elaborate editions of established works. Rivington's three-volume edition of More's Cheap Repository Tracts offers one example. Another appeared in 1794, when the Anglican minister and scholar Thomas Scott wrote a biographical preface to one of the prior century's best-loved narratives, now restored to its entire length, advertised in an "elegant edition," and printed in octavo with some ten illustrations. Appearing fifty years after Wesley's stripped down abridgments, and setting the standard for nearly fifty more, readers enjoyed printing after printing of Scott's *The Pilgrim's Progress*.[98]

IV

By the 1790s, the subtraction of books of piety from the London market leaves readers awash in a commercial sea of novels that, moral authorities assure them, are the worst kind of popular reading. While there is no historical reason to deny the popularity that novels assume for readers at a number of different social levels, there is every reason to emphasize that this popularity has to do with the fact that novels are what is left in a print market from which books of piety have been subject to a focused subtraction. Gradually, through the course of the nineteenth century, novels attain a more enduring association with middle-class reading, but this relative prestige for the novel was also not inevitable. It results in part from an additional contraction in the London print market that took place toward the very end of the 1790s: that of books of poetry. With the heralding of what comes to be known as Romanticism, turn-of-the-century poetic discourse asserted the aesthetic value of poetry, often targeting novels as a generic rival.[99] As we will see, however, books of poetry were subject to the same printing economics as books of prose, and what poetry gained in this period in terms of cultural prestige it could not as well maintain in terms of publishing economics. If books of piety were one rival that the novel had to defeat in its generic ascent, books of poetry were another.

Distinct from the novel's competition with books of piety, however, in the competition with poetry, poetry often fired the first shots. Condemning "the devotees of the circulating libraries" in his *Biographia Literaria* (1817), Samuel Taylor Coleridge refuses to "compliment their *pass-time,* or rather *kill-time,* with the name *reading*" and likened "novels and tales of chivalry in prose or rhyme, (by which last I mean neither rhythm nor metre)" to "gaming, swinging, or swaying on a chair or gate; spitting over a bridge; smoking; snuff-taking; tete a tete quarrels after dinner between husband and wife; conning word by word all the advertisements of the daily advertizer in a public house on a rainy day, &c. &c. &c."[100] Echoing Coleridge's judgment that there is little meaningful distinction between reading a novel and quarreling with a spouse, Ralph Waldo Emerson complained in his journal that Jane Austen's *Pride and Prejudice* (1813) and *Persuasion* (1818) "seem to me vulgar in tone, sterile in artistic invention, imprisoned in the wretched conventions of English society, without genius, wit, or knowledge of the world." Before arriving at his hyperbolic conclusion that "suicide is more respectable" than reading these stories, Emerson objects to the theme of courtship: "'Tis 'the nympholepsy of a fond despair,' say rather, of an English boarding-house."[101] Much like Coleridge's, Emerson's objection to Romantic-era novels is framed by his perception of them as the opposite of Romantic poetry, and he goes so far as to condemn Austen by way of a line from Lord Byron's *Childe Harold's Pilgrimage* (1812–1818).[102]

Opposing poetry to novels in this way, Coleridge, Emerson, and their peers made clear that poetry was also opposed to the forms of clubbing and associationism that novels and libraries provided their readers. Seeking to elevate the reading of poetry to the more visionary vocation of "The Poet" in 1844, Emerson proposed that "readers of poetry see the factory-village, and the railway, and fancy that the poetry of the land-scape is broken up by these; for these works of art are not yet consecrated in their reading; but the poet sees them fall within the great Order not less than the beehive, or the spider's geometrical web."[103] Emerson con-jures a natural order that is transcendent, and yet, despite his metaphors of factories, villages, and trains, that natural order is also unpopulated. As he imagines it, the natural world commands a poet, but it would seem that the poem this poet writes requires little in the way of an audience.

Of course, Romantic-era poets not only had audiences, but in many cases they had the kinds of audiences afforded by the impersonal circu-lation of printed texts for metropolitan markets. Coleridge's 1798 col-laboration with William Wordsworth, *Lyrical Ballads,* for example, was first printed in Bristol by Joseph Cottle, with the rights subsequently sold, at Wordsworth's instruction, to John and Arthur Arch in London, where the text was reprinted.[104] A second volume appeared in 1800 in London, intended as a companion to the first, but the first volume was also reprinted in a limited edition, meaning that there are actually two issues of the first edition. Such a phenomenon was not entirely un-common; as Joseph Rezek has demonstrated, the size and scope of the London market, and its audiences' growing hunger for provincial tales, made London into the place where once regionally published authors found the "metropolitan successes [that] established them as national heroes."[105] But such material considerations—arguably weighty for sub-sequent prose authors like Walter Scott, Maria Edgeworth, or Washington Irving—were entirely written out of these earlier poets' considerations. Though Wordsworth's preface to the 1800 London edition of *Lyrical*

Ballads famously defined "all good poetry" as "the spontaneous over-flow of powerful feelings," he elsewhere in the same preface sought to distinguish poetry from "the literature and theatrical exhibitions of the country" that have "conformed themselves" to the "life and manners" of "the encreasing accumulation of men in cities, where the uniformity of their occupations produces a craving for extraordinary incident which the rapid communication of intelligence hourly gratifies."[106] The me-chanical conditions of this book's printing—rapid, mechanized, urban—are positioned at odds with the view of poetry that it espouses—rarefied, spontaneous, pastoral.

Lyrical Ballads is exemplary, though by no measure unique, in its en-capsulation of these ironic contradictions between nineteenth-century printed books and a timeless poetic manifesto. As Mark L. Greenberg elaborates, "One of the fundamental ironies of romanticism involves au-thors delivering their criticism of industrial culture through typographi-cally set, mechanically reproduced writing printed upon industrially manufactured paper by laborers, and offered for sale (to a public limited by its rate of literacy and ability to afford the productions of the press) by commercial booksellers."[107] What bears emphasis, however, are not just the ironies of natural images disseminated by means of mechanized print, but, more specifically, that such a disavowal of the material condi-tions of printing occurs in a poetry *book*. On both sides of the Atlantic, nineteenth-century readers and writers came into contact with poems printed in a variety of ephemeral platforms, including the broadsheet and the newspaper.[108] Additionally, manuscript poetry continued to circulate much later than arguably any other literary form, including in circumstances where "manuscript" was not a synonym for "unpub-lished."[109] Printed books of poetry, by contrast, were particular and generally more prestigious venues. By the early nineteenth century, well-reputed poets such as Byron or Scott, working with well-capitalized London firms such as Murray's or Longman's, could expect significant sums for their copyrights.[110] Even a century before, the same had not been true. Looking at the case of Alexander Pope, David Foxon has de-tailed the ways in which the author had to go to enormous lengths to wrest profits from the sales of his books—including "choosing his own printer and publisher and directing operations himself."[111] As a seventeenth-century patronage system otherwise yielded to a nineteenth-century market system, poetry became a generally less lucrative endeavor than other kinds of writing for publication. Writing poetry was not often a professional activity—that is, it was not one by means of which a person could earn an independent living—and through to the end of the nineteenth century poetry was, according to William Charvat, "something that was not marketed but inflicted on friends and libraries."[112] The irony of the 1800 *Lyrical Ballads,* then, has to do with both the material technology by which the preface extolls spontaneous nature *and* the prestige format in which it presents its disregard.

One reason that nonephemeral printed books became a relatively prestigious format for publishing poetry had to do with the fact that books of poetry tended to be printed with less type on each page than a prose narrative (especially one designed for continuous reading), and they often took less time to read.[113] If a reader was in some sense getting "less" with a book of poetry, printers and publishers could not sell these books at a lower price because poetry books used just as much paper as prose narratives of comparable length, and paper has always been the costliest aspect of book production.[114] Books of poetry wanted for some consumer justification, and this, indirectly, came to be supplied by poets themselves, who linked the rising cultural prestige of poetry (as opposed to novels) with oblique concerns for the material conditions of poetic publication.[115]

Indeed, the more successful Romantic-era poets defined their craft not in the economic and social terms of markets and audiences, but rather in the epistemological terms of what poetry could help one know. As Percy Bysshe Shelley argued in his *Defense of Poetry* (written in 1821 but only posthumously published in 1840), "The functions of the poetical faculty are twofold: by one it creates new materials of knowledge, and power, and pleasure; by the other it engenders in the mind a desire to reproduce and arrange them according to a certain rhythm and order, which may be called the beautiful and the good."[116] Romantic-era poetry offered both an expressive form and, equally significantly, a frame through which to see the world. For Shelley and his contemporaries, as Mary Poovey summarizes, "the general and systematic nature of the knowledge that poetry produced was at least as important as was poetry's ability to convey the appearance of the phenomenal world."[117] Such an accounting of Romantic poetry implicitly echoes Wordsworth's disavowal of his book and his audience, for, by this understanding, what makes poetry *poetry* is formal: how it expresses the particular things it knows, not the material means through which a reader encounters it. At the same time, Shelley's view implicitly takes Wordsworth's further, insofar as it less ironically works around the kind of prestigious "author-function" that enabled a collection of poems like *Lyrical Ballads* to get into a printed codex format to begin with.[118]

The epistemology of Romantic poetry may have been, as some distinguished critics have suggested, an "aesthetic ideology" as much as anything else.[119] It is certainly the case not only that this poetry had audiences, but furthermore that evidence exists to show that some readers read poetry much like novels, for identification with characters and feelings. One notable example comes from Anne Lister's diaries, in which Byron's swaggering strategies for seducing women offer Lister a model for her own homoerotic explorations.[120] In one moment, Lister observes Byron's death with sadness, and in another gives a copy of his "Cornelia" to a neighbor, Miss Browne, in a coded expression of sexual interest in her.[121] Lister's creative reading practices mark the gap in poetic discourse between what readers of poetry did with poems and what the ideology of Romantic poetry, as espoused by poets themselves, claimed as poetry's goals.[122]

In addition to those by well-reputed authors presenting a particular epistemology, the early nineteenth century saw the proliferation of books of anonymous poems. These poems too were often understood epistemologically, offering in verse a particular kind of knowledge about the world, though as Andrew Piper observes, the period's poetic miscellanies were designed to place emphasis on the pleasure and instruction of their readers, rather than their authors.[123] The kinds of verse in circulation in the early nineteenth century, ranging from established poets to anonymous folk ballads, suggests that the category "poetry," like "novel," was not yet as unified as it would presumptuously become toward the century's close.[124] Indeed, as Steve Newman reminds us, "the lesser lyric of the ballad challenged lyric poetry as a whole, and, in doing so, helped to transform 'literature' from polite writing in general into the body of imaginative writing that becomes known as the English literary canon."[125] Ballad collections, and especially those that gathered poems in historical or allegedly disappearing dialects, provided readers throughout the British Empire with the culturalist grounds on which a past collectivity could be imagined and a future empire could be modeled. From the mid-eighteenth century, as Katie Trumpener writes, "nationalist antiquarians in Ireland, Scotland, and Wales had developed a historical model of national literary life which stressed the primacy of national institutions rather than the imagination of individual writers."[126] While this complex ideological work performed by anonymous poetry deserves more attention than present space allows, suffice it to say that the ironies attendant upon the preface to *Lyrical Ballads* are noticeably less present here. Anonymous poets represented folk voices and thus it was left to editors (and, later, scholars) to write the framing prefaces. To attentive readers, any such prefaces would be understood as something prepared explicitly for publication. Miscellanies, ballad collections, and other anonymous verse thus offers an instance in which the often disembodied voice of Romantic poetry could appear to speak yet further from the taint of the mechanical and material apparatus of the printed book, which, nevertheless, the readers of that same voice held in their hands.[127]

Poetry's champions downplayed material texts and instead insisted on the alternative epistemology that poetry organized and presented. In so doing, they were, sometimes explicitly but more often implicitly, asserting a distinction between poetry and novels. Between the two, poetry possessed the more elevated formal and cultural vantage, while novels amounted to little more than—to reprise Coleridge's judgment—a "*pass-time,* or rather *kill-time.*" It was with a similar patronizing air that the London *Athenaeum* in 1828 lamented that "a novel-reading public will never be a poetry-reading public."[128]

If, however, such judgments proved to be less than totally accurate, that circumstance owed something not only to the readers who enjoyed both novels and poetry, but also to the writers who wrote and published in more than one genre. Few nineteenth-century poets, especially as the print market expanded and the century progressed, could turn poetry into bread, and the list of those who tried their hands at both genres includes those best known as poets like Charlotte Smith, Letitia Elizabeth

Landon, Edgar Allan Poe, and Frances E. W. Harper, who also penned novels, and those best known as prose writers like Walter Scott, Emily Brontë, Herman Melville, Rudyard Kipling, and Thomas Hardy, who also composed poems. Even Henry Wadsworth Longfellow, one of the most commercially successful poets of the first half of the nineteenth century, still didn't make enough money from poems to live. Longfellow supplemented his income by working as a translator and modern language professor at Harvard College.[129] Following up on his reputation-making verse epic, *Evangeline: A Tale of Acadie,* in 1847, Longfellow brought out a novel, *Kavanagh,* in 1849 with the same publisher, the esteemed Boston firm of Ticknor, Reed, and Fields. Poetry granted Longfellow and others enormous cultural prestige, without a comparable economic reward.

The gradual establishment over the course of the nineteenth century and into the twentieth of the novel as a prestige genre in its own right— linked in complex ways around the world with the rise of nationalism— was far from inevitable when the term "novel" belatedly came into circulation in the 1790s.[130] While the "rise of the novel" story has so often been told as the emergence and development of this literary form, the present chapter has instead shown some of the ways that the novel emerges as a kind of market niche not so much on its own terms, as a new kind of formal or expressive creation, but in relation to the economic subtraction of religious publishing from the London marketplace of print, the competition with religious publishing that ensued, and the economic nonviability of poetry, which for a period of time successfully distinguished itself from novels as a prestige literary form. The success of the novel as a signature genre of modernity, in material terms, owes less than scholars have assumed to its own generic accomplishments or innovations and much more to the limitations and failures of competing genres.

V

Well after the generic split between literary and religious works at the end of the eighteenth century, *The Pilgrim's Progress* remained a steady seller and continued to be printed under the auspices of both religious and literary publishing. After its founding in 1825 and all through the nineteenth century, for example, the American Tract Society kept *The Pilgrim's Progress* on its list of perennially in-print titles (along with other seventeenth- and eighteenth-century Protestant devotional works including Richard Baxter's *Call to the Unconverted* [1658] and Philip Doddridge's *Rise and Progress of Religion in the Soul* [1795]), which circulated in thousands of copies of closely printed and sometimes abridged editions, at little or no cost to readers.[131] Most of these editions circulated without elaborate paratexts to frame them or to dictate the terms of pious reading, as had similar texts (such as editions of *Brainerd*) in the century prior. Instead, nineteenth-century editions of *The Pilgrim's Progress* published under the auspices of religious publishing houses quite reasonably presumed that the piety of the text was not up for dispute, that it would and could speak for itself.

On the other hand, the for-profit, market-minded, and, increasingly, "literary" publishers who brought out editions of *The Pilgrim's Progress* after the 1790s gradually repackaged and repositioned the text according to the emergent norms of a marketplace from which religious publishing had been subtracted. Of course no one involved with these editions attempted to deny that *The Pilgrim's Progress* was a pious text. But the material text that delivered this piety was brought into line with the not necessarily pious novels that were rapidly becoming one staple of this market. Thomas Scott's 1794 edition is a case in point, as it presents Bunyan's text in the same reader-friendly octavo format typically used for novels (instead of the duodecimo size popular for late eighteenth-century pamphlets). Even more pertinently, Scott's edition included a biography of the author. This sketch of Bunyan's life, largely based on the events of *Grace Abounding*, conforms to the efflorescence at the end of the eighteenth century of what Margreta de Grazia has called the authorial "apparatus," the alignment of text and author through forms of editorial authentication including the identification of writerly intentions and the establishment of a biography.[132]

The Pilgrim's Progress offers a strong example of the ways in which, after the late eighteenth century bifurcation between the market conditions for novels and books of piety, the residual market for literary publishing attempts to incorporate piety back in. Into the nineteenth century, such attempts mutate seventeenth-century devotional literature, reimagining it in material (and, as we will see in the Conclusion, generic) terms increasingly associated with novels. These mutations often progressed in many small steps. Scott's edition of *The Pilgrim's Progress,* for instance, was reissued into the 1860s, but the first (1794) edition was reprinted wholesale in 1817 in Hallowell, Maine, by a local printer named Nathaniel Cheever.[133] No evidence exists to prove that his only son, George Barrell Cheever, read the book his father printed, but more than three decades later, in 1851, the ascendant New York publishing house of George Putnam brought out a handsome new edition of Bunyan's work, which the younger Cheever, now a minister, had edited.[134] Based on his celebrated *Lectures on the Pilgrim's Progress* (1845), Cheever's edition does Scott one better and not only bases Bunyan's biography on *Grace Abounding* but gently conflates its events with those of *The Pilgrim's Progress* as well.[135] Cheever presents a mutation of the figure of character, whereby a person, and the representations of persons he creates, might align. Cheever's interpretation grants Bunyan's life a narrative arc, much like *The Pilgrim's Progress* has; and it grants that work a character capable of psychological depth, much like Bunyan himself was.

If readers in 1678 could identify with Bunyan's Christian, doing so did not require that they knew anything about Bunyan. A century and a half later, the author could be described as though he were a character in his own story. Writing in New York in 1845, there is every reason to imagine that Cheever had learned some things about character from the novels of Scott, or even Dickens. The mutation of character that appears in his preface to *The Pilgrim's Progress* was, accordingly, something that the growing dominance of novels in the nineteenth century surely facilitated. At the same time, the absence of any substantial discussion of character in the present chapter, along with the extended comparison between reading novels and reading spiritual autobiographies in Chapter 3, together betrays my own sense that reading in order to identify with characters was not a habit that novels invented.

Conclusion

The Retroactive Rise of the Novel

T he preceding chapters revise the story of the rise of the novel, arguing that the development of this genre in the Anglophone world shares a mutually informing history with the development of the book as a media platform. Woven through this revision is a skepticism about linear transmission and development. To bolster that skepticism, the foregoing chapters have tried to shine light on the uneven and inconsistent ways in which media platforms antecedent to the printed book (such as manuscripts, scrolls, and performances) persist into the era of printed books; additionally, they have taken as axiomatic that culture happens in the space between what people say they do and what people actually do, and so have lain interpretive emphasis on the ironic aspects of processes like transmission and development. These processes may prove to be effective (features of the past are indeed transmitted into the present), but these processes also beget mutants, creating a present that often bears little resemblance to the one that textual producers of the past intended to transmit. As applied to cultures and texts, "reproduction" is an overly polite and mostly unhelpful way of describing these mutations.[1] The media history theorized in the preceding chapters has attempted to locate irony, mutation, and nonlinearity at the heart of scholarly histories of the material transmission of the printed book and the generic development of the Anglophone novel.

Like any revisionist study, this one invites a major question: If this revised history is true, why don't we already know it? Given the widespread attention that the history of the Anglophone novel has and continues to receive in literary scholarship, even readers sympathetic to the present argument might harbor reservations about how unfamiliar this account may seem. To the extent that the foregoing pages offer any answer, it is buried in a recurrent sense that the formal features of texts—what and how they figure—matter more to authors, to readers, to stories, to arguments, to detractors, and to scholars' definitional exercises than do the material conditions by which these same formal features are mediated. The broadening access to printed books in the Anglophone world that snapped into place by the beginning of the nineteenth century (in addition to the fact that no other media platform significantly competed with it in this period) meant that readers and writers could take this platform for granted. As nineteenth-century readers and writers developed a critical language by which to anatomize novels, they had comparatively little need for any similar language by which to anatomize print.[2] Thus, the reason we do not already know the history detailed in the preceding chapters has something to do with the ironies of historical transmission. If, as I argued above, irony is a key historiographic concept for understanding the ways that texts are transmitted, irony is likewise important for understanding how the critical discourses surrounding texts are also transmitted. The following paragraphs offer a brief conclusion to my story, aiming to draw out the emergence of this critical discourse around novels and, in an effort to justify my attempt at undoing this discourse, to demonstrate its own revisionist tendencies.

As early into the nineteenth century as 1804, Anna Laetitia Barbauld christened Samuel Richardson "the father of the modern novel."[3] Richardson's own career, however, does not suggest he would entirely have recognized the compliment. In 1755, Richardson had gutted the plots and the epistolary form of his three novels to produce *A Collection of the Moral and Instructive Sentiments, Maxims, Cautions, and Reflexions,*

Contained in the Histories of Pamela, Clarissa, and Sir Charles Grandison, and under cover of an anonymous preface referred to these works variously as "Letters" and "*Histories*" that "may be considered as the LIVES of so many eminent persons."[4] Richardson uses these various generic monikers interchangeably, as though any critical distinction between letters, histories, and lives of eminent persons hardly matters. Furthermore, when Richardson suggests that the author of his texts ("an author modestly *anonymous*") "has found the expedient of engaging the *private attention* of those, who put themselves out of reach of *public exhortation;* pursuing to their *closets* those who fly from the *pulpit;* and there, under the gay air, and captivating semblance of a *Novel,* tempting them to the perusal of many a persuasive *Sermon,*" Richardson denies not only the differences between literary genres, but the differences between secular entertainment and religious instruction.[5]

If Richardson penned and printed his texts without maintaining much concern for the niceties of genre, his early readers read those texts in much the same manner. The same year that Barbauld touted Richardson's generic paternity, former US president John Adams used Richardson's fictional characters to understand something about political realities. Writing to his distant cousin William Cunningham in 1804, Adams observed,

> Democracy is Lovelace, and the people are Clarissa. The artful villain will pursue the innocent lively girl to her ruin and death.—We know that some gentleman will arise at last, who will put the guilty wretch to death in a duel. But this will be no friend of the lady. Perhaps a son, a pupil or a bosom friend of Lovelace, himself. The time will fail me to enumerate all the Lovelaces in the United States. It would be an amusing romance to compare their actions and characters with his.[6]

Thinking with novelistic characters in this abstract way, Adams cuts incongruously across several commonsense ontologies. He does not worry, for instance, that an abstraction is not a person, that a character is not plural, that fiction is not politics, and that populism is not rape. Yet despite these incongruities (or, indeed, as a result of them), this comparison also

A

COLLECTION

Of the Moral and Instructive

SENTIMENTS, MAXIMS, CAUTIONS, *and* REFLEXIONS,

Contained in the

Histories of PAMELA, CLARISSA, and Sir CHARLES GRANDISON.

Digested under Proper HEADS,

With References to the Volume, and Page, both in Octavo and Twelves, in the respective Histories.

To which are subjoined,

Two LETTERS from the Editor of those Works: The one, in ANSWER to a Lady who was solicitous for an additional Volume to the History of Sir CHARLES GRANDISON.

The other, in REPLY to a Gentleman, who had objected to Sir CHARLES's offer'd Compromise in the Article of Religion, had he married a Roman Catholic Lady.

LONDON:

Printed for S. Richardson;

And Sold by C. HITCH and L. HAWES, in *Pater-noster Row*;
J. and J. RIVINGTON, in *St. Paul's Church-Yard*;
ANDREW MILLAR, in the *Strand*;
R. and J. DODSLEY, in *Pall-Mall*; And
J. LEAKE, at *Bath*.

M.DCC.LV.

performs an equally commonsense act of identification. Adams draws an analogy between the deceptive beauty of Lovelace and the flattering ideal of democracy, between the unfortified character of a young girl and the anti-elitist demands of an untried nation. Discrepant as these terms are, the success of the analogy does not require an overwhelming similarity among them. Instead, its success requires only a particular style of reading, familiar enough to anyone who has found something of their own reflection in the lives of fictional people. Reading is a creative act, and texts inspire readers to think all kinds of things. Many times, those thoughts may matter to individual readers, like Richardson or Adams, far more than the specific genres or properties of the inspiring texts themselves, which Barbauld takes hefty rhetorical measures to codify.

Ultimately, however, it is Barbauld's position that becomes dominant, due in part to the enterprise of literary criticism that was slowly emerging from the publishing industry toward the turn of the nineteenth century.[7] Early in the nineteenth century, established London publishers began to circulate literary periodicals, such as the *Quarterly Review,* founded by John Murray II in 1809, which included writings by Walter Scott and Charles Lamb, or *Bentley's Miscellany,* founded by Richard Bentley in 1836, which included writings by Charles Dickens. Successful New York publishers followed suit, with the first issue of *Harper's New Monthly Magazine,* consisting mostly of reprinted British writings alongside advertisements for New York-published books, appearing in June 1850. These and similar publications generated some of the most widely circulating contemporary commentaries on nineteenth-century novels, often penned by popular novelists themselves. In the nineteenth century, novels and novel criticism grew up as twins, both underwritten by the same increasingly mechanized and profitable publishing industry.[8]

Figure C.1. A Collection of the Moral and Instructive Sentiments, Maxims, Cautions, and Reflexions, Contained in the Histories of Pamela, Clarissa, and Sir Charles Grandison. Digested under Proper Heads, with References to the Volume, and Page, Both in Octavo and Twelves, in the Respective Histories (London: S. Richardson, 1755), ix. (Fales Library, New York University)

It is little wonder, then, that the generic parameters of the novel became relatively important to critics after Barbauld in a way they had not
been for novelists like Richardson or readers like Adams, for those rules
of genre were the very qualities that differentiated novels from the other
kinds of writing that novelists and critics performed, often for the same
publishers and in cognate publications. Because their material conditions of publishing were overwhelmingly similar, the rules of genre came
to differentiate the novel, understood as a vehicle for imagination, from
criticism, understood as a vehicle for judgment. By the end of the nineteenth century, the fact that these generic distinctions could always be
less than crisp (in the manner that Richardson implies, Adams performs, and Barbauld downplays) seemed not so much like a generic or
epistemological conundrum as much as comedy gold. In the "Portrait of
Mr. W. H." (not coincidentally published in the prestigious *Blackwood's
Edinburgh Magazine* in 1889), Oscar Wilde, tongue firmly in cheek, rid-
iculed the notion of reading criticism with the kind of absorption with
which readers read novels: "To die for one's theological beliefs is the
worst use a man can make of his life, but to die for a literary theory! It
seemed impossible."[9] The distinction between novels and criticism, between fiction and nonfiction, is the heir of a commercial book market
that consigns fiction to leisure, diversion, and unreality. Criticism helped
to give novels their generic identity.

To be fully differentiated from nineteenth-century literary criticism,
however, it seems that novels further required their own, more independent history. In the eyes of nineteenth-century critics, the novel should
not be *too* new. Of course, by the middle of the nineteenth century the
vogue for novels was widely recognized—and to some extent it was recognized *as* a vogue, such that in 1850 a midcentury London magazine,
the *Prospective Review,* could declare that "the ground once covered by
the Epic and Drama is now occupied by the multiform and multitudi-
nous novel."[10] More often, however, that vogue was projected backward
in time as though it were an enduring trend. The long history of prose
fiction was, thereby, quietly rewritten in the image of the nineteenth-
century novel. The terminological drag in which Barbauld dresses Richardson's legacy is one example. As with that example, the history of the
novel was in many cases narrated from its origin, which was always lo-

cated firmly in the past, and never as part of an emergent critical discourse. Although, as Chapter 2 demonstrated, a reader in 1678 would likely have recognized an affinity between *The Pilgrim's Progress* and other seventeenth-century devotional texts, by 1785 Clara Reeve's *The Progress of Romance* instead gathered *The Pilgrim's Progress* alongside *Robinson Crusoe* and *Don Quixote* on its list of "Novels and Stories Original and uncommon."[11] Such generic disregard did not prevent Walter Scott, a generation later, from acknowledging the impact of Bunyan's life and faith on his works (an edition of which, prefaced by a critical biography, had been edited that year by Robert Southey), but assessments such as Reeve's may have encouraged Scott to speak equivocally of Bunyan's religious "allegory" and his prose "romance," just as they created the precedent by which Henry Hallam's four-volume *Introduction to the Literature of Europe in the Fifteenth, Sixteenth, and Seventeenth Centuries* (1839) would designate the author of *The Pilgrim's Progress* as "the father of our novelists."[12] These and other generic assessments of the early nineteenth century advanced a trend—privileging both the novel as a genre and, not incidentally, filiopietistic reproduction as its mode of transmission—which hardened into critical orthodoxy by the 1870s.[13]

Through much of the nineteenth century, criticism conspired with novels to narrate this story of their mutual distinctness. But where criticism worked to classify and redescribe earlier prose texts as novels, nineteenth-century novels themselves told a story about character, and it is in such stories that John Adams's incongruous readings find their fuller, nineteenth-century expression. The prose narratives of earlier centuries appeared in the prose narratives of the later one, wherein they were often read with the kind of sentimental devotion that Victorian writers and readers widely agreed was suitable for novels.[14] Dickens's Little Nell, for example, found an "old copy of the Pilgrim's Progress, with strange plates, upon a shelf at home, over which she had often pored whole evenings, wondering whether it was true in every word, and where those distant countries with the curious names might be," countries she projects onto the landscape as she sits with her grandfather.[15] The heroine of Susan Warner's *The Wide, Wide World* (1851) listens to her teacher and lover read from Bunyan, while, consistent with the pedagogical erotics of her story, "the listless, careless mood in which she sat down was changed for one of rapt delight; she devoured every word that fell from her reader's lips."[16] George Eliot's Maggie Tulliver rescues her childhood copy—"Our dear old Pilgrim's Progress"—from among the household inventory that her bankrupt father sells off; whereas Huckleberry Finn, who didn't have books to enjoy in childhood, discovers *The Pilgrim's Progress*—"about a man that left his family it didn't say why"— at the comparatively genteel Kentucky home of the Grangerford clan.[17] Meanwhile, the unnamed governess in Henry James's *The Turn of the Screw* (1898)—far less pious a reader—peruses "Fielding's *Amelia*" among "a roomful of old books at Bly—last-century fiction" that "appealed to the unavowed curiosity of my youth."[18] These fictional people read the lives of prior fictional people, identifying with those prior people and projecting past experiences onto present ones. These acts of reading are backward-looking, bringing prior writings into the present; but they are also revisionist, reading that prior writing with much the same sentiment and dedication that nineteenth-century audiences were encouraged to read their contemporary novels. No less than novel criticism, nineteenth-century novels themselves projected a history of the novel, offering an exemplary instance of the more general pattern that Eric Hobsbawm long ago observed, in which one of the great inventions of the European nineteenth century was tradition.[19]

Thus created by stories that both nineteenth-century fiction and criticism told about their mutual differences, the "rise of the novel" developed as a distinctly retroactive critical position. Moreover, the retroactive projections of a history or tradition for the novel back onto the eighteenth century were underwritten by the fact that one thing that was not at all new in this period were books themselves. Even as serial publication came into prominence after the 1830s in London and after the 1860s in Boston and New York, nineteenth-century readers continued to encounter novels in codex format. Not only were nineteenth-century books usually more prestigious publication venues than periodicals and other printed ephemera, but their material properties were—at least in terms of the ways readers interacted with them—overwhelmingly unchanged from the eighteenth century, enabling a sense of continuity with the bibliotechnical artifacts of the century prior.

Because books themselves were not new, nineteenth-century critics of the novel spared little attention for the fact that book production was nonetheless changing considerably in their time: more titles appeared in larger editions, as the beneficiaries of faster, mechanized printing processes; larger numbers of libraries and schools expanded readership, as did the rise not only of criticism and its amplifying, reflexive discourse, but also of serial publications (daily newspapers as well as novels by installment); international copyright laws decreased rates of international piracy, particularly between Anglophone countries (even though the United States only ratified these laws in 1910), arguably accelerating the rates at which publishing markets were becoming increasingly more national and less regional.[20] Yet size formats did not significantly change. Books therefore appeared to stay the same, and so changes to the material conditions by which books reached readers' hands became something for which critics and historians of the novel as a genre failed to find significance.

Even a material event that could not be ignored—for instance, the "speedy death" of the triple-decker after major London circulating libraries refused any longer to buy them in 1894, and the subsequent move toward publishing novels in a single volume—mattered to publishers who sold to libraries and relied on the triple-decker as a prestige format and price point, and to authors who paced their plot twists across the interstitial space between volumes.[21] But it hardly mattered to Victorian readers and critics, who were overwhelmingly dismissive. Walter Besant concluded that most people were "very little concerned in three-volume novels," unless they also ran a circulating library, while the *American Bookmaker* imagined that three-volume novels only really mattered to "English readers hold[ing] fast to things with which they are familiar."[22] Almost instantly the triple-decker became the butt of jokes. The revelation of Wilde's *The Importance of Being Earnest* (1895) turns on the discovery of the governess Miss Prism's authorship of a work mockingly described at once as unpublished and as a "three-volume novel," suggesting the latter to be a genre rather than a format designation.[23] A generation later, the triple-decker continued to index foolishness when Minta Doyle in *To the Lighthouse* (1927) fears and avoids Mr. Ramsay's

369   THE CIRCULA'

"Pray, my dear M.ʳ Page," cried a pretty lisper, looking over a Catalogue "w:
will do for one. N.° 1889, Cruel Disappointment, for another, Reuben, or Suicide, higho
thing. Unguarded Moments, ah we all have our unguarded moments. True Delicacy, N.°
enough of that. Test of Filial Duty, at any rate she puts me to that test pretty often. Ment
Assignation, Frederick or the Libertine, just add these M.ʳ Page, & I shall not have to come ag

Figure C.2. The Circulating Library (London: Laurie and Whittle, 1804).
Note that "Novels," "Romances," and "Tales" have all been checked out,
while more serious subjects remain. (British Library)

TING LIBRARY.

ill you let me have that dear Man of Feeling, I have so long waited for: Well, this
! Nº 4746, I suppose he killed himself for love. Seduction, yes, I want that more than any
? that must be a silly thing by the title. School of Virtue, heaven knows mamma gives me
al Pleasures, worse & worse! I'll look no longer. Oh! stay a moment _ Mutual Attachment,
in until the day after to-morrow." _____ Publish'd Oct. 1804, by LAURIE & WHITTLE, 53, Fleet Street, London.

polite literary inquiries because "she had left the third volume of *Middle-march* in the train and she never knew what happened in the end."[24]

With material textuality rarely amounting to more than a nineteenth-century punchline, it should come as little surprise that the most influential inheritors of this discourse in and beyond the twentieth century told the story of the novel as a story about literary form, in which they paid considerable attention to the kinds of things that novels represented, and minimal attention to the ways in which novels were themselves materially mediated. No less authoritative an account than *The Rise of the Novel* itself stakes its claims on precisely this kind of formalist argument: "If the novel were realistic merely because it saw life from the seamy side, it would only be an inverted romance; but in fact it surely attempts to portray all varieties of human experience, and not merely those suited to one particular literary perspective: the novel's realism does not reside in the kind of life it presents, but in the way it presents it."[25] Valuable though this definition has proven for generations of scholars who have sought to anatomize the English novel since these words were published in 1957, the present study has performed a sustained contestation of this recourse to literary form, on the grounds that such a formalism measures the significance of the novel in terms of the world beyond the novel ("all varieties of human experience"), while at the same time occluding attention to the very conditions of creation, manufacture, circulation, mediation, transmission, and mutation by which that world beyond the novel is encountered and apprehended. Ian Watt is, of course, not alone in making such claims, and the stakes of my own argument have to do with the fact that, indeed, neither are scholars of the novel. As Lisa Gitelman argues, a reflexive accounting for media is often precisely what drops out of historical scholarship, as though we who engage archives and write histories could somehow tell stories *about* media and not also by means of it.[26]

In the particular case of academic histories of the novel, however, the helpmeet of this occlusion has often been a disciplinary bias among literary scholars (one which, as the above quotation makes clear, *The Rise of the Novel* shares) that attention to literary form tells us all we need to know about the history and significance of genre. Indeed, to the extent that a go-it-alone literary formalism is valuable for our professional literary inquiries, it is so because it performs the work that Michel Foucault describes as subjugating knowledge, by which "historical contents have been buried or masked in functional coherences or formal systematizations."[27] Studies of the novel qua novel, which nonetheless brave conclusions about the world beyond the novel, make functional and coherent an account of the novel that matters very much to the discipline of literary studies and very little to anyone outside this narrow professional niche. The reason we do not know the revisionist history detailed in the preceding chapters, in other words, is that we have been telling a disciplinary genre history at the expense of an interdisciplinary media history, and such a media history, at its best, offers an "insurrection of subjugated knowledges."[28] The most optimistic conclusion to be drawn from any revisionist history is, moreover, the one Foucault makes, that "it is the reappearance of what people know, at a local level, of these disqualified knowledges, that made critique possible."[29]

Why this knowledge might return at this particular historical juncture is more than I can say.[30] It is worth observing, however, that this knowledge never completely went away, and, in any case, that it would be wrong to insist that readers even into the nineteenth century harbored absolutely no appreciation for the physicality of books. Rather, by the late nineteenth century, "books" equivocally denoted both physical objects and abstract ideas—as phrases like "book learning" or the verbs for reservation-making, "to book" or "to get booked," come into vernacular usage.[31] That equivocality, as we have already seen with the example of Wilde, directed what appreciation there was of material texts in the nineteenth century toward the kind of minor critical space opened by comedy.[32]

Indeed, the readiest critique of the book's material abstraction came from simply reinserting materiality back into the range of the word's reference. Ishmael, the narrator of Herman Melville's *Moby-Dick* (1851), for instance, relishes just such a metonymic conceit, classifying whales not according to species but, like books, according to size: folio, quarto, octavo, duodecimo. "I promise nothing complete," he writes of his catalog, "because any human thing supposed to be complete, must for that very reason infallibly be faulty."[33] Where Melville's Ishmael uses the materiality of books to make fun of humanity, the narrator of Henry James's

The Portrait of a Lady (1881) uses it to make fun of particular people. With a narrowed focus and amplified cattiness, this narrator qualifies the intellectual abilities of his heroine, introducing her by way of an un-read aunt's dubious misrecognition that Isabel Archer was the kind of person who "was writing a book."[34] With arguably the greatest gusto of all, however, one of Dorothy Parker's "Constant Reader" columns for the *New Yorker* took the considerable length of Theodore Dreiser's auto-biographical *Dawn* as indicative of its tiresome verbosity: "Nearly six hundred sheets to the title of *Dawn:* God help us one and all if Mr. Dreiser ever elects to write anything called 'June Twenty-first!'"[35] Well into the twentieth century, the material properties of books proved largely extra-neous to evaluative literary criticism, unless perhaps one sought to land a particularly sharp zinger.

NOTES

ACKNOWLEDGMENTS

INDEX

Notes

Introduction

1. W. Jackson Bate, *Samuel Johnson* (New York: Harcourt Brace Jovanovich, 1975), 336.

2. Generally speaking, the following chapters will use "format" to talk about the physical features of a text in terms of its production, akin to what G. Thomas Tanselle identifies as a way "to express the relationship between the physical structure of finished books and some of the printing-shop routines that led to that structure" ("The Concept of Format," *Studies in Bibliography* 53 [2000]: 68–117, citation at 68).

3. The English translation of the *Turkish Spy* was printed in London in a 1741 edition and reprinted in 1753; the French original first appeared in 1684.

4. Bate, *Samuel Johnson*, 337. "Print" and "publish" are generally synonyms in our world, but through nearly the whole of the eighteenth century, a book's *printer* designated the person or firm that pressed type to page, while that same book's *publisher* designated the (often distinct) person or firm that invested and thereby risked the capital to pay for the supplies and labor that printing required. The mid-eighteenth-century publication of a large and expensive work like Johnson's *Dictionary* required the cooperation and financial partnership of multiple printers. Such relationships are discussed further in Chapters 3 and 4.

5. G. J. Kolb hypothesizes a connection between *The History of the Marchioness de Pompadour* and *Rasselas* in "Johnson's 'Little Pompadour': A Textual Crux and a Hypothesis," in *Restoration and Eighteenth-Century Literature: Essays in Honor of Alan Dugald McKillop*, ed. Carroll Camden (Chicago: University of Chicago Press for William Marsh Rice University, 1963), 131–142.

6. Margreta de Grazia, *Shakespeare Verbatim: The Reproduction of Authenticity and the 1790 Apparatus* (New York: Oxford University Press, 1991); see also Roger Chartier, *The Order of Books: Readers, Authors, and Libraries in Europe between the Fourteenth and Eighteenth Centuries* [1992], trans. Lydia G. Cochrane (Stanford, CA: Stanford University Press, 1994).

7. Samuel Johnson, *A Dictionary of the English Language*, 2 vols. (London: W. Strahan, for J. and P. Knapton; T. and T. Longman; C. Hitch and L. Hawes; A. Millar; and R. and J. Dodsley, 1755).

8. *Samuel Johnson: Selected Poetry and Prose,* ed. Frank Brady and William Wimsatt (Berkeley: University of California Press, 1978).

9. Though the first edition of *Pamela* was printed in duodecimo, a deluxe illustrated edition in octavo appeared in 1742.

10. Lisa Gitelman, *Paper Knowledge: Toward a Media History of Documents* (Durham, NC: Duke University Press, 2014), 2.

11. Carolyn R. Miller, "Genre as Social Action," *Quarterly Journal of Speech* 70 (1984): 151–167. While this remains my preferred definition, one would do well to note the alternative, noncommunicate theory of media offered by Craig Dworkin in *No Medium* (Cambridge, MA: MIT Press, 2013).

12. Meredith L. McGill, "Echocriticism: Repetition and the Order of Texts," *American Literature* 88, no. 1 (March 2016): 1–29, citation at 3.

13. Henry James, *The Tragic Muse* [1890; rev. ed., 1905], ed. Philip Horne (New York: Penguin, 1990), 4.

14. The major alternative to book publication, especially during the second half of the nineteenth century, was serial publication. Touchstone studies that consider novels in relation to their serialized appearances include J. A. Sutherland, *Victorian Novelists and Publishers* (Chicago: University of Chicago Press, 1976); Linda K. Hughes and Michael Lund, *The Victorian Serial* (Charlottesville: University of Virginia Press, 1991); *Literature in the Marketplace: Nineteenth-Century British Publishing and Reading Practices,* ed. John O. Jordan and Robert L. Patten (Cambridge: Cambridge University Press, 1995); *Periodical Literature in Nineteenth-Century America,* ed. Kenneth M. Price and Susan Belasco Smith (Charlottesville: University of Virginia Press, 1995); Patricia Okker, *Social Stories: The Magazine Novel in Nineteenth-Century America* (Charlottesville: University of Virginia Press, 2003); Christopher Looby, "Southworth and Seriality: *The Hidden Hand* in the *New York Ledger,*" *Nineteenth-Century Literature,* 59, no. 2 (2004): 179–211.

15. Throughout this study, "material text" refers to the diverse properties of the physical object by which a textual content circulates, many of which properties are available to interpretation and inquiry as much as their textual contents. For an elaboration of this term, see Peter Stallybrass, "The Library and Material Texts," *PMLA* 119, no. 5 (October 2004): 1347–1352.

16. Terminology here is tricky, because words like "format," "medium," and "genre" have overlapping meanings and are often evoked with different nuances, even among specialists in the same fields. Generally speaking, the following chapters will use "format" to talk about the physical features of a text in terms of its production (see

Tanselle, "The Concept of Format"). By "media" I refer to the early modern sense of "an intervening or intermediate agency" (Raymond Williams, *Keywords: A Vocabulary of Culture and Society,* rev. ed. [New York: Oxford University Press, 1985], 203). In this account, books are media insofar as they exist in relation to both their creators' designs and their readers' responses—insofar, in other words, as they allow for connections between creators and readers, without necessarily bringing the two into immediate contact. See John Guillory, "Genesis of the Media Concept," *Critical Inquiry* 36, no. 2 (Winter 2010): 321–362. Among the advantages of such consideration is that it requires scholars who care about books to be mindful that the empirically verifiable features of a book's history (such as page size, type, binding, paper quality, place of production and sale, and other significant details that preoccupy descriptive bibliographers) are not the entirety of the story. See, for example, Thomas Tanselle, "Bibliography and Science," *Studies in Bibliography* 27 (1974): 55–89; D. F. McKenzie, *Bibliography and the Sociology of Texts* (Cambridge: Cambridge University Press, 1986); Hugh Amory, "The Trout and the Milk: An Ethnobibliographic Talk," *Harvard Library Bulletin* 7 (1996): 50–65. This point has also been influentially made in Robert Darnton, "What Is the History of Books?," *Daedalus* (Summer 1982): 65–83. Works by Roger Chartier and Peter Stallybrass, cited throughout the following chapters, have also been crucial to my thinking about how texts can be assessed at the intersection of their material and immaterial qualities.

17. Important exceptions in novel studies include Robert B. Winans, "The Growth of a Novel-Reading Public in Late-Eighteenth-Century America," *Early American Literature* 9, no. 3 (Winter 1975): 267–275; Robert B. Winans, "Bibliography and the Cultural Historian: Notes on the Eighteenth-Century Novel," in *Printing and Society in Early America,* ed. William L. Joyce, David D. Hall, Richard D. Brown, and John B. Hench (Worcester, MA: American Antiquarian Society, 1983), 174–185; Cathy N. Davidson, *The Revolution and the Word: The Rise of the Novel in America* (New York: Oxford University Press, 1986); Janine Barchas, *Graphic Design, Print Culture, and the Eighteenth-Century Novel* (Cambridge: Cambridge University Press, 2003); Leah Price, *The Anthology and the Rise of the Novel: From Richardson to George Eliot* (Cambridge: Cambridge University Press, 2005); Leah Price, *How to Do Things with Books in Victorian Britain* (Princeton, NJ: Princeton University Press, 2013); Rachel Sagner Buurma, "Anonymity, Corporate Authority, and the Archive: The Production of Authorship in Late-Victorian England," *Victorian Studies* 50, no. 1 (Autumn 2007): 15–42; Elizabeth Carolyn Miller, *Slow Print: Literary Radicalism and Late Victorian Print Culture* (Stanford, CA: Stanford University Press, 2013); Joseph Rezek, *London and the Making of Provincial Literature: Aesthetics and the Transatlantic Book Trade, 1800–1850* (Philadelphia: University of Pennsylvania Press, 2015).

Exceptions in media studies include Keith Negus, *Music Genres and Corporate Cultures* (New York: Routledge, 1999); Lucas Hildebrand's discussion of "analog aesthetics" in *Inherent Vice: Bootleg Histories of Videotape and Copyright* (Durham, NC: Duke University Press, 2009); Jonathan Sterne, *MP3: The Meaning of a Format* (Durham, NC: Duke University Press, 2012); Ben Kafka, *The Demon of Writing:*

Powers and Failures of Paperwork (New York: Zone Books, 2012); Gitelman, *Paper Knowledge.*

Though somewhat different in its aim, de Grazia's *Shakespeare Verbatim* remains in my estimation a foundational precursor for these concerns. Virginia Jackson's *Dickinson's Misery: A Theory of Lyric Reading* (Princeton, NJ: Princeton University Press, 2005) also offers an invaluable model.

18. Ian Watt, *The Rise of the Novel: Studies in Defoe, Richardson and Fielding* (London: Chatto and Windus, 1957).

19. Though few if any scholars working today are prepared to emphasize the formalism in the "rise of the novel" story in the purely aesthetic sense that is often associated (reductively) with post–World War II New Critical pedagogies, what scholars mean by "literary form" is nevertheless far from agreed upon. For important definitional exercises, some of which diagnose and some of which embrace the multiple meanings of "form," see Marjorie Levinson, "What Is New Formalism?," *PMLA* 122, no. 2 (March 2007): 558–569; Caroline Levine, *Forms: Whole, Rhythm, Hierarchy, Network* (Princeton, NJ: Princeton University Press, 2015); Sandra Macpherson, "A Little Formalism," *ELH* 82, no. 2 (Summer 2015): 385–404; Jonathan Kramnick and Anahid Nersessian, "Form and Explanation," *Critical Inquiry* 43, no. 3 (Spring 2017): 650–669. On the ethics novelistic form, see Jesse Rosenthal, *Good Form: The Ethical Experience of the Victorian Novel* (Princeton, NJ: Princeton University Press, 2016).

20. V21 Collective, "Manifesto of the V21 Collective," 2015, http://v21collective.org/manifesto-of-the-v21-collective-ten-theses, thesis 7; Nancy Armstrong and Leonard Tennenhouse, *Novels in the Time of Democratic Writing: The American Example* (Philadelphia: University of Pennsylvania Press, 2018), 9.

21. Though character is often associated with novels, certainly the performance context for character—and the appearance of characters in printed playtexts beginning in the late fifteenth century—operates in a complex dialectic with the rise of novelistic character. As Julie Stone Peters argues, by the mid-eighteenth century, stage actors and orators drew on novelistic details for their conceptions of character (see *Theatre of the Book, 1480–1880: Print, Text, and Performance in Europe* [New York: Oxford University Press, 2000], 290–293). The bibliography on the development of character in that dialectic is substantial, but for some touchstone works, see Harry Berger Jr., "What Did the King Know and When Did He Know It? Shakespearean Discourses and Psychoanalysis," *South Atlantic Quarterly* 88 (1989): 811–862; David Marshall, *The Surprising Effects of Sympathy: Marivaux, Diderot, Rousseau, and Mary Shelley* (Chicago: University of Chicago Press, 1988); Margreta de Grazia and Peter Stallybrass, "The Materiality of the Shakespearean Text," *Shakespeare Quarterly* 44, no. 3 (Autumn 1993): 255–283; Deidre Shauna Lynch, *The Economy of Character: Novels, Market Culture, and the Business of Inner Meaning* (Chicago: University of Chicago Press, 1998), esp. 70–75; Lisa Freeman, *Character's Theater: Genre and Identity on the Eighteenth-Century English Stage* (Philadelphia: University of Pennsylvania Press, 2001). Martin Puchner traces a longer history of character in philosophical writings in *The Drama of Ideas: Platonic Provocations in Theater and Philosophy*

(New York: Oxford University Press, 2010), esp. 20–36. On printed playtexts, see Zachary Lesser, *Renaissance Drama and the Politics of Publication: Readings in the English Book Trade* (Cambridge: Cambridge University Press, 2004); Zachary Lesser and Peter Stallybrass, "The First Literary *Hamlet* and the Commonplacing of Professional Plays," *Shakespeare Quarterly* 59, no. 4 (Winter 2008): 371–420.

22. The association of characters with depth found important expression in E. M. Forster's *Aspects of the Novel* (1927; repr., New York: Harcourt, 1955), where he distinguishes between "round" and "flat" characters (67). The depth model has been elaborated and qualified in works such as Patricia Ann Meyer Spacks, *Imagining a Self: Autobiography and Novel in Eighteenth-Century England* (Cambridge, MA: Harvard University Press, 1976); J. Paul Hunter, *Before Novels: The Culture of Eighteenth-Century English Fiction* (Chicago: University of Chicago Press, 1990); David A. Brewer, *The Afterlife of Character, 1726–1825* (Philadelphia: University of Pennsylvania Press, 2005); Blakey Vermeule, *Why Do We Care about Literary Characters?* (Baltimore: Johns Hopkins University Press, 2009); David Kurnick, *Empty Houses: Theatrical Failure and the Novel* (Princeton, NJ: Princeton University Press, 2012); Claire Jarvis, *Exquisite Masochism: Marriage, Sex, and the Novel Form* (Baltimore: Johns Hopkins University Press, 2016). Other scholars have countered this tradition by discussing some of the ways that "flat" or superficial characterization serves equally important (though not identical) figurative aims. For some of the most persuasive accounts, see Lynch, *The Economy of Character;* Sandra Macpherson, *Harm's Way: Tragic Responsibility and the Novel Form* (Baltimore: Johns Hopkins University Press, 2010); Marta Figlerowicz, *Flat Protagonists: A Theory of Novel Character* (New York: Oxford University Press, 2016); Daniel M. Stout, *Corporate Romanticism: Liberalism, Justice, and the Novel* (New York: Fordham University Press, 2017). The present study focuses on characterological depth, due to the emphasis on depth in all of the primary texts examined herein. My personal view, however, is that deep and superficial, round and flat figures work together, even as they do not receive equal discursive emphasis. Here I am persuaded by the model put forth in Alex Woloch, *The One vs. the Many: Minor Characters and the Space of the Protagonist in the Novel* (Princeton, NJ: Princeton University Press, 2003). See also Jeremy Rosen's *Minor Characters Have Their Day: Genre and the Contemporary Literary Marketplace* (New York: Columbia University Press, 2016), which provides a suggestive theory of genre in which character is less a figurative practice than a type of readerly negotiation.

23. Ian Green, *Print and Protestantism in Early Modern England* (New York: Oxford University Press, 2000), 349.

24. Georg Lukács, *The Theory of the Novel: A Historico-Political Essay on the Forms of Great Epic Literature* [1963], trans. Anna Bostock (London: Merlin Press, 1971), 88.

25. Carlo Ginzburg, *The Cheese and the Worms: The Cosmos of a Sixteenth-Century Miller* [1976], trans. John and Anne Tedeschi (Baltimore: Johns Hopkins University Press, 1992), xxi. See also Lauren Berlant, "On the Case," *Critical Inquiry* 33, no. 4 (Summer 2007): 663–672.

26. Precisely why *The Rise of the Novel* appears so tone-deaf to gender is unclear. Much more clear is the fact that the literary contributions of Frances Burney, Charlotte

Lennox, Ann Radcliffe, Jane Austen, and other women writers were widely recognized by studies that predate Watt's, including Ernest A. Baker's ten-volume *History of the English Novel* (1924–1939), which, on the syllabus for a Stanford course (Summer 1956), Watt himself identifies as "still" the standard history of "The English Novel through the Eighteenth Century." Ian Watt Papers, Special Collections Department of the Stanford University Archives, ACCN 1990-131 SC 401, Box 49.

The body of scholarship undertaken to revise Watt's contracted canon is substantial, but touchstone contributions include Sandra Gilbert and Susan Gubar, *The Madwoman in the Attic: The Woman Writer and the Nineteenth-Century Literary Imagination* (New Haven, CT: Yale University Press, 1979); Nina Baym, "Melodramas of Beset Manhood: How Theories of American Fiction Exclude Women Authors," *American Quarterly* 33 (1981): 123–139; Jane Tompkins, *Sensational Designs: The Cultural Work of American Fiction 1790–1860* (New York: Oxford University Press, 1985); Terry Castle, *Masquerade and Civilization: The Carnivalesque in Eighteenth-Century English Culture and Fiction* (Stanford, CA: Stanford University Press, 1986); Catherine Gallagher, *Nobody's Story: The Vanishing Acts of Women Writers in the Marketplace, 1670–1820* (Berkeley: University of California Press, 1994); Margaret Anne Doody, *The True Story of the Novel* (New Brunswick, NJ: Rutgers University Press, 1996); Paula McDowell, *The Women of Grub Street: Press, Politics, and Gender in the London Literary Marketplace 1678–1730* (Oxford: Clarendon Press, 1998); Jody Greene, "Revenge of the Straw Woman," in *The Trouble with Ownership: Literary Property and Authorial Liability in England, 1660–1730* (Philadelphia: University of Pennsylvania Press, 2005), esp. 150–194; Paula R. Backscheider, *Elizabeth Singer Rowe and the Development of the English Novel* (Baltimore: Johns Hopkins University Press, 2013).

27. Jan Fergus, *Provincial Novel Readers in Eighteenth-Century England* (Oxford: Oxford University Press, 2006).

28. On race and seventeenth- and eighteenth-century communications media, see Matt Cohen, *The Networked Wilderness: Communicating in Early New England* (Minneapolis: University of Minnesota Press, 2010); Joseph Rezek, "The Orations on the Abolition of the Slave Trade and the Uses of Print in the Early Black Atlantic," *Early American Literature* 45, no. 3 (2010): 655–682; Matt Cohen and Jeffrey Glover, eds., *Colonial Mediascapes* (Lincoln: University of Nebraska Press, 2014); Elizabeth Maddock Dillon, "Atlantic Aesthesis: Books and 'Sensus Communis' in the New World," *Early American Literature* 51, no. 2 (2016): 367–395; Mary Caton Lingold, "Peculiar Animations: Listening to Afro-Atlantic Music in Caribbean Travel Narratives," *Early American Literature* 52, no. 3 (2017): 623–650; Nicole N. Aljoe, "Testimonies of the Enslaved in Caribbean Literary History," in *Literary Histories of the Early Anglophone Caribbean: Islands in the Stream,* ed. Nicole N. Aljoe, Brycchan Carey, and Thomas W. Krise (Cham, Switzerland: Palgrave Macmillan, 2018), 107–123. For thinking about discourses of race in the history of eighteenth-century English fiction, see Srinivas Aravamudan, *Tropicopolitans: Colonialism and Agency, 1688–1804* (Durham, NC: Duke University Press, 1999) and *Enlightenment Orientalism: Resisting the Rise of the Novel* (Chicago: University of Chicago Press, 2012).

29. The vast majority of books read in the British North American colonies were printed in London (or pirated from London by way of Dublin), and the British North American colonies were a crucial export market for the London book trade (at least until the 1770s). See Giles Barber, "Books from the Old World and for the New: The British International Trade in Book in the Eighteenth Century," *Studies on Voltaire and the Eighteenth Century* 151 (1976): 185–224; Winans, "Bibliography and the Cultural Historian"; Stephen Botein, "The Anglo-American Book Trade before 1776: Personnel and Strategies," in Joyce et al., *Printing and Society in Early America,* 48–82; James N. Green, "English Books and Printing in the Age of Franklin," in *A History of the Book in America,* vol. 1, *The Colonial Book in the Atlantic World,* ed. Hugh Amory and David D. Hall (Chapel Hill: University of North Carolina Press, 2000), 248–297; James Raven, *London Booksellers and American Customers: Transatlantic Literary Community and the Charleston Library Society, 1748–1811* (Charleston: University of South Carolina Press, 2002), esp. 6–7.

   Though British colonial North America was the major London export market, a full consideration of that market would also engage exporting to India. That work exceeds the scope of this study, but see B. S. Kesavan, *History of Printing and Publishing in India: A Study of Cultural Reawakening* (New Delhi: National Book Trust, 1985); Vinay Dharwadker, "Print Culture and Literary Markets in Colonial India," in *Language Machines: Technologies of Literary and Cultural Production,* ed. Jeffrey Masten, Peter Stallybrass, and Nancy Vickers (New York: Routledge: 1997), 108–133; Kenneth R. Hall, "The Eighteenth- and Early Nineteenth-Century Evolution of Indian Print Culture and Knowledge Networks in Calcutta and Madras," in *Print Culture Histories Beyond the Metropolis,* ed. James J. Connolly, Patrick Collier, Frank Felsenstein, Kenneth R. Hall, and Robert G. Hall (Toronto: University of Toronto Press, 2016), 88–122.

30. See, for example, Timothy Brennan, "The National Longing for Form," in *Nation and Narration,* ed. Homi K. Bhabha (New York: Routledge, 1990), 44–70; Doris Sommer, *Foundational Fictions: The National Romances of Latin America* (Berkeley: University of California Press, 1991); Lawrence Buell, *The Dream of the Great American Novel* (Cambridge, MA: Harvard University Press, 2014), 10–12. The rise of novels in relation to "new world" nationalisms has been influentially expounded by Benedict Anderson, *Imagined Communities: Reflections on the Origin and Spread of Nationalism,* rev. ed. (New York: Verso, 1991), 47–65.

31. Rezek, *London and the Making of Provincial Literature.*

32. Kermit Vanderbilt, *American Literature and the Academy: The Roots, Growth, and Maturity of a Profession* (Philadelphia: University of Pennsylvania Press, 1986); Gerald Graff, *Professing Literature: An Institutional History* (Chicago: University of Chicago Press, 1987); Gauri Viswanathan, *Masks of Conquest: Literary Study and British Rule in India* (New York: Columbia University Press, 1989); Nina Baym, "Early Histories of American Literature: A Chapter in the Institution of New England," *American Literary History* 1, no. 3 (Autumn 1989): 459–488; David R. Shumway, *Creating American Civilization: A Genealogy of American Literature as an*

Academic Discipline (Minneapolis: University of Minnesota Press, 1994); Elizabeth Renker, *The Origins of American Literature Studies: An Institutional History* (Cambridge: Cambridge University Press, 2010); Rachel Sagner Buurma and Laura Heffernan, "The Common Reader and the Archival Classroom: Disciplinary History for the 21st Century," *New Literary History* 43, no. 1 (Spring 2012): 113–135; "The Classroom in the Canon: T. S. Eliot's Modern English Literature Extension Course for Working People and *The Sacred Wood*," *PMLA* 133, no. 2 (2018): 264–281. For my own attempts to tell episodes from this story, see Jordan Alexander Stein, "Are 'American Novels' Novels? *Mardi* and the Problem of Boring Books," in *The Oxford Handbook of Nineteenth-Century American Literature,* ed. Russ Castronovo (New York: Oxford University Press, 2011), 42–58; and "Secular Aesthetics: Form, Theme, and Method in the Study of American Literature," *Comparative Literature* 65, no. 3 (Summer 2013): 325–344.

33. For generative arguments that pursue transatlantic approaches, see Robert Weisbuch, *Atlantic Double-Cross: American Literature and British Influence in the Age of Emerson* (Chicago: University of Chicago Press, 1986); Paul Gilroy, *The Black Atlantic: Modernity and Double Consciousness* (Cambridge, MA: Harvard University Press, 1993); Amanda Claybaugh, *The Novel of Purpose: Literature and Social Reform in the Anglo-American World* (Ithaca, NY: Cornell University Press, 2007) and "New Fields, Conventional Habits, and the Legacy of *Atlantic Double-Cross*," *American Literary History* 20, no. 3 (2008): 439–448; Leonard Tennenhouse, *The Importance of Feeling English: American Literature and the British Diaspora, 1750–1850* (Princeton, NJ: Princeton University Press, 2007); Elisa Tamarkin, *Anglophilia: Deference and Devotion in Antebellum American Literature* (Chicago: University of Chicago Press, 2008); Omise'eke Natasha Tinsley, "Black Atlantic, Queer Atlantic: Queer Imaginings of the Middle Passage," *GLQ: A Journal of Lesbian and Gay Studies* 14, nos. 2–3 (2008): 191–216; Julia Lee, *The American Slave Narrative and the Victorian Novel* (New York: Oxford University Press, 2010); Elizabeth Maddock Dillon, *New World Drama: The Performative Commons in the Atlantic World, 1649–1849* (Durham, NC: Duke University Press, 2014). Daniel Hack, *Reaping Something New: African American Transformations of Victorian Literature* (Princeton, NJ: Princeton University Press, 2017).

34. Exceptions include Davidson, *The Revolution and the Word;* Lynch, *The Economy of Character;* Price, *The Anthology and the Rise of the Novel* and *How to do Things with Books in Victorian Britain;* Christina Lupton, *Knowing Books: The Consciousness of Mediation in Eighteenth-Century Britain* (Philadelphia: University of Pennsylvania Press, 2012).

35. *The Cambridge History of the Book in Britain,* 6 vols., ed. Richard Gameson et al. (Cambridge: Cambridge University Press, 1998–2014); *The Oxford History of the Irish Book,* 5 vols., ed. Raymond Gillespie and Andrew Hadfield et al. (New York: Oxford University Press, 2006–); *The Edinburgh History of the Book in Scotland,* 4 vols., ed. Stephen W. Brown and Warren McDougall et al. (Edinburgh: Edinburgh University Press, 2007–); *Histoire de l'édition française,* 4 vols., ed. Henri-Jean Martin et Roger Chartier, en collaboration avec Jean-Pierre Vivet (Paris: Promodis, 1984–1989); *A History of the Book in America,* 5 vols., ed. David D. Hall (Chapel Hill: University of North Carolina Press, 2000–2010).

36. The most influential introductory summary of the field remains Darnton, "What Is the History of Books?" For reconsiderations of Darnton's model, see Thomas R. Adams and Nicholas Barker, "A New Model for the History of the Book," in *A Potencie of Life: Books in Society,* ed. Nicholas Barker (London: British Library, 1993), 5–42; Robert Darnton, "'What Is the History of Books?' Revisited," *Modern Intellectual History* 4 (2007): 495–508. For a more recent discussion, see Meredith L. McGill, "Literary History, Book History, and Media Studies," in *Turns of Event: American Literary Studies in Motion,* ed. Hester Blum (Philadelphia: University of Pennsylvania Press, 2016), 23–39. A different set of models emerges from the debate between Elizabeth L. Eisenstein, *The Printing Press as an Agent of Change: Communications and Cultural Transformations in Early Modern Europe,* 2 vols. (Cambridge: Cambridge University Press, 1979), and Adrian Johns, *The Nature of the Book: Print and Knowledge in the Making* (Chicago: University of Chicago Press, 1998); see esp. their exchange: Eisenstein, "An Unacknowledged Revolution Revisited," *American Historical Review* 101, no. 7 (February 2002): 87–105; Johns, "How to Acknowledge a Revolution," *American Historical Review* 101, no. 7 (February 2002): 106–125; Eisenstein, "Reply," *American Historical Review* 101, no. 7 (February 2002): 126–128. For an altogether different and searching model, see Juliet Fleming, *Cultural Graphology: Writing after Derrida* (Chicago: University of Chicago Press, 2016).

37. Franco Moretti, "On *The Novel,*" in *The Novel,* vol. 1, *History, Geography, and Culture,* ed. Franco Moretti (Princeton, NJ: Princeton University Press, 2006), ix–x, citation at ix.

38. Stephen Greenblatt and Catherine Gallagher, *Practicing New Historicism* (Chicago: University of Chicago Press, 2000), 16.

39. Lawrence Grossberg, Cary Nelson, and Paula A. Treichler, eds., *Cultural Studies* (New York: Routledge, 1992), 11.

40. Alan Liu, "The Power of Formalism: The New Historicism," *ELH* 56, no. 4 (Winter 1989): 721–771, citation at 754–755.

41. Brook Thomas, *The New Historicism and Other Old-Fashioned Topics* (Princeton, NJ: Princeton University Press, 1991), 10–12.

42. David Scott Kastan, *Shakespeare after Theory* (New York: Routledge, 1999), 18.

43. Meredith L. McGill, *American Literature and the Culture of Reprinting, 1834–1853* (Philadelphia: University of Pennsylvania Press, 2003), 6. See also the introduction to *The Book in History, The Book as History: New Intersections of the Material Text,* ed. Heidi Brayman, Jesse M. Lander, and Zachary Lesser (New Haven, CT: Yale University Press, 2016).

44. Matthew P. Brown, "Book History, Sexy Knowledge, and the Challenge of the New Boredom," *American Literary History* 16, no. 4 (Winter 2004): 688–706, citation at 691.

45. Watt, *The Rise of the Novel,* 33.

46. A notable example comes from Nancy Armstrong's scholarship, which definitively challenged the narrow bias of Watt's masculine canon, and yet which determinedly isolates the novel's causal power in effecting modern persons. Her influential 1987

monograph, *Desire and Domestic Fiction,* for instance, argues unequivocally that "the domestic novel antedated—was indeed necessarily antecedent to—the way of life it represented" (*Desire and Domestic Fiction: A Political History of the Novel* [New York: Oxford University Press, 1987], 9). Armstrong expanded this claim two decades later in *How Novels Think,* postulating that the British novel "came into being, I believe, as writers sought to formulate a kind of subject that had not yet existed in writing. Once formulated in fiction, however, this subject proved uniquely capable of reproducing itself not only in authors but also in readers, in other novels, and across British culture in law, medicine, moral and political philosophy, biography, history, and other forms of writing that took the individual as their most basic unit" (*How Novels Think: The Limits of British Individualism, 1719–1900* [New York: Columbia University Press, 2005], 3). As before, the novel brought into being "the way of life it represented," but in the second account, that being proved epistemologically and disciplinarily saturating for British culture as a whole. The novel in Armstrong's view is clearly a causal agent, but its effects are dizzyingly widespread, moving at the quick pace of two sentences from an isolated literary form to the defining characteristics of a culture.

Despite some real differences between Watt's and Armstrong's accounts, the fact that the epistemology of fiction extends beyond the novel and into the world is, for both of them, something for which we must credit the novel. These are not the only influential scholars who make this move. D. A. Miller justified his exquisite readings of the culturally consequential effects of Victorian novels in *The Novel and the Police* by observing that "perhaps no openly fictional form has ever sought to 'make a difference' in the world more than the Victorian novel, whose cultural hegemony and diffusion well qualified it to become the primary spiritual exercise of an entire age" (*The Novel and the Police* [Berkeley: University of California Press, 1988], x). While the ambition of the novel is surely as great as Miller says, it is nonetheless difficult to agree that its reach is simply the result of that ambition. Indeed, one does not have to dispute the Foucauldian insight that action is shaped by the parameters of the thinkable in order to observe that representations of the thinkable do not catapult all thoughts to the status of world-historical agents. Even Michael McKeon's ambitious dialectical investigation into *The Origins of the English Novel* does less to solve this problem than simply to embrace it, asserting that "genre theory cannot be divorced from the history of genres, from the understanding of genres in history" (*The Origins of the English Novel, 1660–1740* [Baltimore: Johns Hopkins University Press, 1986], 1). Meanwhile, Franco Moretti, in a series of provocative attempts to diversify the novelistic canon (and so the interpretive claims made under the sign "novel"), envisions the evolution of the novel's form as full of "branches, formal choices, that don't replicate each other but rather move *away* from each other, turning the genre into a wide field of diverging moves" (*Distant Reading* [New York: Verso, 2013], 77. See also *Graphs, Maps, Trees: Abstract Models for Literary History* [New York: Verso, 2005], esp. 67–91). While this account is admirable in its emphasis on divergence (atypical in a field that prefers to think in terms of homology or influence) and in its determination to demonstrate the wide historical and geographic scope of this divergence, it nonetheless falls into the same circular thinking as Watt's account, mapping the global reach of literary forms in order to understand that what stands behind them are formal choices.

47. Gilles Deleuze and Félix Guattari, *A Thousand Plateaus: Capitalism and Schizophrenia* [1980], trans. Brian Massumi (Minneapolis: University of Minnesota Press, 1987), 15, 229–230.

48. For this reason, one recurrent topos for the analysis in each of the following chapters is jokes—those variously knowing and unknowing, intentional and unintentional, instances of parabasis that open a window onto culture. My understanding of irony as "permanent parabasis" comes from Paul de Man, "The Concept of Irony," in *Aesthetic Ideology,* ed. with an introduction by Andrzej Warminski (Minneapolis: University of Minnesota Press, 1996), 163–184, citation at 179.

49. Philip Fisher, *Hard Facts: Setting and Form in the American Novel* (New York: Oxford University Press, 1985); Tompkins, *Sensational Designs.*

50. This axiom underpins the modern study of cultural anthropology, particularly among what's sometimes (half-jokingly) called the Functional School. The differences between action and explanation, and between specialist knowledge and folk knowledge, are charted most influentially in Bronislaw Malinowski, "Baloma: The Spirits of the Dead in the Trobriand Islands," *Journal of the Royal Anthropological Institute of Great Britain and Ireland* 46 (1916): 353–430.

51. Lara Langer Cohen, *The Fabrication of American Literature: Fraudulence and Antebellum Print Culture* (Philadelphia: University of Pennsylvania Press, 2012), 4. I have adapted from Cohen's phrase, the "bummer school of American literature" (244). See also Trish Loughran in *The Republic in Print: Print Culture in the Age of U.S. Nation Building, 1770–1870* (New York: Columbia University Press, 2007); Kafka, *The Demon of Writing.*

1. Paper Selves

1. E. M. Forster, *Aspects of the Novel* (1927; repr., New York: Harcourt, 1955), 43.

2. Recent scholarship has pointed to the brief proliferation of "it" narratives in the late eighteenth century, which figure objects rather than persons as characters. See Deidre Shauna Lynch, *The Economy of Character: Novels, Market Culture, and the Business of Inner Meaning* (Chicago: University of Chicago Press, 1998); Jonathan Lamb, "The Crying of Lost Things," *ELH* 71, no. 4 (2004): 949–967; Mark Blackwell, ed., *The Secret Life of Things: Animals, Objects, and It-Narratives in Eighteenth-Century England* (Lewisburg, PA: Bucknell University Press, 2007); Julie Park, *The Self and It: Novels and Objects in Eighteenth-Century England* (Stanford, CA: Stanford University Press, 2009). A few scholars have connected the proliferation of these narratives with the media history of books more generally. See Leah Price, "From History of a Book to a 'History of the Book,'" *Representations* 108 (Fall 2009): 120–138; Christina Lupton, *Knowing Books: The Consciousness of Mediation in Eighteenth-Century Britain* (Philadelphia: University of Pennsylvania Press, 2012). A particularly powerful

move in this conversation has been the analysis of figuration itself, especially though tropes of personification. See, in particular, Heather Keenleyside, *Animals and Other People: Literary Forms and Living Beings in the Long Eighteenth Century* (Philadelphia: University of Pennsylvania Press, 2016); Monique Allewaert, "Insect Poetics: James Grainger, Personification, and Enlightenments Not Taken," *Early American Literature* 52, no. 2 (2017): 299–332.

3. On the nature of character, see Erich Auerbach, "Figura," [1944], trans. Ralph Manheim, in *Scenes from the Drama of European Literature* (Minneapolis: University of Minnesota Press, 1984), 11–78; Aaron Kunin, "Characters Lounge," *MLQ* 70, no. 3 (Spring 2009): 291–318; John Frow, *Character and Person* (New York: Oxford University Press, 2014). See also notes 21 and 22 of the Introduction.

4. Eve Kosofsky Sedgwick, *Epistemology of the Closet* (Berkeley: University of California Press, 1990), 22.

5. Nancy Ruttenburg, *Democratic Personality: Popular Voice and the Trial of American Authorship* (Stanford, CA: Stanford University Press, 1998), 82.

6. My preferred term of art in this chapter and those that follow will be "Reformed Protestants" rather than "Puritans." I prefer the former term as a corrective to the often too-neat arguments that draw lines of intellectual and cultural dissent from white settler colonists in New England to the United States (a mythology that has been productively illuminated if not exactly overturned by Sacvan Bercovitch's magisterial study *The Puritan Origins of the American Self* [New Haven, CT: Yale University Press, 1975]). Of course, scholars have used "Puritan" in dynamic ways. As John Coffey and Paul C. H. Lim observe, "Puritanism is the name we give to a distinctive and particularly intense variety of early modern Reformed Protestantism which originated within the unique context of the Church of England but spilled out beyond it, branching off into divergent streams, and overflowing into other lands and foreign churches" ("Introduction," in *The Cambridge Companion to Puritanism* [Cambridge: Cambridge University Press, 2008], 1–15, citation at 1–2). However, even with such a broad definition in play, the lines of intellectual influence and theological affiliation that emerge over this and the next three chapters are still not clearly "Puritan."

My thinking about these terms owes much to other scholars who have found various ways of accounting for nuances of position without affirming a theological consensus. Foundational for these concerns is Patrick Collinson's *The Elizabethan Puritan Movement* (Berkeley: University of California Press, 1967), which paints a dynamic relation between doctrine and practice. With particular sophistication, Janice Knight distinguishes between two variants of late sixteenth-century Cambridge theology: the "Intellectual Fathers" who follow in the tradition of William Perkins and William Ames, and the "Spiritual Brethren" who follow in the tradition of Richard Sibbes and John Preston; see Knight's *Orthodoxies in Massachusetts: Rereading American Puritanism* (Cambridge, MA: Harvard University Press, 1994); T. D. Bozeman offers the term "Contra-Puritan" to describe a different set of intellectual fissures in "The Glory of the 'Third Time': John Eaton as Contra-Puritan," *Journal of Ecclesiastical History* 47 (1996): 638–654. For a particularly helpful overview of the scholarly use of the term "Puritan," see Michael P. Winship, "Were There Any Puritans in New England?," *New England Quarterly* 74, no. 1 (March 2001): 118–138. Jorge Cañizares-Esguerra further complicates the term, positing parallels between the Protestant and Catholic colonization efforts, in *Puritan Conquistadors: Iberianizing the Atlantic, 1550–1700* (Stanford, CA: Stanford University Press, 2006). For historical contexts, see Emory Elliot, "The Dream of a Christian Utopia," in *The Cambridge History of American Literature,* vol. 1, *1590–1820* (Cambridge: Cambridge University Press, 1994), 183–204, esp. 183–185; and the synthetic framing offered by Sarah Rivett and Abram Van Engen in "Postexceptionalist Puritanism," *American Literature* 90, no. 4 (December 2018): 675–692. On the terminological complexities of "religion" more generally, one would do well to start with Jonathan Z. Smith, "Religion, Religions, Religious," in *Critical Terms for Religious Studies,* ed. Mark C. Taylor (Chicago: University of Chicago Press, 1998), 269–284.

7. A canonical formulation of this point can be found in Perry Miller, *The New England Mind: The Seventeenth Century* (Cambridge, MA: Harvard University Press, 1939), 78–84; for a more elaborated version, see John Morgan, *Godly Learning: Puritan Attitudes towards Reason, Learning and Education, 1560–1640* (Cambridge: Cambridge University Press, 1988).

8. Ann Kibbey, *The Interpretation of Material Shapes in Puritanism: A Study of Rhetoric, Prejudice, and Violence* (Cambridge: Cambridge University Press, 1986), 11.

9. For one powerful statement among many of this view, see Paul de Man, "Semiology and Rhetoric," *Diacritics* 3, no. 3 (Autumn 1973): 27–33.

10. Sarah Rivett proposes a broader cultural connection between the agendas and rhetorical practices of plain-style ministers, Cambridge Platonists, and early Royal Society scientists and historians in the seventeenth century in *The Science of the Soul in Colonial New England* (Chapel Hill: University of North Carolina Press for the Omohundro Institute of Early American History and Culture, 2012), 56. See also Brian Cummings, *The Literary Culture of the Reformation: Grammar and Grace* (New York: Oxford University Press, 2003).

11. T. H. Breen, *The Character of the Good Ruler: A Study of Puritan Political Ideas in New England, 1630–1730* (New Haven, CT: Yale University Press, 1970), 61.

12. Gilles Deleuze and Félix Guattari, *A Thousand Plateaus: Capitalism and Schizophrenia* [1980], trans. Brian Massumi (Minneapolis: University of Minnesota Press, 1987), 15.

13. Gayatri Chakravorty Spivak, *A Critique of Postcolonial Reason: Toward a History of the Vanishing Present* (Cambridge, MA: Harvard University Press, 1999), 256.

14. Heb. 11:1; *The Humble Advice of the Assembly of Divines, Now by Authority of Parliament Sitting at Westminster, concerning a Confession of Faith* (London: Printed for the Company of Stationers, 1646).

15. A valuable starting point for understanding this debate remains Peter Brown, *Augustine of Hippo* (Berkeley: University of California Press, 1967), 340–353.

16. St. Augustine of Hippo, *Confessions* [c. 397], trans. R. S. Pine-Coffin (New York: Penguin, 1961), 64. All translations into English are from this edition.

17. Saint Augustine, Bishop of Hippo, *Confessiones* [c. 397], ed. with commentary by James J. O'Donnell (Oxford: Clarendon Press, 1992), 29. All citations to the Latin text are from this edition.

18. Lisa Freinkel, *Reading Shakespeare's Will: The Theology of Figure from Augustine to the Sonnets* (New York: Columbia University Press, 2002).

19. Augustine, *Confessions*, 117; *Confessiones*, 62.

20. Augustine, *Confessions*, 227; *Confessiones*, 131.

21. Jean-François Lyotard, *The Confession of Augustine* [1998], trans. Richard Beardsworth (Stanford, CA: Stanford University Press, 2000), 49.

22. Charles Taylor, *Sources of the Self: The Making of Modern Identity* (Cambridge, MA: Harvard University Press, 1989), 130–131. See also J. B. Schneewind, *The Invention of Autonomy: A History of Modern Moral Philosophy* (Cambridge: Cambridge University Press, 1998).

23. John Locke, *Second Treatise of Government* [1690], ed. C. B. MacPherson (Indianapolis: Hackett, 1980), 46.

24. Augustine, *Confessions*, 177; *Confessiones*, 101.

25. Augustine, *Confessions*, 178; *Confessiones*, 101. Pine-Coffin gives "passage" for the Latin "capitulum," though "chapter" is preferred in Henry Chadwick's translation, *Confessions* (New York: Oxford University Press, 2008), 153.

26. Augustine, *Confessions*, 178; *Confessiones*, 101.

27. Thomas Lechford, *Plain Dealing; or, News from New-England* (London: Printed by W. E. and I. G. for N. Butter, 1642), 5.

28. Edmund Morgan, *Visible Saints: The History of a Puritan Idea* (1963; repr., Ithaca, NY: Cornell University Press, 1965), 93. Morgan disputes the assumption made by prior historians that this practice originated in Holland and thus came to New England via the gathered churches at Plymouth in the 1620s (64–67). Harry S. Stout argues that the "the prototype for all church covenants in New England was that of the Salem church founded in 1629" (*The New England Soul: Preaching and Religious Culture in Colonial New England* [New York: Oxford University Press, 1986], 18).

29. On the spread on confessional narratives, see D. Bruce Hindmarsh, *The Evangelical Conversion Narrative: Spiritual Autobiography in Early Modern England* (New York: Oxford University Press, 2005).

30. Much of that disagreement is nationalist, leading, on the one hand, Owen C. Watkins to claim that confessions can be understood as "the outcome of conditions that were distinctly English" (*The Puritan Experience* [London: Routledge and Keegan Paul, 1972], 2) and, on the other hand, Patricia Caldwell to argue that New England colonists worked in advance of their counterparts in the European metropole, making New England confessional narratives "the prototype of the form" (*The Puritan Conversion Narrative: The Beginnings of American Expression* [Cambridge: Cambridge University Press, 1983], 35). Caldwell further notes that "in England, conversion narrative can only blossom after the Civil War, when the gathered churches are free to depart from the parochial system of general membership" (35), a political context that Watkins largely ignores in favor of cultural sources.

Compounding this nationalist disagreement is a dispute over the kinds of social crisis that would have precipitated the proliferation of confessional narratives. Historians of New England have postulated that the Antinomian controversy of 1636–1638 may have been a crucial event that led to the wide adoption of public testimonies as a condition for church membership. For background on this controversy, see Morgan, *Visible Saints,* 141–152; Knight, *Orthodoxies in Massachusetts;* Theodore Dwight Bozeman, *The Pre-scientist Strain: Disciplinary Religion and Antinomian Backlash in Puritanism to 1638* (Chapel Hill: University of North Carolina Press for the Omohundro Institute of Early American History and Culture, 2004). Meanwhile, Kathleen Lynch cogently links the "surge" of confessional publication in England after 1653 with "the uncertain fate of the Commonwealth after Cromwell's purging of the Rump Parliament" (*Protestant Autobiography in the Seventeenth-Century Anglophone World* [New York: Oxford University Press, 2012], 21).

Drawing attention to the literary form (and, to a lesser extent, the medium of expression), other scholars have offered a number of competing interpretations of how the Augustinian strain of piety spread. Kenneth Murdock argues that among English Dissenters "all religious progress centered on the individual" and that "personal writings" (including diaries and biographies, as well as confessional narratives) were exemplary of this trend (*Literature and Theology in Colonial New England* [1949; repr., New York: Harper and Row, 1965], 99). For William Haller (in *The Rise of Puritanism, or, The Way to the New Jerusalem as Set Forth in Pulpit and Press from Thomas Cartwright to John Lilburne and John Milton* [New York: Columbia University Press, 1938]) and William York Tindall (in *John Bunyan, Mechanick Preacher* [New York: Columbia University Press, 1934]), confessional narratives were a genre of seventeenth-century popular expression. Diary keeping, suggests Haller, was a dissenting substitute for the Catholic confessional, in which "the devout Puritan turned his back on stage plays and romances, but only in order to look in his own heart and write what happened there" (*The Rise of Puritanism,* 96). Keith Thomas makes a related argument when he posits that the loss of auricular confession presents problems to Protestants after the Reformation, particularly regarding the enforcement of religious morality and the dispensation of pastoral advice, which diaries were a partial means of correcting (*Religion and the Decline of Magic* [New York: Charles Scribner's Sons, 1971], 154–158). In a recent intervention, Sarah Rivett convincingly demonstrates how the evidence revealed in confessional testimonies was "as much a part of seventeenth- and eighteenth-century philosophy, metaphysics, and empiricism as it was a part of an evolving post-Reformation theological tradition" (*The Science of the Soul,* 5).

31. *Thomas Shepard's Confessions,* ed. George Selement and Bruce C. Woolley (Boston: Colonial Society of Massachusetts, 1981), 129.

32. *Thomas Shepard's Confessions,* 143.

33. *Thomas Shepard's Confessions,* 151.

34. Mary Rhinelander McCarl, "Thomas Shepard's Record of Relations of Religious Experience, 1648–1649," *William and Mary Quarterly,* 3rd ser., 48, no. 3 (July 1991): 432–466, citation at 442.

35. McCarl, "Thomas Shepard's Record," 443.

36. McCarl, "Thomas Shepard's Record," 444. A manicule is a small pointing hand, a nonalphabetic mark whose meaning and function scholars of seventeenth-century manuscripts have debated. For one of the most detailed discussions, see William H. Sherman, *Used Books: Marking Readers in Renaissance England* (Philadelphia: University of Pennsylvania Press, 2008), 25–52.

37. McCarl, "Thomas Shepard's Record," 451–452.

38. McCarl, "Thomas Shepard's Record," 466.

39. Charles E. Hambrick-Stowe, *The Practice of Piety: Puritan Devotional Disciplines in Seventeenth-Century New England* (Chapel Hill: University of North Carolina Press for the Institute of Early American History and Culture, Williamsburg, Virginia, 1982), 26.

40. Perry Miller, *The New England Mind: From Colony to Province* (Cambridge, MA: Harvard University Press, 1953), 56. "The Augustinian Strain of Piety" is the title of the first chapter of Miller's *The New England Mind: The Seventeenth Century* (1939; repr., Cambridge, MA: Harvard University Press, 1954), wherein he calls Puritan piety Augustinian "simply because Augustine is the arch-exemplar of a religious frame of mind of which Puritanism is only one instance out of many in fifteen hundred years of religious history" (4).

41. John Calvin, *Institutes of the Christian Religion*, 2 vols., ed. John T. McNeil and trans. Ford Lewis Battles (Philadelphia: Westminster Press, 1960), 1:634.

42. William Perkins, *A Golden Chain; or, the Description of Theology* (Cambridge: Iohn Legat, 1600), 1.

43. Miller, *The New England Mind: From Colony to Province*, 56.

44. Ivy Schweitzer traces the Pauline rationale for conversion to Rom. 8:29–30 in *The Work of Self-Representation: Lyric Poetry in Colonial New England* (Chapel Hill: University of North Carolina Press, 1991), 44. See also John S. Coolidge, *The Pauline Renaissance in England: Puritanism and the Bible* (Oxford: Clarendon Press, 1970). The contrast between Augustinian and Pauline conversion is a difference of degree rather than kind. According to Jacob Taubes, the function of the "I" for both Paul and Augustine is not to overcome the will so much as to undermine it. See *The Political Theology of Paul* [1993], trans. Dana Hollander (Stanford, CA: Stanford University Press, 2004), 87.

45. *The Journal of John Winthrop, 1630–1649*, ed. Richard S. Dunn, James Savage, and Laetitia Yeandle (Cambridge, MA: Harvard University Press, 1996), 263.

46. Judith Butler, *Giving an Account of Oneself* (New York: Fordham University Press, 2005), 21.

47. Michel Foucault, *The History of Sexuality*, vol. 1, *An Introduction* [1976], trans. Robert Hurley (New York: Vintage, 1990), 59.

48. Rivett, *The Science of the Soul in Colonial New England*, 4; Lynch, *Protestant Autobiography in the Seventeenth-Century Anglophone World*, 7.

49. See, for example, Margreta de Grazia, "The Secularization of Language in the Seventeenth Century," in *Language and the History of Thought*, ed. Nancy Struever (Rochester, NY: University of Rochester Press, 1995), 16–26.

50. On the development of "the social" as an analytic, see Mary Poovey, "The Liberal Civil Subject and the Social in Eighteenth-Century British Moral Philosophy," *Public Culture* 14, no. 2 (Winter 2002): 125–145. On the historiographic problems of distinguishing between religion and culture, see Jordan Alexander Stein and Justine S. Murison, "Religion and Method," *Early American Literature* 45, no. 1 (Spring 2010): 1–29.

51. Morgan, *Visible Saints,* 41–42.

52. *God's Plot: Puritan Spirituality in Thomas Shepard's Cambridge,* ed. Michael Mc-Giffert (Amherst: University of Massachusetts Press, 1994), 137.

53. This aspect of print comes to be exploited more self-consciously into the eighteenth century. See, for example, Jody Greene, "Francis Kirkman's Counterfeit Authority: Autobiography, Subjectivity, Print," *PMLA* 121, no. 1 (January 2006): 17–32.

54. Norman Pettit, *The Heart Prepared: Grace and Conversion in Puritan Spiritual Life* (New Haven, CT: Yale University Press, 1966), 80–81.

55. Extant church records are incomplete, and a precise number of members is difficult to determine. In Massachusetts Bay between 1631 and 1664 (the period when church membership made a man eligible for freemanship, among the privileges of which were voting rights) Richard Archer estimates that "no less than 20.7 percent of adult males from all parts of New England were church members, while no less than 47.2 percent of office holders were church members. In towns that still have at least fragmentary evidence of church membership, between 14.3 percent and 45.7 percent of the male population and between 27.3 percent and 75.5 percent of deputies [i.e., town representatives to the colonial government] belonged to the church" (*Fissures in the Rock: New England in the Seventeenth Century* [Hanover: University Press of New England for the University of New Hampshire, 2001], 69). David Cressy estimates the white settler population of New England at 1,800 in 1630, 13,500 in 1640, and 22,400 in 1650. See *Coming Over: Migration and Communication between England and New England in the Seventeenth Century* (Cambridge: Cambridge University Press, 1987), 70. Another valuable source of data on freemanship is *Records of the Governor and Company of the Massachusetts Bay in New England,* 5 vols., ed. Nathaniel B. Shurtleff (Boston: William Whyte, 1853–1854). Harry Stout rightly observes that "there were far more church goers than church members" (*The New England Soul,* 4).

56. The number of extant narratives depends somewhat on how one counts. My numbers are restricted to confessions made in church as a condition for membership, recorded by ministers. These numbers grow considerably when one includes confessional narratives recorded in congregants' own diaries. See Hambrick-Stowe, *The Practice of Piety,* 85–90; Margaret Spufford, "First Steps in Literacy: The Reading and Writing Experiences of the Humblest Seventeenth-Century Spiritual Autobiographers," *Social History* 4, no. 3 (October 1979): 407–435. For primary texts not discussed in the works above, see Robert Strong, "Two Seventeenth-Century Conversion Narratives from Ipswich, Massachusetts Bay Colony," *New England Quarterly* 82, no. 1 (March 2009): 136–169; "The Commonplace Book of Joseph Green (1675–1715)," ed. Samuel Eliot Morison, *Transactions of the Colonial Society of Massachusetts* 34 (1943), esp. 241–244. On Native American confessions, see Neal Salisbury,

"Red Puritans: The 'Praying Indians' of Massachusetts Bay and John Eliot," *William and Mary Quarterly*, 3rd ser., 31, no. 1 (January 1974): 49–50; Kristina Bross, *Dry Bones and Indian Sermons: Praying Indians in Colonial America* (Ithaca, NY: Cornell University Press, 2004), 77–83. A different, eighteenth-century account is available as *Experience Mayhew's Indian Converts: A Cultural Edition*, ed. Laura Arnold Leibman (Amherst: University of Massachusetts Press, 2008). Sarah Rivett discusses the genre of deathbed confessions in "Tokenography: Narration and the Science of Dying in Puritan Deathbed Testimonies," *Early American Literature* 42, no. 3 (2007): 471–494.

57. *Thomas Shepard's Confessions;* McCarl, "Thomas Shepard's Record."

58. *The Diary of Michael Wigglesworth, 1653–1657: The Conscience of a Puritan,* ed. Edmund S. Morgan (New York: Harper and Row, 1946), 107–125.

59. *The Notebook of the Reverend John Fiske, 1644–1675,* ed. Robert G. Pope (Boston: Colonial Society of Massachusetts, 1974).

60. Rogers prefaces his congregants' confessions with the caveat that "I must *contract* much their *experiences* as they were *taken*, least they be too *voluminous*" (*A Tabernacle for the Sun* [London: R. I. and G. and H. Eversden, 1653], 392). Another edited version of these confessions is available with additional commentary as J. H. Taylor, "Some Seventeenth-Century Testimonies," *Transactions of the Congregational Historical Society* 16 (1949–1951): 64–77. Patricia Caldwell discusses a different British confessional narrative, published as *The Experience of God's Gracious Dealing with Mrs. Elizabeth White* (1698), at some length in the introduction to *The Puritan Conversion Narrative*.

61. *Thomas Shepard's Confessions,* viii.

62. "Thomas Shepard's Confessions," Mss. 553, R. Stanton Avery Special Collections, New England Historic Genealogical Society.

63. *Thomas Shepard's Confessions,* 210.

64. *Thomas Shepard's Confessions,* 118, 102–105.

65. *Thomas Shepard's Confessions,* 212.

66. Charles Lloyd Cohen, *God's Caress: The Psychology of Puritan Religious Experience* (New York: Oxford University Press, 1986), 139.

67. Meredith Marie Neuman, *Jeremiah's Scribes: Creating Sermon Literature in Puritan New England* (Philadelphia: University of Pennsylvania Press, 2013). On auditory "sermon culture," see also Arnold Hunt, *The Art of Hearing: English Preachers and Their Audiences, 1590–1640* (Cambridge: Cambridge University Press, 2010).

68. McCarl, "Thomas Shepard's Record," 434.

69. Headnotes were common enough for manuscript books; some manuscript books (in the seventeenth century as now) were graced with hand-drawn title pages, and others had more than one title page. See the example discussed in Neuman, *Jeremiah's Scribes,* 21–28.

70. Ann Blair, "Note Taking as an Art of Transmission," *Critical Inquiry* 31, no. 1 (Autumn 2004): 85–107, citation at 85. Furthermore, as Neuman shows, note-taking was widespread but differentially executed. There was no single established convention for note-taking, with regard to shorthand, type of paper, topic to be studied, or usage

after the fact. Some auditors and notetakers built indexes, suggesting that they referred back (or at least intended to refer back) to their notes later; others followed the possible practice of Shepard's extant Cambridge confessions and recopied what they heard in a neater hand; still others appear to have just taken notes in an abbreviated way; and some employed a combination of these strategies. See *Jeremiah's Scribes*. On the interactions between print and manuscript in early modern note-taking, see Ann Moss, *Printed Commonplace-Books and the Structuring of Renaissance Thought* (Cambridge: Cambridge University Press, 1996).

71. Harold Love, *The Culture and Commerce of Texts: Scribal Publication in Seventeenth-Century England* (Oxford: Clarendon Press, 1993).

72. J. W. Saunders "The Stigma of Print: A Note on the Social Bases of Tudor Poetry," *Essays in Criticism* 1, no. 2 (1951): 139–164; W. J. Cameron, "A Late Seventeenth-Century Scriptorium," *Renaissance and Modern Studies* 7 (1963): 25–52. These historical arguments were superseded in the next generation by Jonathan Goldberg's powerful deconstructive argument in *Writing Matter: From the Hands of the English Renaissance* (Stanford, CA: Stanford University Press, 1990).

73. Michael Warner, *The Letters of the Republic: Publication and the Public Sphere in Eighteenth-Century America* (Cambridge, MA: Harvard University Press, 1990).

74. Arthur F. Marotti, *Manuscript, Print, and English Renaissance Lyric* (Ithaca, NY: Cornell University Press, 1995), 211.

75. George Selement, "Publication and the Puritan Minister," *William and Mary Quarterly*, 3rd ser., 37, no. 2 (April 1980): 219–241, citation at 223.

76. On the impersonality of media circulation, see Michael Warner, "Publics and Counterpublics," *Public Culture* 14, no. 1 (2002): 49–90.

77. Thomas Shepard, "Relations of Conversion by Various Members of the Church of Cambridge," Mather Family Papers, 1613–1819, American Antiquarian Society, Box 11, Folder 7.

78. The attribution to Thomas follows McCarl, "Thomas Shepard's Record," 433.

79. Five leaves makes for an incomplete gathering, though no pages are obviously missing from the "Relation." These leaves have all been separated along the spine of the book, though I have not been able to determine whether this separation is an effect of design or age.

80. McCarl, "Thomas Shepard's Record," 433.

81. Shepard's bound notebook containing fifty-one Cambridge confessions was donated to the New England Historic Genealogical Society (NEHGS) in 1848 by Charlotte Ewer, wife of Charles Ewer, one of the five founding members of the NEHGS. There is no clear evidence that this book belonged to her family—she may easily have acquired it for the purposes of donating it to the society. I am grateful to Tim Salls, librarian at the NEHGS, for information about the provenance of this book.

82. *The Diary of Isaiah Thomas, 1805–1828*, 2 vols., ed. Benjamin Thomas Hill (Worcester, MA: American Antiquarian Society, 1909), 1:253–254. Hill notes that the library "contained a great number and variety of manuscript productions of the Mathers" including "miscellaneous parcels, memorandum books and a large mass of

material written by the Mathers for public and private use" (254n2). See also Philip F. Gura, *The American Antiquarian Society, 1812–2012: A Bicentennial History* (Worcester, MA: American Antiquarian Society, 2012), 2–4.

83. Augustine, *Confessions*, 278; *Confessiones*, 163. For a history of this term's multiple meanings, see Raymond Williams, "Media," and "Mediation," in *Keywords: A Vocabulary of Culture and Society*, rev. ed. (New York: Oxford, 1985), 200–207.

84. Lisa Gitelman, *Always Already New: Media, History, and the Data of Culture* (Cambridge, MA: MIT Press, 2006), 7.

85. John Guillory, "Genesis of the Media Concept," *Critical Inquiry* 36, no. 2 (Winter 2010): 321–362, citation at 321.

86. Giles Firmin, *The Real Christian, or A Treatise of Effectual Calling* (London: Dorman Newman, 1670), 214.

87. Firmin, *The Real Christian*, 214, 215.

88. *God's Plot*, 71.

89. John A. Albro, "Life of Thomas Shepard," in *The Works of Thomas Shepard*, 3 vols. (1853; repr., New York: AMS Press, 1967), 1:136.

90. Jonathan Beecher Field, *Errands into the Metropolis: New England Dissidents in Revolutionary London* (Hanover, NH: University of New England Press for Dartmouth College Press, 2009), esp. 17–25.

91. David D. Hall, *Ways of Writing: The Practice and Politics of Text-Making in Seventeenth-Century New England* (Philadelphia: University of Pennsylvania Press, 2008), 99–103.

92. Thomas Shepard, *Theses Sabbaticae* (London: T. R. and E. M. for John Rothwell, 1649), n.p.

93. Warner, *Letters of the Republic*, 23.

94. John Milton, *Areopagitica* [1644], in *Complete Poems and Major Prose*, ed. Merrit Y. Hughes (New York: Macmillan, 1957), 716–749, citation at 733.

95. Gilles Deleuze, *Difference and Repetition* [1968], trans. Paul R. Patton (New York: Columbia University Press, 1994), 3.

96. Bob Dylan, "I Dreamed I Saw St. Augustine," *John Wesley Harding* (Columbia Records, 1967).

97. For details of Augustine's initial publications, see Harry Y. Gamble, *Books and Readers in the Early Church: A History of Early Christian Texts* (New Haven, CT: Yale University Press, 1995), esp. 132–140.

98. Claire Sotinel, "Ancient Christianity and the Techniques of Information," *Studia Patristica* 44 (2010): 77–84.

99. Augustine, *Revisions* [c. 427], trans. Boniface Ramsey and ed. Roland Teske, SJ (Hyde Park, NY: New City Press, 2010), 114; *Retractationum*, ed. Almut Mutzenbecher (Turnholt: Typographi Brepolis, 1984), 94.

100. Clemens Weidman, "Augustine's Works in Circulation," in *A Companion to Augustine*, ed. Mark Vessey, with the assistance of Shelley Reid (Malden, MA: Wiley-Blackwell, 2012), 431–449, esp. 433–434.

101. Tzvetan Todorov, *Theories of the Symbol* [1977], trans. Catherine Porter (Ithaca, NY: Cornell University Press, 1982), 36.

102. Brian Stock, *After Augustine: The Meditative Reader and the Text* (Philadelphia: University of Pennsylvania Press, 2001).

103. Pierre Hadot, *What Is Ancient Philosophy?* [1995], trans. Michael Chase (Cambridge, MA: Harvard University Press, 2002), 3–4.

104. Michel Foucault, "The Hermeneutics of the Subject," in *Ethics: Subjectivity and Truth,* ed. Paul Rabinow, trans. Robert Hurley et al. (New York: New Press, 1997), 93–106, citations at 103, 104.

105. Michael M. Gorman, "The Manuscript Tradition of St. Augustine's Major Works," *Studia Ephemeridis Augustinianum* 24 (1987): 381–410, citation at 402.

106. Weidman, "Augustine's Works in Circulation," 440.

107. Arnoud S. Q. Visser, *Reading Augustine in the Reformation: The Flexibility of Intellectual Authority in Europe, 1500–1620* (New York: Oxford University Press, 2011), 5.

108. The English translation was undertaken by an English statesman and courtier, Sir Tobie Matthew, who converted to Roman Catholicism. On the printed debates this translation engendered in London, see Molly Murray, *The Poetics of Conversion in Early Modern English Literature: Verse and Change from Donne to Dryden* (Cambridge: Cambridge University Press, 2009), 25.

109. Lucien Febvre and Henri-Jean Martin, *The Coming of the Book: The Impact of Printing, 1450–1800* [1958], trans. David Gerard (London: Verso, 2010), 254.

110. Irena Backus, "The 'Confessionalization' of Augustine in the Reformation and Counter-Reformation," in *The Oxford Guide to the Historical Reception of Augustine,* ed. Karla Pollman (New York: Oxford University Press, 2013), 74–82.

2. The Character of Steady Sellers

1. Peter Stallybrass, "Printing and the Manuscript Revolution," in *Explorations in Communication History,* ed. Barbie Zelizer (New York: Routledge, 2008), 111–118.

2. Mary Rhinelander McCarl, "Thomas Shepard's Record of Relations of Religious Experience, 1648–1649," *William and Mary Quarterly,* 3rd ser., 48, no. 3 (July 1991): 432–466, citation at 452.

3. My sense of the term "steady seller" comes from David D. Hall, *Worlds of Wonder, Days of Judgment: Popular Religious Belief in Early New England* (Cambridge, MA: Harvard University Press, 1989), 48–52. C. John Sommerville, in *Popular Religion in Restoration England* (Gainesville: University Presses of Florida, 1977), estimates that print runs for seventeenth-century English books were typically under 1,000 copies, though reprint runs tended to be larger, sometimes as large as 2,000 copies, depending on the speed at which the first run sold (9–11). Some of the methodological challenges of translating numbers of extant copies into assessments of initial popularity are explored in Charles C. Mish, "Best Sellers in Seventeenth-Century Fiction," *Papers of the Bibliographic Society of America* 47 (1953): 356–373. Trish Loughran, in *The Republic in Print: Print Culture in the Age of U.S. Nation Building, 1770–1870* (New York: Columbia University Press, 2007), has conclusively demonstrated the pitfalls of the term "best seller" in relation to preindustrial books (esp. 40–42, 57–58).

4. Robert B. Winans, "Bibliography and the Cultural Historian: Notes on the Eighteenth-Century Novel," in *Printing and Society in Early America,* ed. William L. Joyce, David D. Hall, Richard D. Brown, and John B. Hench (Worcester, MA: American Antiquarian Society, 1983), 175.

5. Fredson Bowers defines an edition as *"the whole number of copies of a book printed at any time or times from substantially the same setting of type-pages" (Principles of Bibliographic Description* [Princeton, NJ: Princeton University Press, 1949], 39). An edition therefore includes all issues and variant states existing within its basic typesetting, as well as all impressions or reprintings. In the case of steady sellers, I use the term "reprinting" to refer to both authorized impressions and piracies.

6. David D. Hall, "The Uses of Literacy in New England, 1600–1850," in Joyce et al., *Printing and Society in Early America,* 1–47, esp. 28–29.

7. Margaret Spufford, *Small Books and Pleasant Histories: Popular Fiction and Its Readership in Seventeenth-Century England* (London: Methuen, 1981), 197; see also Tessa Watt, *Cheap Print and Popular Piety, 1550–1640* (Cambridge: Cambridge University Press, 1991), 259–260.

8. Matthew P. Brown, *The Pilgrim and the Bee: Reading Rituals and Book Culture in Early New England* (Philadelphia: University of Pennsylvania Press, 2007), 7.

9. Stephen Foster, *The Long Argument: English Puritanism and the Shaping of New England Culture, 1570–1700* (Chapel Hill: University of North Carolina Press for the Institute of Early American History and Culture, Williamsburg, Virginia, 1991), 87. See also Brown, *The Pilgrim and the Bee,* 6–7.

10. Brown, *The Pilgrim and the Bee,* esp. 31–34.

11. Bradin Cormack and Carla Mazzio, *Book Use, Book Theory, 1500–1700* (Chicago: University of Chicago Library, 2005), 5.

12. Ian Green, *Print and Protestantism in Early Modern England* (New York: Oxford University Press, 2000), 349.

13. No single note can do justice to the vast literature on this topic. In addition to works cited subsequently, however, useful general studies of the English Bible as a book include Gerald Hammond, *The Making of the English Bible* (Manchester: Carcanet New Press, 1982); Christopher Hill, *The English Bible and the Seventeenth-Century Revolution* (London: Penguin, 1993); Paul Saegner and Kimberly van Kampen, eds., *The Bible as Book: The Earliest Printed Editions* (London: British Library, 1999); Christopher De Hamel, *The Book: A History of the Bible* (London: Phaidon, 2001). On North American Bibles, see Margaret T. Hills, ed., *The English Bible in America: A Bibliography of Editions of the Bible and the New Testament Published in America, 1777–1957* (New York: American Bible Society and New York Public Library, 1961); Paul C. Gutjahr, *An American Bible: A History of the Good Book in the United States, 1777–1880* (Stanford, CA: Stanford University Press, 1999); Seth Perry, *Bible Culture and Authority in the Early United States* (Princeton, NJ: Princeton University Press, 2018).

14. M. H. Black, "The Printed Bible," in *Cambridge History of the Bible* (Cambridge: Cambridge University Press, 1963), 408–475. Many seventeenth-century French printers were Huguenots, and with the revocation of the Edict of Nantes in 1685,

many flee France for Holland and England where they resume work as printers. See Henri-Jean Martin, *The French Book: Religion, Absolutism, and Readership, 1585–1715*, trans. Paul Saenger and Nadine Saenger (Baltimore: Johns Hopkins University Press, 1996), 52–53; Julian Roberts, "The Latin Trade," in *The Cambridge History of the Book in Britain*, vol. 4: *1557–1695*, ed. John Barnard and D. F. McKenzie, with the assistance of Maureen Bell (Cambridge: Cambridge University Press, 2002), 141–173, esp. 168–169.

15. Herbert Palmer, *The Glasse of Gods Providence towards His Faithful Ones* (London: G. M. for Th. Underhill, 1644), n.p.

16. Erich Auerbach, "Figura," [1944], trans. Ralph Manheim, in *Scenes from the Drama of European Literature* (Minneapolis: University of Minnesota Press, 1984), 11–78.

17. William Guild, *Moses Unveiled; or Those Figures which Served unto the Patterne and Shaddow of Heauenly Things . . .* (London: G. P. for John Budge, 1620), n.p.

18. Samuel Mather, *The Figures or Types of the Old Testament, by Which Christ and Heavenly Things of Gospel Were Preached and Shadowed to the People of God of Old* (London: N. Hillier, 1705), 9.

19. John Cotton, *A Brief Exposition of the Whole Book of Canticles, or Song of Solomon* (London: Philip Nevil, 1642).

20. Edward Taylor, *Upon the Types of the Old Testament*, 2 vols., ed. Charles W. Mignon (Lincoln: University of Nebraska Press, 1989). See also Charles W. Mignon, "The Nebraska Edward Taylor Manuscript: 'Upon the Types of the Old Testament,'" *Early American Literature* 12, no. 3 (Winter 1977/1978): 296–301.

21. Thomas M. Davis, "The Traditions of Puritan Typology," in *Typology and Early American Literature*, ed. Sacvan Bercovitch (Amherst: University of Massachusetts Press, 1972), 38.

22. Patrick Collinson, "The Coherence of the Text: How It Hangeth Together: The Bible in Reformation England," *The Bible, the Reformation, and the Church: Essays in Honor of James Atkinson*, ed. W. P. Stephens (Sheffield: Sheffield Academic Press, 1995), 84–108, citation at 87. Carl Bridenbaugh estimates 150 editions of Bibles printed in England between 1603 and 1640, with between 2,500 and 3,000 copies per print run, as well as 57 editions printed abroad and "surreptitiously introduced" into Britain. See Carl Bridenbaugh, *Vexed and Troubled Englishmen 1590–1642* (New York: Oxford University Press, 1968), 278n6.

23. William H. Sherman, *Used Books: Marking Readers in Renaissance England* (Philadelphia: University of Pennsylvania Press, 2008), 71.

24. Frances E. Dolan, *Dangerous Familiars: Representations of Domestic Crime in England, 1550–1700* (Ithaca, NY: Cornell University Press, 1994), 8.

25. Foster, *The Long Argument*, 91; Francis R. Johnson, "Notes on English Retail Book Prices, 1550–1640," *The Library*, 5th series, 5 (1950): 83–112, esp. 93.

26. Marjorie Plant, *The English Book Trade: An Economic History of the Making and Sale of Books* (London: George Allen and Unwin, 1965), 240–242. On English prayer book ownership, see Judith Maltby, *Prayer Book and People in Elizabethan and Early Stuart England* (Cambridge: Cambridge University Press, 1998), esp. 24–29.

27. Hugh Amory, *Bibliography and the Book Trades: Studies in the Print Culture of Early New England,* ed. David D. Hall (Philadelphia: University of Pennsylvania Press, 2005), 58–79.

28. Karen E. Rowe, *Saint and Singer: Edward Taylor's Typology and the Poetics of Meditation* (Cambridge: Cambridge University Press, 1986).

29. Barbara Kiefer Lewalski, "Typological Symbolism and the 'Progress of the Soul' in Seventeenth-Century Literature," in *Literary Uses of Typology: From the Late Middle Ages to the Present,* ed. Earl Miner (Princeton, NJ: Princeton University Press, 1977), 79–114, citation at 81.

30. William Haller, *The Rise of Puritanism, or, The Way to the New Jerusalem as Set Forth in Pulpit and Press from Thomas Cartwright to John Lilburne and John Milton* (New York: Columbia University Press, 1938), 33.

31. I discuss this literalization of figure in "Mary Rowlandson's Hunger and the Historiography of Sexuality," *American Literature* 81, no. 3 (September 2009): 469–495, esp. 480–484. For other significant arguments, see Larzer Ziff, "The Literary Consequences of Puritanism," *ELH* 30 (September 1963): 293–305; Ann Kibbey, *The Interpretation of Material Shapes in Puritanism: A Study of Rhetoric, Prejudice, and Violence* (Cambridge: Cambridge University Press, 1986); Lisa M. Gordis, *Opening Scripture: Bible Reading and Interpretive Authority in Puritan New England* (Chicago: University of Chicago Press, 2003).

32. See C. B. MacPherson, *The Political Theory of Possessive Individualism: Hobbes to Locke* (1964; repr., New York: Oxford University Press, 1992).

33. Janice Knight, *Orthodoxies in Massachusetts: Rereading American Puritanism* (Cambridge, MA: Harvard University Press, 1994), 175.

34. Roger Chartier, "Texts, Printing, Readings," in *The New Cultural History,* ed. Lynn Hunt (Berkeley: University of California Press, 1989), 154–171, citation at 156.

35. Gérard Genette, *Narrative Discourse: An Essay in Method* [1972], trans. Jane E. Lewin (Ithaca, NY: Cornell University Press, 1980).

36. D. A. Miller, *The Novel and the Police* (Berkeley: University of California Press, 1988).

37. Admittedly, two narrative works appear to have enjoyed continuing interest: Arthur Dent's *The Plaine Mans Path-Way to Heaven* (1601), which reached twenty-five editions by 1640, and Thomas Tymme's *A Silver Watch-Bell* (1605), with at least eighteen printings by 1640. These exceptions, however, would seem to prove the rule. See Elizabeth K. Hudson, "The Plaine Mans Pastor: Arthur Dent and the Cultivation of Popular Piety in Early Seventeenth-Century England," *Albion: A Quarterly Journal Concerned with British Studies* 25, no. 1 (Spring 1993): 23–36.

38. Lewis Bayly, *The Practice of Piety: Directing a Christian How to Walke That He May Please God* (London: John Hidgetts, 1619), 244.

39. Bayly, *The Practice of Piety,* 245–246.

40. William Perkins, *The Arte of Prophecying* (London: s.n., 1606). This work was originally published in Latin in 1592. The three parts of Perkins's sermon template include the *opening* or citation of scripture, *doctrine* or the interpretation of scripture, and *use* or the application of scripture to local affairs.

41. Richard Bernard, *The Faithfull Shepheard: Or the Shepheard's Faithfulnesse: Wherein Is . . . Set Forth the Excellencie and Necessitie of the Ministerie, etc.* (London: Arnold Hatfield for John Bill, 1607), 72.

42. David D. Hall, *Ways of Writing: The Practice and Politics of Text-Making in Seventeenth-Century New England* (Philadelphia: University of Pennsylvania Press, 2008), 100.

43. Thomas Shepard, *The Sincere Convert, Discovering the Paucity of True Beleevers and the Great Difficulty of Saving Conversion* (London: T. Paine, 1640), 21.

44. The severity of Shepard's theological style and manner is discussed by Cotton Mather in *Magnalia Christi Americana, or The Ecclesiastical History of New England* [1702], 2 vols., ed. Thomas Robbins (Hartford: Silas Andrus and Son, 1853), 1:142–158, and in Samuel Eliot Morison, *Builders of the Bay Colony* (Boston: Houghton Mifflin, 1930), 105–134.

45. Spufford, *Small Books and Pleasant Histories,* 207.

46. Samuel Hieron, *A Helpe unto Devotion* (London: H. L. for Samuel Macham, 1608), n.p.

47. Henry Scudder, *The Christian's Daily Walke in Holy Securitie and Peace* (London: I. D. for William Sheffard, 1627), n.p.

48. A particularly helpful concept-metaphor for capturing the dynamic relation among these moving parts has been what Neil Postman influentially calls a media ecology, "the interaction between people and their communications technology." Postman further explains that a "media ecology looks into the matter of how media of communication affect human perception, understanding, feeling, and value; and how interaction with media facilitates or impeded our chances of survival." The reciprocal influences of an ecology such as Postman outlines allow scholars to track multiple lines of cause and effect. The elements of an ecology, by definition, exist in balance with one another, and, conversely, do not have an integral or entirely independent existence outside of that ecology. See "The Reformed English Curriculum," in *High School 1980: The Shape of the Future in American Secondary Education,* ed. Alvin C. Eurich (New York: Pitman, 1970), 160–168, all citations at 161.

49. Brown, *The Pilgrim and the Bee,* 16.

50. Stephen Greenblatt, *Renaissance Self-Fashioning: From More to Shakespeare* (Chicago: University of Chicago Press, 1980), 86.

51. Brown, *The Pilgrim and the Bee,* 7.

52. McCarl, "Thomas Shepard's Record," 452.

53. *The Diary of Michael Wigglesworth, 1653–1657: The Conscience of a Puritan,* ed. Edmund S. Morgan (New York: Harper and Row, 1946), 101.

54. John Bunyan, *Grace Abounding, with Other Spiritual Autobiographies,* ed. John Stanchniewski and Anita Pacheco (New York: Oxford University Press, 1998), 9.

55. John Eliot's Algonquin translations of several Christian texts were printed in Cambridge beginning in 1663. For a detailed discussion, see George Parker Winship, "The Eliot Indian Tracts," in *Bibliographical Essays: A Tribute to Wilberforce Eames,* ed. Bruce Rogers (Cambridge, MA: Harvard University Press, 1924), 179–192. Additional Eliot tracts were printed in Boston in the 1680s. Samuel Sewall, who

became the overseer of the Indian mission for many years, worked with Boston printer Samuel Green and a Native American compositor, James Printer, to issue a second (1685) edition of the Bible translated into Algonquin by Eliot, in a privately financed print run of about 2,000 copies. In 1685 or 1686, a new edition of Bayly's *Practice of Piety* "probably" followed the Bible (referred to in a letter of August 29, 1686, by Eliot); followed by a new issue of the *Indian Primer* (original 1669); by Perkins's *Foundation of the Christian Religion Gathered into Six Principles* (referred to in a letter by Increase Mather to Professor Leusden of Utrecht, July 12, 1687); then by Richard Baxter's *Call to the Unconverted* (1688); and Thomas Shepard's *The Sincere Convert (Sampwutteahae Quinnuppekompauenin)* in 1689. Eliot died in 1690, and the following year, his collaborators, including Samuel Green Jr.'s brother Bartholomew Green, brought out a translation of John Cotton's *Spiritual Milk for Babes* (1691). See George Parker Winship, *The Cambridge Press, 1638–1692* (Philadelphia: University of Pennsylvania Press, 1945), 355–357. Notably, these publications keep getting smaller, with the Eliot Bible at 1,220 pages, *The Practice of Piety* at 335, *The Sincere Convert* at 161, and *Spiritual Milk* at a mere 13. See also Philip Round, *Removable Type: Histories of the Book in Indian Country, 1663–1880* (Chapel Hill: University of North Carolina Press, 2010).

56. Collinson, "The Coherence of the Text," 92. The annotator is identified in Collinson's copy of the Geneva Bible only as "T. Grashop."

57. On paratexts, see Gérard Genette, *Paratexts: Thresholds of Interpretation* [1987], trans. Jane E. Lewin (Cambridge: Cambridge University Press, 1997).

58. John Owen, *The Reason of Faith, or, An Answer unto That Enquiry, Wherefore We Believe the Scripture to Be the Word of God* (London: Nathaniel Ponder, 1677), 47.

59. John Locke, *A Paraphrase and Notes on the Epistles of St. Paul . . . to Which is Prefix'd, An Essay for the Understanding of St. Paul's Epistles, by Consulting St. Paul Himself,* 5th ed. (London: S. Brit et al., 1751), vi.

60. Jordy Rosenberg persuasively discusses how Lockean empiricism connects with biblical historicism in *Critical Enthusiasm: Capital Accumulation and the Transformation of Religious Passion* (New York: Oxford University Press, 2011), esp. 46–48.

61. Lucien Febvre and Henri-Jean Martin, *The Coming of the Book: The Impact of Printing, 1450–1800* [1958], trans. David Gerard (London: Verso, 2010), 243.

62. For discussion of the steady sixteenth-century rise in almanac sales and the use of their calendars as private diaries, see Bernard Capp, *English Almanacs, 1500–1800: Astrology and the Popular Press* (Ithaca, NY: Cornell University Press, 1979), 23–42 and 61–62; see also T. J. Tomlin, *A Divinity for All Persuasions: Almanacs and Early American Religious Life* (New York: Oxford University Press, 2014). Among many other useful observations, Tomlin notes that "in 1639, an almanac became the second item printed in British North America" after the Bible (11).

63. Keith Thomas, *Religion and the Decline of Magic* (New York: Charles Scribner's Sons, 1971), 294.

64. Stuart Sherman, *Telling Time: Clocks, Diaries, and English Diurnal Form, 1660–1785* (Chicago: University of Chicago Press, 1996), 50.

65. Alison A. Chapman, "Now and Then: Sequencing the Sacred in Two Protestant Calendars," *Journal of Medieval and Early Modern Studies* 33, no. 1 (Winter 2003): 91–123, citation at 93.

66. Benedict Anderson, *Imagined Communities: Reflections on the Origin and Spread of Nationalism,* rev. ed. (New York: Verso, 1991), 22–36; Walter Benjamin, "Theses on the Philosophy of History," in *Illuminations* [1955], trans. Harry Zohn and ed. with an introduction by Hannah Arendt (New York: Schocken, 1968), 253–264, citation at 262.

67. On ownership, see Thomas R. Adams and Nicholas Barker, "A New Model for the History of the Book," *A Potencie of Life: Books in Society,* ed. Nicholas Barker (London: British Library, 1993), 5–42; esp. 34; on imitations, see David E. Smith, *John Bunyan in America* (Bloomington: Indiana University Press, 1966); on translations, see Isabel Hofmeyr, *The Portable Bunyan: A Transnational History of the Pilgrim's Progress* (Princeton, NJ: Princeton University Press, 2004).

68. For a touchstone discussion, see Stanley E. Fish, *Self-Consuming Artifacts: The Experience of Seventeenth-Century Literature* (Berkeley: University of California Press, 1972), 224–264.

69. John Bunyan, *The Pilgrim's Progress,* ed. R. W. Owens (New York: Oxford University Press, 2003), 10. All citations are to this edition unless otherwise specified.

70. The complexities and ambivalences attendant upon this association are explored wonderfully by James Kearney in *The Incarnate Text: Imagining the Book in Reformation England* (Philadelphia: University of Pennsylvania Press, 2009).

71. Colin H. Roberts and T. C. Skeat, *The Birth of the Codex* (London: British Academy for Oxford University Press, 1983), 44. See also Guglielmo Cavallo, "Between *Volumen* and Codex: Reading in the Roman World," in *A History of Reading in the West* [1995], ed. Guglielmo Cavallo and Roger Chartier, trans. Lydia G. Cochrane (Amherst: University of Massachusetts Press, 1999), 64–89; Anthony Grafton and Megan Williams, *Christianity and the Transformation of the Book: Origen, Eusebius, and the Library at Caeserea* (Cambridge, MA: Harvard University Press, 2003).

72. Peter Stallybrass, "Book and Scrolls: Navigating the Bible," in *Books and Readers in Early Modern England,* ed. Jennifer Anderson and Elizabeth Sauer (Philadelphia: University of Pennsylvania Press, 2002), 43. See also Peter Katz, "The Early Christians' Use of Codices Instead of Rolls," *Journal of Theological Studies* 46 (1945): 63–65; Kathleen Biddick, *The Typological Imaginary: Circumcision, Technology, History* (Philadelphia: University of Pennsylvania Press, 2003).

73. Bunyan, *The Pilgrim's Progress,* 11.

74. Bunyan, *The Pilgrim's Progress,* 11.

75. As Irven M. Resnick has demonstrated, this difference of format is arguably encoded into these texts. For example, in Ps. 40:7, the Psalmist remarks, "I am come with the roll of a book which is prescribed for me." The Hebrew phrase for "roll of a book" *(b'megillat sefer)* signifies a scroll; but as the Septuagint translates this phrase into Greek, it offers a different interpretation *(en kephalidi bibliou),* placing emphasis on the book. It is the spirit of the Greek translation, rather than the Hebrew original, that appears in the Latin Vulgate *(in capite libri),* which may be translated "at the beginning [or head] of a book." See Resnick, "The Codex in Early Jewish and Christian

Communities," *Journal of Religious History* 17, no. 1 (June 1992): 12. By 1577, the Geneva translation of the Psalms renders this phrase "volume of the boke." This translation rationalizes the poetic redundancy of the original, equating roll with volume and suggesting that each might be part of a larger work. Nevertheless, it loses any media specificity that may have been contained in the Hebrew and that seems to have been effaced in its early Greek translation. Though the codex had achieved dominance over the scroll throughout Europe by the late sixteenth century, the association of sacred texts and codices was, for these translators, still strong.

The fact that media terms are poorly translated in the transmission of antique texts is part of a larger phenomenon by which, as Chapter 1 discusses at greater length, the concept of "medium" was largely absent from European thought between antiquity and the early modern period. One additional example comes from Giorgio Agamben, who observes that Aristotle's discussion of a wax writing tablet *(grammateion)* in *De Anima* becomes for Latin translators the blank slate or "white sheet" *(tabula rasa)* used so influentially as a metaphor by John Locke in his *Essay concerning Human Understanding* (1690). See Giorgio Agamben, *Potentialities: Collected Essays in Philosophy,* ed. and trans. Daniel Heller-Roazen (Stanford, CA: Stanford University Press, 1999), 244.

76. For critical discussion of the persistence of the scroll after the triumph of the codex, see Roger Chartier, *Forms and Meanings: Texts, Performances, and Audiences from Codex to Computer* (Philadelphia: University of Pennsylvania Press, 1995), 19; Kearney, *The Incarnate Text,* 160–163.

77. Bunyan, *The Pilgrim's Progress,* 10.

78. Hugh Amory, "Printing and Bookselling in New England, 1638–1713," in *A History of the Book in America,* vol. 1, *The Colonial Book in the Atlantic World,* ed. Hugh Amory and David D. Hall (Chapel Hill: University of North Carolina Press, 2000), 83–116, citation at 104.

79. Winship, *The Cambridge Press,* 346.

80. "Appendix: Sewall's Imprints," in *The Diary of Samuel Sewall,* 2 vols., ed. M. Halsey Thomas (New York: Farrar, Straus and Giroux, 1973), 1107–1111.

81. *Records of the Governor and Company of the Massachusetts Bay in New England. Printed by Order of the Legislature,* 5 vols., ed. Nathaniel B. Shurtleff, M.D. (Boston: William White, 1854), 5:323.

82. The convention since the 1878 published edition of the *Diary* has been to supply details of the events of Sewall's life from commonplace books, interleaved almanacs, and other sources. (See the editor's note in the 1973 edition, p. 45). None of these sources, so far as I have been able to determine, include any information as to why *The Pilgrim's Progress* was printed in 1681.

83. On Owen's centrality to English debates about Congregationalism, see Geoffrey F. Nuttall, *Visible Saints: The Congregational Way 1640–1660* (Oxford: Basil Blackwell, 1957), esp. 16–19, and on his relationship with Bunyan, 39–40.

84. Francis J. Bremer, "Increase Mather's Friends: The Trans-Atlantic Congregational Network of the Seventeenth Century," *Proceedings of the American Antiquarian Society* 94, no. 1 (April 1985): 59–96.

85. Thomas Goddard Wright, *Literary Culture in Early New England, 1620–1730* (New Haven, CT: Yale University Press, 1920), 110–114.

86. One of the only scholars to ascribe any significance to the fact that *The Pilgrim's Progress* was printed in Boston, Worthington Chauncey Ford incorrectly observes that Cotton Mather was opposed the book's production, having "already gone far in smothering true piety under his flood of soporific denunciations" (*The Boston Book Market, 1679–1700* [Boston: The Club of Odd Volumes, 1917], 61). This claim is noteworthy, however, for its indication that by 1917, *The Pilgrim's Progress* was presumed to be the kind of work to which ministers would be opposed, a circumstance detailed in chapter 4 of the present study.

87. John Bunyan, *The Pilgrim's Progress from This World to That Which Is to Come: Delivered under the Similitude of a Dream* (Boston: Samuel Green, 1681), n.p.

88. Mary Rowlandson, *The Sovereignty and Goodness of God, Together with the Faithfulness of His Promises Displayed Being a Narrative of the Captivity and Restoration of Mrs. Mary Rowlandson* [1682], ed. Neal Salisbury (Boston: Bedford / St. Martin's, 1997), 107.

89. Teresa A. Toulouse, *The Captive's Position: Female Narrative, Male Identity, and Royal Authority in Colonial New England* (Philadelphia: University of Pennsylvania Press, 2007), 23.

90. Nancy Armstrong and Leonard Tennenhouse have argued that the English novel is the outgrowth of texts like Rowlandson's, which are colonial in origin. Their claim is suggestive, but it is not the one I am making. See their "The American Origins of the English Novel," *American Literary History* 4, no. 3 (1992): 386–410. On the novel as a "New World" phenomenon, see M. M. Bakhtin, *The Dialogic Imagination: Four Essays*, ed. Michael Holquist, trans. Caryl Emerson and Michael Holquist (Austin: University of Texas Press, 1981); William C. Spengemann, "The Earliest American Novel: Aphra Behn's *Oroonoko*," *Nineteenth-Century Fiction* 38, no. 4 (1984): 384–414.

91. Rowlandson herself dips into the Bible. In the middle of her captivity, grieving for a dead child, she writes, "I opened my Bible to read, and the Lord brought that precious Scripture to me, *Jer.* 31.16 *Thus saith the Lord, refrain thy voice from weeping, and thine eyes from tears, for thy work shall be rewarded, and they shall come again from the land of the enemy.* This was a sweet Cordial to me, when I was ready to faint; many and many a time have I sat down and wept sweetly over this Scripture" (*The Sovereignty and Goodness of God*, 78). For a sharp discussion of this passage, see Michael Warner, "Uncritical Reading," in *Polemic: Critical or Uncritical*, ed. Jane Gallop (New York: Routledge, 2004), 13–38.

92. Wilkie Collins, *The Moonstone* [1868], ed. Sandra Kemp (New York: Penguin, 1998), 21.

93. Collins, *The Moonstone*, 179.

94. Daniel Defoe, *Robinson Crusoe* [1719], ed. Michael Shinagel (New York: Norton, 1975), 70–71.

95. Jean-Jacques Rousseau, *Émile, or Education* [1762], trans. Allan Bloom (New York: Basic Books, 1979), 184–188; Karl Marx, *Capital*, vol. 1, *A Critique of Political Economy* [1867], trans. Ben Fowkes (New York: Penguin, 1977), esp. 169–170.

96. Ian Watt, *The Rise of the Novel: Studies in Defoe, Richardson and Fielding* (London: Chatto and Windus, 1957), 63.

97. Maximillian E. Novak, "Robinson Crusoe's 'Original Sin,'" *Studies in English Literature, 1500–1900* 1, no. 3 (Summer 1961): 19–29; G. A. Starr, *Defoe and Spiritual Autobiography* (Princeton, NJ: Princeton University Press, 1965); J. Paul Hunter, *The Reluctant Pilgrim: Defoe's Emblematic Method and Quest for Form in Robinson Crusoe* (Baltimore: Johns Hopkins University Press, 1966); Peter Hulme, *Colonial Encounters: Europe and the Native Caribbean, 1492–1797* (London: Methuen, 1986); Lydia H. Liu, "Robinson Crusoe's Earthenware Pot," *Critical Inquiry* 25, no. 4 (Summer 1999): 728–757; Jonathan Lamb, *The Things Things Say* (Princeton, NJ: Princeton University Press, 2011), esp. 160–169.

98. Indeed, scholarly conceptions of eighteenth-century economics have also become considerably more sophisticated since the 1950s. For relevant recent interventions in relation to studies of the Anglophone novel, see Catherine Gallagher, *The Body Economic: Life, Death, and Sensation in Political Economy and the Victorian Novel* (Princeton, NJ: Princeton University Press, 2006); Mary Poovey, *Genres of the Credit Economy: Mediating Value in Eighteenth-Century Britain* (Chicago: University of Chicago Press, 2008). See also Michelle Burnham, *Folded Selves: Colonial New England Writing in the World System* (Hanover, NH: University Press of New England, 2007).

99. Fredric Jameson, "Reification and Utopia in Mass Culture," *Social Text* 1 (Winter 1979): 130–148.

100. Fredric Jameson, *The Political Unconscious: Narrative as a Socially Symbolic Act* (Ithaca, NY: Cornell University Press, 1981), 279. For Jameson's most important passage on the transitional, see his *Postmodernism, or, the Cultural Logic of Late Capitalism* (Durham, NC: Duke University Press, 1991), 417.

101. Toni Morrison, *Beloved: A Novel* (New York: Alfred Knopf, 1987).

102. Henry Clinton Hutchins posits four printings in *Robinson Crusoe and Its Printing 1719–1731: A Bibliographical Study* (New York: Columbia University Press, 1925), and this number was revised to six in Keith I. Maslen, "The Printers of *Robinson Crusoe*," *The Library,* 5th ser., 7 (1952): 124–131.

103. K. I. D. Maslen, "Edition Quantities for *Robinson Crusoe,* 1719," *The Library,* 5th ser., 24 (1969): 145–150; quotation at 150.

104. Paula McDowell, *The Women of Grub Street: Press, Politics, and Gender in the London Literary Marketplace 1678–1730* (Oxford: Clarendon Press, 1998), 4–5; J. Paul Hunter, *Before Novels: The Cultural Contexts of Eighteenth-Century English Fiction* (New York: Norton, 1990), 65; William B. Warner, *Licensing Entertainment: The Elevation of Novel Reading in Britain, 1684–1750* (Berkeley: University of California Press, 1998), 138; Marshall McLuhan, *The Gutenberg Galaxy: The Making of Typographic Man* (Toronto: University of Toronto Press, 1965), 254.

105. Melissa Free, "Un-Erasing Crusoe: *Farther Adventures* in the Nineteenth Century," *Book History* 9 (2006): 89–130.

106. See Hutchins, *Robinson Crusoe and Its Printing,* 157–158; P. N. Furbank and W. R. Owens, *A Critical Bibliography of Daniel Defoe* (London: Pickering and Chatto,

1998), 196. On the serialization of Defoe's other works, see J. L. Wood, "Defoe Serialised," *Factotum* 19 (October 1984): 21–23; David J. Shaw, "Serialization of *Moll Flanders* in *The London Post* and *The Kentish Post*, 1722," *The Library* 8, no. 2 (June 2007): 182–192. See also Robert D. Mayo, *The English Novel in the Magazines 1740–1815* (Evanston, IL: Northwestern University Press, 1962).

107. On translations, see Herman Ullrich, *Robinson und Robinsonaden: Bibliographie, Geschichte, Kritik* (Weimar: Verlang von Emil Felber, 1898); on illustrated editions, see David Blewett, *The Illustration of Robinson Crusoe 1719–1920* (Gerrards Cross, Buckinghamshire: Colin Smythe, 1995); on bowdlerization, see Leah Price, *The Anthology and the Rise of the Novel: From Richardson to George Eliot* (Cambridge: Cambridge University Press, 2000), 83–90.

3. The Rise of the Text-Network

1. Robert B. Winans, "Bibliography and the Cultural Historian: Notes on the Eighteenth-Century Novel," in *Printing and Society in Early America,* ed. William L. Joyce, David D. Hall, Richard D. Brown, and John B. Hench (Worcester, MA: American Antiquarian Society, 1983), 174–185.

2. Generally speaking, "remediation" names a process whereby a text is translated from one medium into another. Paul Levenson defines this process as generally progressive, a process of improvement, in *The Soft Edge: A Natural History and Future of the Information Revolution* (New York: Routledge, 1997), 111–113. Jay David Bolter and Richard Grusin define it alternately as a "formal logic by which new media refashion prior media forms" in *Remediation: Understanding New Media* (Cambridge, MA: MIT Press, 1999), 273.

3. Daniel Selden, "Text Networks," *Ancient Narrative* 8 (2009): 1–30. See also Susan Gillman and Kirsten Silva Gruesz, "Worlding America: The Hemispheric Text-Network," in *A Companion to American Literary Studies,* ed. Caroline F. Levander and Robert S. Levine (Oxford: Wiley-Blackwell, 2011), 228–247; Susan Gillman, "Networking *Uncle Tom's Cabin;* or, Hyper Stowe in Early African American Print Culture," in *Early African American Print Culture,* ed. Lara Langer Cohen and Jordan Alexander Stein (Philadelphia: University of Pennsylvania Press, 2012), 231–249.

4. Lauren Berlant, *The Female Complaint: The Unfinished Business of Sentimentality in American Culture* (Durham, NC: Duke University Press, 2008), 28; Jonathan Gray, *Show Sold Separately: Promos, Spoilers, and Other Media Paratexts* (New York: New York University Press, 2010), 1. On paratexts, see Gérard Genette, *Paratexts: Thresholds of Interpretation* [1987], trans. Jane E. Lewin (Cambridge: Cambridge University Press, 1997).

5. This chronology follows William Merritt Sale Jr., *Samuel Richardson: A Bibliographical Record of His Literary Career with Historical Notes* (New Haven, CT: Yale University Press, 1936), xv–xvi. On the international adaptations, see also James Grantham Turner, "Novel Panic: Picture and Performance in the Reception of Richardson's *Pamela,*" *Representations* 48 (Autumn 1994): 70–96; Thomas Keymer and Peter Sabor, Pamela *in*

the Marketplace: Literary Controversy and Print Culture in Eighteenth-Century Britain and Ireland (Cambridge: Cambridge University Press, 2005).

6. *Gentleman's Progress: The Itinerarium of Dr. Alexander Hamilton, 1744,* ed. Carl Bridenbaugh (Chapel Hill: University of North Carolina Press for the Institute of Early American History and Culture at Williamsburg, Virginia, 1948), 112.

7. Kevin J. Hayes, *A Colonial Woman's Bookshelf* (Knoxville: University of Tennessee Press, 1996), 104.

8. James N. Green and Peter Stallybrass, *Benjamin Franklin: Writer and Printer* (New Castle, DE: Oak Knoll Press, 2006), 69.

9. Leonard W. Labaree et al., eds., *The Papers of Benjamin Franklin,* 42 vols. to date (New Haven, CT: Yale University Press, 1959–2017), 13:114–115.

10. Records of the Society in Scotland for Propagating Christian Knowledge, Minutes of General Meetings, 1736–1759, GD95/1/4, National Archives of Scotland, Edinburgh, Meeting of 5 June 5, 1746.

11. Records of the Society in Scotland for Propagating Christian Knowledge, Minutes of General Meetings, 1736–1759, GD95/1/4, National Archives of Scotland, Edinburgh, Meeting of March 19, 1747.

12. Records of the Society in Scotland for Propagating Christian Knowledge, Minutes of General Meetings, 1736–1759, GD95/1/4, National Archives of Scotland, Edinburgh, Meeting of June 2, 1748.

13. Though Edwards maintained active correspondence with several prominent Scottish Presbyterian ministers, his edition of *Brainerd* appears to have been undertaken without the involvement or knowledge of the SSPCK. For Edwards's motives and the stakes of the project, see George M. Marsden, *Jonathan Edwards: A Life* (New Haven, CT: Yale University Press, 2003), 327–333. More generally, see Harold P. Simonson, "Jonathan Edwards and His Scottish Connections," *Journal of American Studies* 21, no. 3 (December 1987): 353–376; Kenneth P. McKenna, Adriaan C. Neele, and Kelly van Andel, eds., *Jonathan Edwards and Scotland* (Edinburgh: Dunedin Academic Press, 2011).

14. This chronology follows Thomas H. Johnson, *The Printed Writings of Jonathan Edwards, 1703–1758: A Bibliography* [1940], rev. ed. by M. X. Lesser (Princeton, NJ: Princeton Theological Seminary, 2003), 78.

15. For instance, in the years 1791–1800, 35,910 imprints originated in London, about ten times as many as Dublin (4,400), Edinburgh (3,230), and Philadelphia (just over 3,000); nearly thirty times as many as Boston (1,228); and almost eighty times as many as New York (452). The most significant aspect of the figures for this particular decade, however, is not the size of London market compared to colonial ones, but the size of the Philadelphia market compared to the other colonial markets. Forty years earlier, in the 1750s, Dublin had almost nine times as many imprints as Philadelphia (2,410 vs. 275), and in the 1760s Dublin's advantage was still more than five imprints to one (2,400 vs. 440). All these figures follow Richard B. Sher, *The Enlightenment and the Book: Scottish Authors and Their Publishers in Eighteenth-Century Britain, Ireland, and America* (Chicago: University of Chicago Press, 2006), 510, and accordingly revise those presented in Sher, "Corporatism and Consensus in the Late

Eighteenth-Century Book Trade: The Edinburgh Bookseller's Society in Comparative Perspective," *Book History* 1 (1998): 32–90.

16. The same patterns of movement that explain why *Pamela* was illustrated and remediated visually while *Brainerd* was not.

17. Leah Price, *The Anthology and the Rise of the Novel: From Richardson to George Eliot* (Cambridge: Cambridge University Press, 2000). See also Barbara M. Benedict, *Making the Modern Reader: Cultural Mediation in Early Modern Literary Anthologies* (Princeton, NJ: Princeton University Press, 1996), esp. 165–181.

18. Twenty-one of these indexed maxims from *Clarissa* found their way, unattributed, into Franklin's *Poor Richard's Almanac*. See Robert Newcomb, "The Sources of Benjamin Franklin's Sayings of Poor Richard" (PhD diss., University of Maryland, 1957); Robert Newcomb, "Franklin and Richardson," *Journal of English and Germanic Philology* 57 (1958): 27–35. Price notes that "Newcomb tends to overstate this debt by assuming that a parallel between Richardson's and Franklin's maxims shows influence rather than the dependence of both on a common stock of commonplaces" (*The Anthology and the Rise of the Novel*, 161n10).

19. On the "American *Pamela*," see Leonard Tennenhouse, *The Importance of Feeling English: American Literature and the British Diaspora, 1750–1850* (Princeton, NJ: Princeton University Press, 2007), 53–56.

20. Sale, *Samuel Richardson*, 134.

21. The uniform title information for this volume follows Charles Evans, *American Bibliography 1639–1820*, 10 vols. (Chicago: for the author, 1909), s.v. 13145. Evans names Anthony Benezet as editor, but this attribution claims with certainty something that had been doubted by Joseph Smith in *A Descriptive Catalog of Friends' Books*, 2 vols. (London: Joseph Smith, 1867), 1:245.

22. *An Extract of Miss Mary Gilbert's Journal: With Some Account of the Lady Elizabeth Hastings, &c.* (London, Printed: Philadelphia, Reprinted and Sold by David Hall and William Sellers, 1769), 60–66.

23. Gregory S. Jackson, *The Word and Its Witness: The Spiritualization of American Realism* (Chicago: University of Chicago Press, 2009), 96.

24. Terry Eagleton, *The Rape of Clarissa: Writing, Sexuality and Class Struggle in Samuel Richardson* (Oxford: Basil Blackwell, 1982), 5.

25. Naomi Klein, *No Logo* (New York: Picador, 1999).

26. Turner, "Novel Panic," 74.

27. *The Life of David Brainerd*, ed. Norman Pettit, vol. 7 of *The Works of Jonathan Edwards*, 26 vols. (New Haven, CT: Yale University Press, 1985), 42. On the infamy of Brainerd's alleged comment about Whittelsey, see Leonard Bacon, *Thirteen Historical Discourses, on the Completion of Two Hundred Years from the Beginning of the First Church in New Haven* (New Haven, CT: Durrie and Peck, 1839), 245; Norman Pettit, "Prelude to Mission: Brainerd's Expulsion from Yale," *New England Quarterly*, 59 (1986): 28–50.

28. Records of the Society in Scotland for Propagating Christian Knowledge, Letters, Minutes, &c., 1707–1741, GD95/10/2, National Archives of Scotland, Edinburgh, Recommendation of May 12, 1732.

29. Records of the Society in Scotland for Propagating Christian Knowledge, Letters, Minutes, &c., 1707–1741, GD95/10/2, National Archives of Scotland, Edinburgh, Recommendation of May 12, 1732.

30. John A. Grigg, *The Lives of David Brainerd: The Making of an American Evangelical Icon* (New York: Oxford University Press, 2009), 87.

31. Brainerd noted a small number of corrections (mostly to printer's errors, rather than any substantial revision) in a copy of *Mirabilia Dei inter Indicos* (bound with the sequel, *Divine Grace Display'd*) in 1747, which he left in the possession of Edward Bromfield, with whom he stayed in Boston shortly before his death. This copy came into the possession of Thomas Foxcroft, a Congregationalist minister of some reputation, by way of another minister and friend of Brainerd's, Jonathan Dickinson. It passed through several subsequent hands, as it is inscribed "Elizabeth Marsh 1804" and also contains a paper bookplate from the late nineteenth-century New York book collector Herman Le Roy Edgar. It was eventually acquired by Philadelphia book collector William McIntire Elkins for his large collection of Americana, and it now belongs to the rare books collections of the Free Library of Philadelphia.

32. *Boston, June 23. Proposals for Printing by Subscription, an Account of the Life of That Extraordinary Person, the Late Reverend Mr. Brainard* (Boston: Daniel Henchman, 1748).

33. Joseph Conforti, "Jonathan Edwards's Most Popular Work: 'The Life of David Brainerd' and Nineteenth-Century Evangelical Culture," *Church History* 54, no. 2 (June 1985): 188–201. See also Perry Miller, untitled review of *The Life and Diary of David Brainerd* by Jonathan Edwards, *New England Quarterly* 23, no. 2 (June 1950): 277. The comprehensive bibliography of editions of *Brainerd* again treats the book as Edwards's. See Johnson, *The Printed Writings of Jonathan Edwards.*

34. However, SSPCK records indicate that their New York correspondents repeatedly pronounce the success of the mission in letters to Edinburgh. A March 19, 1747, letter, for example, announces to officers in Edinburgh the publication of *Mirabilia Dei inter Indicos,* "which they had caused to be printed, whereby it appears his Labour among the Indeans [*sic*] have been blest with surprising success." Records of the Society in Scotland for Propagating Christian Knowledge, Minutes of General Meetings, 1736–1759, GD95/1/4, National Archives of Scotland, Edinburgh.

    If anything, more recent scholars have been attentive to the ways that Native Americans may have impacted Brainerd. See Richard W. Pointer, "'Poor Indians' and the 'Poor in Spirit': The Indian Impact on David Brainerd," *New England Quarterly* 67, no. 3 (September 1994): 403–426; Paul Harris, "David Brainerd and the Indians: Cultural Interaction and Protestant Missionary Ideology," *American Presbyterian* 72 (1994): 2.

35. Records of the Society in Scotland for Propagating Christian Knowledge, Minutes of General Meetings, 1736–1759, GD95/1/4, National Archives of Scotland, Edinburgh, Minutes of November 3, 1748.

36. Sandra M. Gustafson, *Eloquence Is Power: Oratory and Performance in Early America* (Chapel Hill: University of North Carolina Press for the Omohundro Institute of Early American History and Culture, 2000), 80; Laura M. Stevens, *The Poor Indians:*

British Missionaries, Native Americans, and Colonial Sensibility (Philadelphia: University of Pennsylvania Press, 2004), 142.

37. See Brainerd's manuscript diary in the Beinecke Rare Book and Manuscript Library, Yale University, qtd. in Grigg, *The Lives of David Brainerd*, 10. On Prince, see Grigg, *The Lives of David Brainerd*, 87; Frank Lambert, *Inventing the "Great Awakening"* (Princeton, NJ: Princeton University Press, 1999), 143–150.

38. See Patricia Ann Meyer Spacks, *Imagining a Self: Autobiography and the Novel in Eighteenth-Century England* (Cambridge, MA: Harvard University Press, 1976).

39. See also Lauren Berlant's argument that "for an occasion of banality to be both utopian and sublime its ordinariness must be thrust into a zone of overwhelming disavowal" ("The Subject of True Feeling: Pain, Privacy, Politics," in *Cultural Pluralism, Identity Politics, and the Law,* ed. Austin Sarat and Thomas R. Kearns [Ann Arbor: University of Michigan Press, 1999], 49–84, citation at 60).

40. *The Life of David Brainerd,* 175, 184, 189, 199, 205, 232.

41. *The Life of David Brainerd,* 189. See also David L. Weddle, "The Melancholy Saint: Jonathan Edwards's Interpretation of David Brainerd as a Model of Evangelical Spirituality," *Harvard Theological Review* 81, no. 3 (July 1988): 297–318.

42. *The Life of David Brainerd,* 134.

43. David Brainerd, *Mirabilia Dei inter Indicos; or, The Rise and Progress of a Remarkable Work of Grace amongst a Number of the Indians in the Provinces of New-Jersey and Pennsylvania, Justly Represented in a Journal Kept by Order of the Honourable Society (in Scotland) for Propagating Christian Knowledge. With Some General Remarks* (Philadelphia: William Bradford, 1746); *The Life of David Brainerd,* 89.

44. Brainerd, *Mirabilia Dei inter Indicos,* vi.

45. P[hilip]. Doddridge, ed., *An Abridgement of Mr. David Brainerd's Journal among the Indians; or, the Rise and Progress of a Remarkable Work of Grace among a Number of the Indians. In the Provinces of New-Jersey and Pensylvania [sic]* (London: John Oswald, 1748), ii–iii.

46. "To the Editor of the Theological Magazine," *Theological Magazine* 3, no. 2 (January–February 1798): 117–123, citation at 122.

47. *Meditations and Spiritual Exercises of Mr. Thomas Shepard, Late Worthy and Dear Pastor of the Church of Christ in Cambridge, in New-England, from November 25. 1640–to December 27. 1641. Transcribed Out of His Own Book, Written in His Own Hand; and Left by Him to His Son Thomas Shepard, with This Word Prefixed—Try All Things, and Hold Fast That Which Is Good* (Boston: Rogers and Fowle, 1747), v.

48. *Meditations and Spiritual Exercises,* v.

49. Grigg, *The Lives of David Brainerd,* 156. See also Ann Taves, *Fits, Trances, and Visions: Experiencing Religion and Explaining Experience from Wesley to James* (Princeton, NJ: Princeton University Press, 1999), 374n20.

50. John Wesley, *An Extract of the Life of the Late Rev. Mr. David Brainerd, Missionary to the Indians,* 2nd ed. (Bristol: William Pine, 1771), n.p.

51. Theodor W. Adorno, "Commitment" [1962], trans. Francis McDonagh, in *The Essential Frankfurt School Reader,* ed. Andrew Arato and Eike Gebhardt, introduction by Paul Piccone (New York: Continuum, 1982), 300–318, citation at 308.

52. Joseph Conforti, "David Brainerd and the Nineteenth Century Missionary Movement," *Journal of the Early Republic* 5, no. 3 (Autumn 1985): 309–329.

53. John Sargent, *Memoir of the Rev. Henry Martyn, B.D. Late Fellow of St. John's College, Cambridge, and Chaplain to the Honourable East India Company,* 6th ed. (London: J. Hatchard and Son, 1821), 84, 101.

54. Eustace Carey, *Memoir of William Carey , D.D. Late Missionary to Bengal; Professor of Oriental Languages in the College of Fort William, Calcutta* (London: Jackson and Walford, 1836), 7.

55. Carey, *Memoir of William Carey,* 130.

56. J. B. Marsden, ed., *Memoirs of the Life and Labors of the Rev. Samuel Marsden, of Paramatta, Senior Chaplain of New South Wales; and of His Early Connexion with the Missions to New Zealand and Tahiti* (London: Religious Tract Society, 1858), 8.

57. *Memoirs of the Life and Labours of Robert Morrison, D.D., Compiled by His Widow; with Critical Notices of His Chinese Works, by Samuel Kidd,* 2 vols. (London: Longman, Orme, Brown, Green, and Longmans, 1839), 70. Eliot's connection to the print ecology of the steady seller is discussed above, in Chapter 2, note 55.

58. David A. Brewer, *The Afterlife of Character, 1726–1825* (Philadelphia: University of Pennsylvania Press, 2005), 101.

59. According to Arthur Fawcett, *Brainerd* became "one of the greatest inspirations behind missionary enterprise" that included in subsequent years the founding of the Methodist Missionary Society in 1786, the Baptist Missionary Society in 1792, and the London Missionary Society in 1795 (*The Cambuslang Revival: The Scottish Evangelical Revival of the Eighteenth Century* [London: Banner of Truth Trust, 1971], 217).

60. *The Life of David Brainerd,* 18.

61. *Catalogues of Books,* ed. Peter J. Thuesen, vol. 26 of *The Works of Jonathan Edwards,* 26 vols. (New Haven, CT: Yale University Press, 2008), 343–345. On *Christian History* more generally, see Timothy E. W. Gloege, "The Trouble with *Christian History:* Thomas Prince's 'Great Awakening,'" *Church History* 82, no. 1 (March 2013): 125–165.

62. *The Journal of Esther Edwards Burr, 1754–1757,* ed. Carol F. Karlsen and Laurie Crumpacker (New Haven, CT: Yale University Press, 1984), 99, 102.

63. Alan Dugald McKillop, *Samuel Richardson: Printer and Novelist* (Chapel Hill: University of North Carolina Press, 1936), 47.

64. Brian W. Downs, *Richardson* (London: George Routledge and Sons, 1928), 48; *The Life of Pamela* [1741] (New York: Garland, 1974), 340.

65. *Apocalyptic Writings,* ed. Stephen J. Stein, vol. 5 of *The Works of Jonathan Edwards,* 26 vols. (New Haven, CT: Yale University Press, 1977), 292n1.

66. Samuel Richardson, *Pamela; or, Virtue Rewarded,* ed. Thomas Keymer (New York: Oxford, 2001), 3.

67. Richardson, *Pamela,* 5, 9.

68. Richardson, *Pamela,* 106.

69. Richardson, *Pamela,* 172.

70. Ira Konigsberg, "The Dramatic Background of Richardson's Plots and Characters," *PMLA* 83, no. 1 (March 1968): 42–53; Keymer and Sabor, Pamela *in the Marketplace,*

85. See also John Richetti, *Popular Fiction before Richardson: Narrative Patterns 1700–1739* (Oxford: Clarendon Press, 1969); Lennard J. Davis, *Factual Fictions: The Origins of the English Novel* (New York: Columbia University Press, 1983).

71. *Selected Letters of Samuel Richardson,* ed. with an introduction by John Carroll (Oxford: Clarendon Press, 1964), 41.

72. Morris Golden, "Public Contexts and Imagining Self in *Pamela* and *Shamela*," *ELH* 52 (1986): 311–329.

73. P. Salzman, "*Virtue Rewarded* and *Pamela*," *Notes and Queries* 26 (1979): 554–556; Hubert McDermott, "*Virtue Rewarded*: The First Anglo-Irish Novel," *Studies: An Irish Quarterly Review* 75, no. 298 (Summer 1986): 177–185, esp. 182–184.

74. Philip Sydney, *The Countess of Pembroke's Arcadia: The Old Arcadia,* ed. Jean Robertson (Oxford: Clarendon Press, 1973).

75. Richardson, *Pamela,* 204.

76. Richardson, *Pamela,* 205.

77. For a version of that alternative argument, see Cynthia Griffin Wolff, *Samuel Richardson and the Eighteenth-Century Puritan Character* (New York: Archon, 1972).

78. *Selected Letters of Samuel Richardson,* 47.

79. Henry Fielding, *Joseph Andrews* [1742], in *Joseph Andrews and Shamela,* ed. Douglas Brooks-Davies (New York: Oxford, 1999), 75.

80. Turner, "Novel Panic," 78.

81. *Pamela Censured: In A Letter to the Editor* (London: J. Roberts, 1741), 21.

82. Thomas Keymer and Peter Sabor argue that Richardson may have promoted sales of the text with the understanding that it appealed as pornography. See Pamela *in the Marketplace,* 31–37. For the classic study of *Pamela* as sexual fiction, see Terry J. Castle, "P/B: *Pamela* as Sexual Fiction," *Studies in English Literature* 22, no. 3 (Summer 1982): 469–489.

83. On Highmore's *Twelve Prints,* see Pamela *in the Marketplace,* 163–164.

84. Henry Fielding, *Shamela* [1741], in *Joseph Andrews and Shamela,* ed. Douglas Brooks-Davies (New York: Oxford, 1999), 312–313.

85. Bernard Kreissman, *Pamela-Shamela: A Study of the Criticisms, Burlesques, Parodies, and Adaptations of Richardson's "Pamela"* (Lincoln: University of Nebraska Press, 1960), 53.

86. Albert O. Hirschman, *The Passions and the Interests: Political Arguments for Capitalism before Its Triumph* [1977] (Princeton, NJ: Princeton University Press, 1997), 43.

87. Nancy Glazner, "Benjamin Franklin and the Limits of Secular Civil Society," *American Literature* 80, no. 2 (2008): 203–231, citation at 214.

88. Eliza Haywood, *Anti-Pamela; or, Feign'd Innocence Detected* [1741], in *Anti-Pamela and Shamela,* ed. Catherine Ingrassia (Peterborough, Ontario: Broadview Press, 2004), 66, 164.

89. William B. Warner, *Licensing Entertainment: The Elevation of Novel Reading in Britain 1684–1750* (Berkeley: University of California Press, 1998), xv.

90. Samuel Richardson, *Clarissa; or, The History of a Young Lady* [1748], ed. Angus Ross (New York: Penguin, 1985), 61, 83.

91. The question of interest in *Clarissa,* I would aver, exists apart from the question of intention, which has concerned many of the novel's recent critics. Much criticism of the last four decades has explored the distribution of responsibility in the novel: specifically, whether Clarissa in some sense desired her own violation (for example, William Beatty Warner, *Reading Clarissa: The Struggles of Interpretation* [New Haven, CT: Yale University Press, 1979]) or whether her desires were irrelevant to her actions (for example, Frances Ferguson, "Rape and the Rise of the Novel," *Representations* 20 [Fall 1987]: 88–112). More recently, Sandra Macpherson has argued that the *Clarissa* distributes the agency and responsibility for the violations of its plot across different characters (in *Harm's Way: Tragic Responsibility and the Novel Form* [Baltimore: Johns Hopkins University Press, 2010], 59–97). See also Jonathan Kramnick, *Actions and Objects from Hobbes to Richardson* (Stanford, CA: Stanford University Press, 2010), 194–203. For one particularly searching interpretation that opens the novel in a queer direction, see Sarah Nicolazzo, "Reading *Clarissa*'s 'Conditional Liking': A Queer Philology," *Modern Philology* 112, no. 1 (August 2014): 205–225.

92. James Boswell, *Life of Johnson* [1791], ed. R. W. Chapman (New York: Oxford University Press, 1998), 480.

93. *Selected Letters of Samuel Richardson,* 40–41. Sale argues that Osborne's son may have been the actual printer (*Samuel Richardson,* 333). See also T. C. Duncan Eaves and Ben Kimpel, "The Publisher of *Pamela* and Its First Audience," *Bulletin of the New York Public Library* 64 (1960): 143–146.

94. Frank Lambert, *"Pedlar in Divinity": George Whitefield and the Transatlantic Revivals* (Princeton, NJ: Princeton University Press, 1994), 84.

95. Lambert, *"Pedlar in Divinity,"* 86.

96. For inconclusive information, see R. A. Austen-Leigh, "William Strahan and His Ledgers," *The Library,* 4th ser., 3, no. 4 (March 1923): 261–287. See also Robert D. Harlan, "William Strahan's American Book Trade, 1744–76," *Library Quarterly* 31 (July 1961): 235–244. According to J. A. Cochrane, Strahan maintained an account with James Hutton from 1740 to 1742 for printing sermons by Whitefield, and with Whitefield himself the account ran from August 1739 to November 1753 to a total amount of over £460. See *Dr. Johnson's Printer: The Life of William Strahan* (London: Routledge and Kegan Paul, 1964), 10, 69.

97. John Nichols, *Literary Anecdotes of the Eighteenth Century* [1812–1816], ed. Colin Clair (Carbondale: Southern Illinois University Press, 1967), 324.

98. Cochrane, *Dr. Johnson's Printer,* 145.

99. Boswell, *Life of Johnson,* 206.

100. Albert Henry Smyth, ed., *The Life and Writings of Benjamin Franklin,* 10 vols. (New York: Macmillan, 1905), 2:278–279.

101. Green and Stallybrass, *Benjamin Franklin,* 66; C. William Miller, *Benjamin Franklin's Philadelphia Printing 1728–1766: A Descriptive Bibliography* (Philadelphia: American Philosophical Society, 1974), 187, 227, 266, 225, 344.

102. *A Catalogue of Choice and Valuable Books, Consisting of Near 600 Volumes, in Most Faculties and Sciences, viz. Divinity, History, Law, Mathematics, Philosophy, Physic, Poetry, &c. Which Will Begin to Be Sold for Ready Money, Only, by Benj. Franklin, at*

the Post-Office in Philadelphia, on Wednesday, the 11th of April 1744. at Nine a Clock in the Morning* (Philadelphia: [B. Franklin] 1744), 14.

103. Michael Warner, "The Preacher's Footing," in *This Is Enlightenment,* ed. Clifford Siskin and William Warner (Chicago: University of Chicago Press, 2010), 368–383. See also John Ladras Modern, *Secularism in Antebellum America* (Chicago: University of Chicago Press, 2011).

104. Ian Maxted, "The London Book Trades 1775–1800: A Topographical Guide," *Exeter Working Papers in Book History* (blog), http://bookhistory.blogspot.com/2007/01/streets-introduction.html.

105. Michael Warner, "Secularism," in *Keywords for American Cultural Studies,* ed. Bruce Burgett and Glenn Hendler (New York: New York University Press, 2007), 209–213. For syntheses of the abundant scholarship on secularism in literary studies, see Jordan Alexander Stein and Justine S. Murison, "Religion and Method," *Early American Literature* 45, no. 1 (Spring 2010): 1–29; Peter Coviello and Jared Hickman, "After the Postsecular," *American Literature* 86, no. 4 (December 2014): 645–654; Colin Jager, "The Secular and the Literary," *Christianity and Literature* 67, no. 3 (2018): 411–418.

106. *Pennsylvania Gazette,* June 12, 1744, qtd. in Green and Stallybrass, *Benjamin Franklin,* 66.

107. Benjamin Franklin, *Autobiography, Poor Richard, and Later Writings,* ed. J. A. Leo Lemay (New York: Library of America, 1997), 669.

108. *George Whitefield's Journals* (Edinburgh: Banner of Truth Trust, 1960), 360.

109. Walter Benjamin, "Unpacking My Library: A Talk about Book Collecting," in *Illuminations* [1955], trans. Harry Zohn and ed. with an introduction by Hannah Arendt (New York: Schocken Books, 1968), 59–67, citation at 60.

4. Letters, Libraries, and Lyrics

1. Richard D. Altick, *The English Common Reader: A Social History of the Mass Reading Public* (Chicago: University of Chicago Press, 1957), 36.

2. Benjamin Franklin, *Autobiography, Poor Richard, and Later Writings,* ed. J. A. Leo Lemay (New York: Library of America, 1997), 586.

3. Jürgen Habermas, *The Structural Transformation of the Public Sphere: An Inquiry into a Category of Bourgeois Society* [1962], trans. Thomas Burger, with the assistance of Frederick Lawrence (Cambridge, MA: MIT Press, 1989), 50. One of the most important correctives to Habermas's theorization of a bourgeois public sphere remains Oskar Negt and Alexander Kluge, *Public Sphere and Experience: Toward an Analysis of the Bourgeois and Proletarian Public Sphere* [1972], foreword by Miriam Hansen and trans. Peter Labanyi, Jamie Owen Daniel, and Assenka Oksiloff (Minneapolis: University of Minnesota Press, 1993).

4. Henry Fielding, *Joseph Andrews* [1742], in *Joseph Andrews and Shamela,* ed. Douglas Brooks-Davies (New York: Oxford, 1999), 69.

5. See, for example, Terry Belanger, "Publishers and Writers in Eighteenth-Century England," in *Books and Their Readers in Eighteenth-Century England,* ed. Isabel

Rivers (London: St. Martin's, 1982), 5–25; David Saunders and Ian Hunter, "Lessons from the 'Literary': How to Historicise Authorship," *Critical Inquiry* 17, no. 3 (Spring 1991): 479–509; Mark Rose, *Authors and Owners: The Invention of Copyright* (Cambridge, MA: Harvard University Press, 1993). Several histories of the Stationers' Company exist, but the classic one is Cyprian Blagden, *The Stationers' Company: A History 1403–1959* (London: George Allen and Unwin, 1960).

6. Jody Greene, *The Trouble with Ownership: Literary Property and Authorial Liability in England, 1660–1730* (Philadelphia: University of Pennsylvania Press, 2005). The legal figure of the author (one who is liable for the contents of his works) seems to appear nearly a century earlier in France than in England. See Joan de Jean, *The Reinvention of Obscenity: Sex, Lies, and Tabloids in Early Modern France* (Chicago: University of Chicago Press, 2002).

7. On copyright's eighteenth-century transformation, see Lyman Ray Patterson, *Copyright in Historical Perspective* (Nashville: Vanderbilt University Press, 1968); Rose, *Authors and Owners;* Adrian Johns, *The Nature of the Book: Print and Knowledge in the Making* (Chicago: University of Chicago Press, 1998), 230–248.

8. On colonies as laboratories of modernity, see Ann Laura Stoler, *Race and the Education of Desire: Foucault's History of Sexuality and the Colonial Order of Things* (Durham, NC: Duke University Press, 1995), 15. The phrase "laboratory of modernity" comes from Paul Rabinow, *French Modern: Norms and Forms of the Social Environment* (Berkeley: University of California Press, 1989), 317.

9. Rosalind Remer, *Printers and Men of Capital: Philadelphia Book Publishers in the New Republic* (Philadelphia: University of Pennsylvania Press, 1996).

10. James N. Green and Peter Stallybrass, *Benjamin Franklin: Writer and Printer* (New Castle, DE: Oak Knoll Press, 2006), 60.

11. See Rollo G. Silver, "Financing the Publication of Early New England Sermons," *Studies in Bibliography* 11 (1958): 163–178. Print runs for late seventeenth- and early eighteenth-century sermons were about 500 for the press at Cambridge, England. See D. F. McKenzie, *Making Meaning: "Printers of the Mind" and Other Essays,* ed. Peter D. McDonald and Michael F. Suarez (Amherst: University of Massachusetts Press, 2002), 24. See also G. Thomas Tanselle, "Press Figures in America: Some Preliminary Observations," *Studies in Bibliography* 19 (1966): 123–160, which concentrates on the 1790s and 1810s.

12. On the United Brethren, see A. J. Lewis, *Zinzendorf, The Ecumenical Pioneer: A Study in the Moravian Contribution to Christian Mission and Unity* (Philadelphia: Westminster Press, 1962), 34–44, 59–69.

13. Green and Stallybrass, *Benjamin Franklin,* 60.

14. See Joanna Brooks and John Saillant, eds., *"Face Zion Forward": First Writers of the Black Atlantic, 1785–1798* (Boston: Northeastern University Press, 2002), 3–33.

15. Scott Mandelbrote, "The Publishing and Distribution of Religious Books by Voluntary Associations: From the Society for Promoting Christian Knowledge to the British and Foreign Bible Society," in *The Cambridge History of the Book in Britain,* vol. 5, *1695–1830,* ed. Michael F. Suarez and Michael L. Turner (Cambridge: Cambridge University Press, 2009), 613–630, citation at 618.

16. Leslie Howsam, *Cheap Bibles: Nineteenth-Century Publishing and the British and Foreign Bible Society* (Cambridge: Cambridge University Press, 1991); David Paul Nord, *Faith in Reading: Religious Publishing and the Birth of Mass Media in America* (Chapel Hill: University of North Carolina Press, 2004).

17. *Selected Letters of Samuel Richardson,* ed. with an introduction by John Carroll (Oxford: Clarendon Press, 1964), 40–41.

18. Mandelbrote, "The Publishing and Distribution of Religious Books by Voluntary Associations," 621.

19. *A Collection of Papers Printed by Order of the Society for the Propagation of the Gospel in Foreign Parts* (London: E. Owen, 1741), 44.

20. W. O. B. Allen and Edmund McClure, *Two Hundred Years: The History of the Society for Promoting Christian Knowledge, 1698–1898* (London: Society for Promoting Christian Knowledge, 1898), 185–187.

21. *An Account of the Society for Promoting Religious Knowledge among the Poor: Began Anno 1750* (London: for Thomas Field, 1769), 50–51.

22. Mandelbrote, "The Publishing and Distribution of Religious Books by Voluntary Associations," 622. On the eighteenth-century British reprint trade, see William Todd, "Bibliography and the Editorial Problem in the Eighteenth Century," *Studies in Bibliography* 4 (1951–1952): 41–55. On North American reprinting after Independence, see Robert A. Gross, "Introduction: An Extensive Republic," in *A History of the Book in America,* vol. 2, *An Extensive Republic: Print, Culture, and Society in the New Nation, 1790–1840,* ed. Robert A. Gross and Mary Kelley (Chapel Hill: University of North Carolina Press, 2010), 1–50, esp. 26–29.

23. In our introduction to *Early African American Print Culture* (Philadelphia: University of Pennsylvania Press, 2012), Lara Cohen and I have outlined this critique of what we call the "print-capitalism thesis" (1–16, esp. 13–14). On the ways that circulation becomes configured an abstract entity unto itself within global capitalist systems, see also Benjamin Lee and Edward LiPuma, "Cultures of Circulation: The Imaginations of Modernity," *Public Culture* 14, no. 1 (2002): 191–213.

24. Records of the Society in Scotland for Propagating Christian Knowledge, Minutes of General Meetings, 1736–1759, GD95/1/4, National Archives of Scotland, Edinburgh, Meeting of June 2, 1748.

25. By contrast, subscription economics didn't generally work for early American novels, as printers could only occasionally drum up enough subscribers (the magic number seems to have been about 200) to make the venture lucrative. See Cathy N. Davidson, *The Revolution and the Word: The Rise of the Novel in America* (New York: Oxford University Press, 1986), 26–27.

26. Isabel Rivers, "Religious Publishing," in *The Cambridge History of the Book in Britain,* 5:579–600, citation at 583–584; Frank Baker, "Wesley's Printers and Booksellers," *Proceedings of the Wesley Historical Society* 22 (1939–1940): 61–65, 97–101, 131–140, 164–168.

27. See also Richard Green, *The Works of John and Charles Wesley: A Bibliography,* 2nd ed. (New York: AMS Press, 1976); Frank Baker, *A Union Catalogue of the Publications of John and Charles Wesley* (Durham, NC: Duke University Divinity School, 1966).

28. *A Ledger of Charles Ackers, Printer of the London Magazine,* ed. D. F. McKenzie and J. C. Ross (Oxford: Oxford University Press for the Oxford Bibliographical Society, 1968), 2–4.

29. Mandelbrote, "The Publishing and Distribution of Religious Books by Voluntary Associations," 618n30.

30. Isabel Rivers, "The First Evangelical Tract Society," *Historical Journal* 50, no. 1 (March 2007): 1–22, citation at 10.

31. Mandelbrote, "The Publishing and Distribution of Religious Books by Voluntary Associations," 618.

32. Anne Stott, *Hannah More: The First Victorian* (New York: Oxford University Press, 2003), 144.

33. Stott, *Hannah More,* 206. The sales figure comes from Ernest Marshall Howse, *Saints in Politics: The "Clapham Sect" and the Growth of Freedom* (Toronto: University of Toronto Press, 1952), 102.

34. Mandelbrote, "The Publishing and Distribution of Religious Books by Voluntary Associations," 624. On Johnson, see *The Joseph Johnson Letterbook,* ed. John Bugg (New York: Oxford University Press, 2016), esp. xix–lxvi.

35. "Cheap Book Society," *Belfast Monthly Magazine* 13, no. 73 (August 31, 1814): 148–149, citation at 148.

36. *The Works of Henry Fielding, Esq: With the Life of the Author,* 12 vols. (London: William Strahan, 1783).

37. William St Clair, *The Reading Nation in the Romantic Period* (Cambridge: Cambridge University Press, 2004); James Raven, *Publishing Business in Eighteenth-Century England* (Woodbridge, Suffolk: Boydell Press, 2014); David McKitterick, *History of Cambridge University Press,* vol. 2, *Scholarship and Commerce, 1698–1872* (Cambridge: Cambridge University Press, 1998), 4.

38. The story I'm telling becomes somewhat more complicated after 1774, when the House of Lords, in *Donaldson v. Becket,* finds printers' claims to perpetual copyright illegal in both Britain and Scotland. As William St Clair observes, this circumstance jumpstarts a reprint trade of polite and literary works at very low cost to consumers, effectively putting these works in the hands of readers who may not otherwise ever have been able to afford them. Here again, however, the rise of the novel as such factors little if at all into what the scholar has called "the explosion of reading." See St Clair, *The Reading Nation in the Romantic Period,* 110–139. On the expansion of provincial publishing as a result of the 1774 decision, see John Feather, *The Provincial Book Trade in Eighteenth-Century England* (Cambridge: Cambridge University Press, 1985), 44–68.

39. The growth in the gross domestic product (GDP) of England in the eighteenth century averaged about 2.8 percent before 1714, dropped to half of that between 1714 and 1745, was restored to about 3 percent to 1760, and then plunged into a negative rate of −1.5 percent to 1781, closing with a relative economic surge of 5.1 percent to 1800. See François Crouzet, "Toward an Export Economy," *Explorations in Economic History* 17 (1980): 48–93. It is important to recognize, as well, that GDP data averages all domestic products and does not isolate books or printing as such. More

focused analyses have shown how an event like the Revolutionary War compromised existing export patterns in the colonial book trade well after the military conflict ended in 1783. See Giles Barber, "Books from the Old World and for the New: The British International Trade in Book in the Eighteenth Century" *Studies in Voltaire and the Eighteenth Century* 151 (1976): 185–224. Though the texts now recognized to be novels emerged in the 1740s and gained popularity in the next several decades, it nonetheless appears that novels impacted unquantifiable things like British culture far more than quantifiable things like the British economy.

40. *Catalogues of Books,* ed. Peter J. Thuesen, vol. 26 of *The Works of Jonathan Edwards,* 26 vols. (New Haven, CT: Yale University Press, 2008), 343–345.

41. Michael Warner, *The Letters of the Republic: Publication and the Public Sphere in Eighteenth-Century America* (Cambridge, MA: Harvard University Press, 1990), 21.

42. Wilson H. Kimnach and Kenneth P. Minkema, "The Material and Social Practices of Intellectual Work: Jonathan Edwards's Study," *William and Mary Quarterly,* 3rd ser., 69, no. 4 (October 2012): 683–730. See also Thomas H. Johnson, "Jonathan Edwards' Background of Reading," *Publications of the Colonial Society of Massachusetts* 28 (1935): 193–222; Wallace E. Anderson, "Editor's Introduction," *Scientific and Philosophical Writings,* vol. 6 of *The Works of Jonathan Edwards,* 26 vols. (New Haven, CT: Yale University Press, 1980), 1–143.

43. Fiona Brideoake, *The Ladies of Llangollen: Desire, Indeterminacy, and the Legacies of Criticism* (Lewisburg, PA: Bucknell University Press, 2017), 123–138.

44. David Gilson, "Jane Austen's Books," *Book Collector* (Spring 1974): 27–39.

45. *Poets and Men of Letters,* vol. 7 of *Sale Catalogues of Libraries of Eminent Persons,* ed. Hugh Amory (London: Mansell with Sotheby Park Bernet Publications, 1975), 51–79.

46. Robert Halsband, "Lady Mary Wortley Montague and Eighteenth-Century Fiction," *Philological Quarterly* 45, no. 1 (1966), 145–156.

47. Donald Greene, *Samuel Johnson's Library: An Annotated Guide* (Victoria, BC: English Literary Studies, University of Victoria, 1975), 34, 97.

48. *Memoirs of the First Forty-Five Years of the Life of James Lackington, the Present Bookseller in Chiswell-Street, Moorfields, London. Written by Himself* (London: for the Author, 1792), 386–387.

49. Altick, *The English Common Reader,* 40. For one interesting rethinking of Altick's conclusions, see Robert D. Hume, "The Value of Money in Eighteenth-Century England: Incomes, Prices, Buying Power—and Some Problems in Cultural Economics," *Huntington Library Quarterly* 77, no. 4 (Winter 2014): 373–416.

50. Samuel Johnson, "Life of Swift," in *Samuel Johnson: Selected Poetry and Prose,* ed. Frank Brady and W. K. Wimsatt (Berkeley: University of California Press, 1977), 454.

51. John Brewer, *The Pleasures of the Imagination: English Culture in the Eighteenth Century* (London: Harper Collins, 1997), 189–190.

52. Karl Marx, *Capital,* vol. 1: *A Critique of Political Economy* [1867], trans. Ben Fowkes (New York: Penguin, 1977); Walter Benjamin, "The Work of Art in the Age of Mechanical Reproduction," in *Illuminations* [1955], trans. Harry Zohn, ed. with an introduction by Hannah Arendt (New York: Schocken Books, 1968), 217–251; Peter

Stallybrass, "Marx's Coat," in *Border Fetishisms: Material Objects in Unstable Spaces,* ed. Patricia Spyer (New York: Routledge, 1998), 183–207, citation at 186.

53. David Cressy, "Books as Totems in Seventeenth-Century England and New England," *Journal of Library History* 21, no. 1 (Winter 1986): 92–106. For an extended case study, see Douglas Anderson, *William Bradford's Books: Of Plimmoth Plantation and the Printed Word* (Baltimore: Johns Hopkins University Press, 2003).

54. William Zachs, *The First John Murray and the Late Eighteenth-Century London Book Trade* (Oxford: Oxford University Press for the British Academy, 1998), 26.

55. Brewer, *The Pleasures of the Imagination,* 173–175.

56. Anna Janney DeArmond, *Andrew Bradford, Colonial Journalist* (Newark: University of Delaware Press, 1949), 21.

57. Qtd. in Paul Kaufman, *Libraries and Their Users: Collected Papers in Library History* (London: Library Association, 1969), 224.

58. For the classic discussion of coffeehouses, see Habermas, *The Structural Transformation of the Public Sphere,* 31–43. According to Giles Barber, the 1767 Revenue Act generated a policy of nonimportation among American booksellers: "It would seem however that the rigours of this policy were progressively weakened as the importation of additional classes of books was allowed and in 1770 the Act was in any case repealed. The non-importation agreements show up clearly in low figures for New England in both 1769 and 1770 but elsewhere imports remained universally high" ("Books from the Old World and for the New," 199).

59. Michael Harris, "Periodicals and the Book Trade," in *Development of the English Book Trade, 1700–1899,* ed. Robin Myers and Michael Harris (Oxford: Oxford Polytechnic Press, 1981), 66–94.

60. Michael Warner, "Publics and Counterpublics," *Public Culture* 14, no. 1 (2002): 49–90, esp. 70–73.

61. Franklin, *Autobiography, Poor Richard, and Later Writings,* 632.

62. David Allan, *Commonplace Books and Reading in Georgian England* (Cambridge: Cambridge University Press, 2010). See also Peter Clark, *British Clubs and Societies 1580–1800: The Origins of an Associated World* (Oxford: Clarendon Press, 2000).

63. Thomas Kelly, *Early Public Libraries: A History of Public Libraries in Great Britain before 1850* (London: Library Association, 1966), 144; James Green, "Subscription Libraries and Commercial Circulating Libraries in Colonial Philadelphia and New York," in *Institutions of Reading: The Social Life of Libraries in the United States,* ed. Thomas Augst and Kenneth Carpenter (Amherst: University of Massachusetts Press, 2007), 53–71, esp. 60–61. See also Paul Kaufman, "The Community Library: A Chapter in English Social History," *Transactions of the American Philosophical Society* 57 (1967), pt. 7, 3–67.

64. Kaufman, *Libraries and Their Users,* 118.

65. K. A. Manley, "Circulating Libraries in Eighteenth-Century England," in *Libraries and the Book Trade: The Formation of Collections from the Sixteenth to the Twentieth Century,* ed. Robin Myers, Michael Harris, and Giles Mandelbrote (New Castle, DE: Oak Knoll Press, 2000), 29–50, citation at 48.

66. Allan, *Commonplace Books and Reading in Georgian England,* 15.

67. Paul Kaufman, *Borrowings from the Bristol Library 1773–1784: A Unique Record of Reading Vogues* (Charlottesville: Bibliographical Society of the University of Virginia, 1960), 121–122.

68. *The Charter, Laws, and Catalogue of Books of the Library Company of Burlington* (Philadelphia: William Dunlap, 1758).

69. The charter and records of the Library Company of Burlington are in possession of the library. Copies of the pre-1800 materials have been privately microfilmed and are in the collection of the Library Company of Philadelphia. On Pepys's reading, see Kate Loveman, *Samuel Pepys and His Books: Reading, Newsgathering, and Sociability, 1660–1703* (Oxford: Oxford University Press, 2015), esp. 135–164. I owe the term "not-nonfiction" to conversation with Jim Green.

70. *A Catalogue of Books Belonging to the Library Company of Philadelphia* (Philadelphia: B. Franklin, 1741).

71. *The Charter, Laws, and Catalogue of Books, of the Library Company of Philadelphia* (Philadelphia: B. Franklin and D. Hall, 1757). The catalog erroneously lists *Gulliver's Travels* in a 1722 edition, which never existed. I have presumed it refers to the 1742 edition which remains in the library's collection.

72. John Feather, "The Book Trade and Libraries," in *The Cambridge History of Libraries in Britain and Ireland*, vol. 2, *1640–1850*, ed. Giles Mandelbrote and K. A. Manley (Cambridge: Cambridge University Press, 2006), 301–323, citation at 301.

73. After the volatility of the 1770s, in terms of the American Revolution's impact on the London export trade, the legal limits put on copyright after 1774, and the expansion of provincial printing (see note 39 above), the relative consistency into which the print trade had settled in the 1790s ended abruptly with the 1801 Act of Union, which created the United Kingdom and extended British copyright to Ireland for the first time. See Charles Benson, "The Dublin Book Trade," "The Irish Trade," and "Printers and Booksellers in Dublin, 1800–1850," in *Spreading the Word: The Distribution Networks of Print, 1550–1850,* ed. Robin Myers and Michael Harris (Winchester, UK: St. Paul's Bibliographies, 1990), 47–59; Joseph Rezek, *London and the Making of Provincial Literature: Aesthetics and the Transatlantic Book Trade, 1800–1850* (Philadelphia: University of Pennsylvania Press, 2015), 31–33. See also Meredith L. McGill, "Copyright," in *A History of the Book in America*, vol. 2, *An Extensive Republic: Print, Culture, and Society in the New Nation, 1790–1840,* ed. Robert A. Gross and Mary Kelley (Chapel Hill: University of North Carolina Press, 2010), 198–211.

74. *The Oxford Dictionary of English Etymology*, ed. C. T. Onions (Oxford: Clarendon Press, 1966), s.v. "novel."

75. *An Essay on the New Species of Writing Founded by Mister Fielding: With a Word or Two upon the Modern State of Criticism* (London: W. Owen, 1751), 12.

76. Henry Fielding, *Tom Jones* [1749], ed. John Bender and Simon Stern (New York: Oxford University Press, 1996), 29, 3, 5.

77. Samuel Johnson, *A Dictionary of the English Language*, 2 vols. (London: W. Strahan for J. and P. Knapton; T. and T. Longman; C. Hitch and L. Hawes; A. Millar; and R. and J. Dodsley, 1745), s.v. "History."

78. On fiction, see Catherine Gallagher, "The Rise of Fictionality," in *The Novel*, vol. 1: *History, Geography, and Culture*, ed. Franco Moretti (Princeton, NJ: Princeton University Press, 2006), 336–363.

79. Daniel Defoe, *Robinson Crusoe* [1719], ed. Michael Shinagel (New York: Norton, 1975), 4; Jonathan Swift, *Gulliver's Travels* [1726], ed. Albert J. Rivero (New York: Norton, 2002), 6.

80. Jean-Jacques Rousseau, *Œuvres Complètes*, 24 vols. (Paris: Éditions Champion, 2012), 15:1216.

81. Susanna Haswell Rowson, *Charlotte Temple* [1791], ed. Cathy N. Davidson (New York: Oxford University Press, 1986), 5.

82. Hannah Webster Foster, *The Coquette* [1797], ed. Cathy N. Davidson (New York: Oxford University Press, 1987).

83. William Godwin, *Things as They Are; or, The Adventures of Caleb Williams* [1794], ed. Maurice Hindle (New York: Penguin, 1987), 3.

84. Maria Edgeworth, *Belinda* [1801], ed. Kathryn J. Kirkpatrick (New York: Oxford University Press, 1994), 3.

85. Alan Dugald McKillop, *Samuel Richardson: Printer and Novelist* (Chapel Hill: University of North Carolina Press, 1936), 47.

86. Vicesimus Knox, *Essays Moral and Literary, Volume the Second* (London: Charles Dilly, 1779), 190.

87. Mary Wollstonecraft, *A Vindication of the Rights of Woman: With Strictures on Political and Moral Subjects*, 2nd ed. (London: J. Johnson, 1792), 427.

88. "Novel Reading, a Cause of Female Depravity," *Monthly Mirror* 4 (1797): 177–179, citation at 177.

89. *New England Quarterly Magazine* 1 (April, May, and June 1802): 172–174; *Atheneum* (1817): 717–720; *Monthly Anthology* 1, no. 363 (June 1804): n.p. Frank Luther Mott describes this essay as "widely reprinted in American periodicals," in *A History of American Magazines: 1741–1850* (Cambridge, MA: Harvard University Press, 1930), 174.

90. Benjamin Rush, *Thoughts upon Female Education* (Philadelphia: Printed by Prichard and Hall, 1787), 12. Rush's reference is to a short novel, part of the international text-network surrounding Goethe's *Die Leiden des jungen Werthers* (1774), published under the title *The Letters of Charlotte, during her Connexion with Werter,* and printed in New York and Boston, among other North American cities, after 1787.

91. For histories of the objection to novel reading see, W. F. Gallaway Jr., "The Conservative Attitude toward Fiction, 1770–1830," *PMLA* 45 (1940): 1041–1059; John Tinnon Taylor, *Early Opposition to the English Novel: The Popular Reaction from 1760 to 1830* (New York: King's Crown Press, 1943).

92. A. W., Esq, *The Enormous Abomination of the Hoop-Petticoat, as The Fashion Now Is, and Has Been for about These Two Years Fully-Display'd* . . . (London: William Russel, 1745), 4.

93. James Miller, *The Picture; or, The Cuckold in Conceit* (London: J. Watts, 1745), 10–11.

94. [Richard Sheridan], *The Rivals, A Comedy* (London: John Wilkie, 1775), 12.

95. It is hardly the case that wrongness and sin were not otherwise widely decried in the 1780s and after. See Joanne Innes, "Politics and Morals: The Reformation of Manners

Movement in Late Eighteenth-Century England," in *The Transformation of Political Culture: England and Germany in the Late Eighteenth Century,* ed. Eckhart Hellmuth (Oxford: Oxford University Press, 1990), 57–118.

96. *Selected Writings of Hannah More,* ed. Robert Hole (London: William Pickering, 1996), 139, 132.

97. Rivers, "Religious Publishing," 5:599.

98. John Bunyan, *The Pilgrim's Progress. With Original Notes by Thomas Scott, Chaplain to the Lock Hospital* (London: J. Saunders, 1794).

99. See David Fairer, *Organising Poetry: The Coleridge Circle, 1790–1798* (New York: Oxford University Press, 2009).

100. Samuel Taylor Coleridge, *Biographia Literaria; or, Biographical Sketches of My Literary Life and Opinions,* ed. James Engell and W. Jackson Bate (Princeton, NJ: Princeton University Press, 1983), 48–49.

101. Ralph Waldo Emerson, *The Journals and Miscellaneous Notebooks of Ralph Waldo Emerson,* 16 vols., ed. William H. Gillman et al. (Cambridge, MA: Harvard University Press, 1960–1982): 15:146.

102. George Gordon, Lord Byron, *Poetical Works,* ed. Frederick Page and John Jump (New York: Oxford University Press, 1970), 242. The correct line is "The nympholepsy of some fond despair."

103. Ralph Waldo Emerson, *Essays and Lectures,* ed. Joel Porte (New York: Library of America, 1983), 445.

104. Robert W. Daniel, "The Publication of the 'Lyrical Ballads,'" *MLR* 33, no. 3 (July 1938): 406–410.

105. Rezek, *London and the Making of Provincial Literature,* 4.

106. W[illiam]. Wordsworth, *Lyrical Ballads, with Other Poems. In Two Volumes,* 2nd ed. (London: T. N. Longman and O. Rees, 1800): 1:iv, xviii–xix.

107. Mark L. Greenberg, "Romantic Technology: Books, Printing, and Blake's *Marriage of Heaven and Hell,*" in *Literature and Technology,* ed. Mark L. Greenberg and Lance Schachterle (Bethlehem, PA: Lehigh University Press, 1992), 154–176, citation at 155–156.

108. See, for example, Eliza Richards, *Gender and the Poetics of Reception in Poe's Circle* (Cambridge: Cambridge University Press, 2004), esp. 11–18; Ingrid Satelmajer, "When a Consumer Becomes an Editor: Susan Hayes Ward and the Poetry of *The Independent,*" *Textual Cultures* 2, no. 1 (Spring 2007): 78–100; Natalie M. Houston, "Newspaper Poems: Material Texts in the Public Sphere," *Victorian Studies* 50, no. 2 (Winter 2008): 233–242. See also James Raven, "Why Ephemera Were Not Ephemeral: The Effectiveness of Innovative Print in the Eighteenth Century," *Yearbook of English Studies* (2015): 56–73.

109. See Chapter 1, note 72. G. Gabrielle Starr attempts to complicate this medium / genre distinction by discussing some of the ways that poetry becomes a sphere of citation for the novel after 1750. See *Lyric Generations: Poetry and the Novel in the Long Eighteenth Century* (Baltimore: Johns Hopkins University Press, 2004). For useful background, see also Harold Love, "Oral and Scribal Texts in Early Modern England," in *The Cambridge History of the Book in Britain,* vol. 4: *1557–1695,* ed. John Barnard and D. F. McKenzie, with the assistance of Maureen Bell (Cambridge:

Cambridge University Press, 2002), 97–121, esp. 109–110; Peter Beal, "John Donne and the Circulation of Manuscripts, in *The Cambridge History of the Book in Britain*, 4:122–126; David D. Hall, *Ways of Writing: The Practice and Politics of Text-Making in Seventeenth-Century New England* (Philadelphia: University of Pennsylvania Press, 2008), 69–80.

110. Tim Chilcott, *A Publisher and His Circle: The Life and Work of John Taylor, Keats's Publisher* (London: Routledge and Kegan Paul, 1972), 20; Lee Erickson, *The Economy of Literary Form: English Literature and the Industrialization of Publishing, 1800– 1850* (Baltimore: Johns Hopkins University Press, 1996), 22.

111. David Foxon, *Pope and the Early Eighteenth-Century Book Trade* (Oxford: Clarendon Press, 1991), 102.

112. William Charvat, *Literary Publishing in America, 1790–1850* (Philadelphia: University of Pennsylvania Press, 1959), 34.

113. On the economics of printing poetry in the eighteenth century, see Michael F. Suarez, "Publishing Contemporary Literature, 1695–1774," in *The Cambridge History of the Book in Britain*, 5:649–666, esp. 654–660.

114. Lucien Febvre and Henri-Jean Martin, *The Coming of the Book: The Impact of Printing, 1450–1800* [1958], trans. David Gerard (London: Verso, 2010), 29–44; John Bidwell, "The Industrialization of the Paper Trade," in *The Cambridge History of the Book in Britain*, 5:200–217. See as well the charts in St Clair, *The Reading Nation in the Romantic Period*, 506–509. For a nineteenth-century example, see Michael Winship, *American Literary Publishing in the Mid-Nineteenth Century: The Business of Ticknor and Fields* (Cambridge: Cambridge University Press, 1995), 94–121.

115. The connections between the rise of a conception of Romantic poetic genius and the economic self-interest of Romantic poets are laid out beautifully in Michael Gamer, *Romanticism, Self-Canonization, and the Business of Poetry* (Cambridge: Cambridge University Press, 2017).

116. Percy Bysshe Shelley, *A Defense of Poetry* [1840], in *The Major Works*, ed. Zachary Leader and Michael O'Neill (New York: Oxford University Press, 2003), 674–701, citation at 696.

117. Mary Poovey, *A History of the Modern Fact: Problems of Knowledge in Sciences of Wealth and Society* (Chicago: University of Chicago Press, 1998), 326.

118. On the author-function, see Michel Foucault, "What Is an Author?," in *Language, Counter-Memory, Practice: Selected Essays and Interviews*, ed. Donald F. Bouchard (Ithaca, NY: Cornell University Press, 1977), 113–138.

119. Paul de Man, *Aesthetic Ideology*, ed. with an introduction by Andrzej Warminski (Minneapolis: University of Minnesota Press, 1996).

120. Terry Castle, *The Apparitional Lesbian: Female Homosexuality and Modern Culture* (New York: Columbia University Press, 1995), esp. 92–106; Anna Clark, "Anne Lister's Construction of Lesbian Identity," *Journal of the History of Sexuality* 7, no. 1 (July 1996): 23–50.

121. *I Know My Own Heart: The Diaries of Anne Lister, 1791–1840*, ed. Helena Whitbread (New York: New York University Press, 1992), 344, 78.

122. See also the longer historical discussion of poetry in the context of "losing literature" in Deidre Shauna Lynch, *Loving Literature: A Cultural History* (Chicago: University of Chicago Press, 2015), 235–275.

123. Andrew Piper, *Dreaming in Books: The Making of the Bibliographic Imagination in the Romantic Age* (Chicago: University of Chicago Press, 2009), esp. 121–152.

124. On the unification of poetry as "lyric," see Virginia Jackson, *Dickinson's Misery: A Theory of Lyric Reading* (Princeton, NJ: Princeton University Press, 2005). On the invention of metrics, see Meredith Martin, *The Rise and Fall of Meter: Poetry and English National Culture, 1860–1930* (Princeton, NJ: Princeton University Press, 2012).

125. Steve Newman, *Ballad Collection, Lyric, and the Canon: The Call of the Popular from the Restoration to New Criticism* (Philadelphia: University of Pennsylvania Press, 2007), 1.

126. Katie Trumpener, *Bardic Nationalism: The Romantic Novel and the British Empire* (Princeton, NJ: Princeton University Press, 1997), 78.

127. See Meredith L. McGill, "What is a Ballad? Reading for Genre, Format, and Medium," *Nineteenth-Century Literature* 70, no. 2 (September 2016): 156–175.

128. Qtd. in Taylor, *Early Opposition to the English Novel,* 105.

129. William Charvat, *The Profession of Authorship in America, 1800–1870,* ed. Matthew J. Bruccoli (Columbus: Ohio State University Press, 1968), 106–167. See also Leon Jackson, *The Business of Letters: Authorial Economies in Antebellum America* (Stanford, CA: Stanford University Press, 2008), 34–35.

130. Lawrence Buell, *The Dream of the Great American Novel* (Cambridge, MA: Harvard University Press, 2014), 10–12. The rise of novels in relation to "New World" nationalisms has been influentially expounded by Benedict Anderson, *Imagined Communities: Reflections on The Origin and Spread of Nationalism,* rev. ed. (New York: Verso, 1991), 47–65. Many scholars attracted instead to Habermas's account of the eighteenth century imagine that novels appear in relation to the rise of a public sphere, rather than a national one. For a useful corrective and complication of that story, see Jonathan Brody Kramnick, *Making the English Canon: Print-Capitalism and the Cultural Past, 1700–1770* (Cambridge: Cambridge University Press, 1998). See also Elizabeth Maddock Dillon's useful distinction between Habermas's "public sphere" and Immanuel Kant's "public sense" in "Atlantic Aesthesis: Books and 'Sensus Communis' in the New World," *Early American Literature* 51, no. 2 (2016): 367–395.

131. Nord, *Faith in Reading,* 113–115, 127.

132. Margreta de Grazia, *Shakespeare Verbatim: The Reproduction of Authenticity and the 1790 Apparatus* (New York: Oxford University Press, 1991).

133. On unauthorized reprinting, see James N. Green, "The Rise of Book Publishing," in *A History of the Book in America,* vol. 2: *An Extensive Republic: Print, Culture, and Society in the New Nation, 1790–1840,* ed. Robert A. Gross and Mary Kelley (Chapel Hill: University of North Carolina Press, 2010), 75–127; Meredith L. McGill, *American Literature and the Culture of Reprinting, 1834–1853* (Philadelphia: University of Pennsylvania Press, 2003).

134. John Bunyan, *The Pilgrim's Progress from This World to That Which Is to Come,* ed. George Barrell Cheever (New York: George Putnam, 1851).

135. George Barrell Cheever, *Lectures on the Pilgrim's Progress, and on the Life and Times of John Bunyan* (New York: Wiley and Putnam, 1845).

Conclusion

1. Scholarship in queer theory is uncommonly precise in distinguishing among creation, transmission, and reproduction, terms too willingly considered as approximate synonyms by much nonqueer scholarship studying change over time. For a particularly helpful exploration, one would do well to start with Elizabeth Freeman, *Time Binds: Queer Temporalities, Queer Histories* (Durham, NC: Duke University Press, 2010).

2. To be clear, my claim is not that nineteenth-century people did not talk about media; rather, it is that their technical and evaluative languages generally diverged, so that when material features of a text were noticed and discussed, those features were not typically estimated as an aspect of the intentions of the text's creator. Below, I offer the example of the Victorian triple-decker, but similar kinds of examples could be drawn from Victorian periodical production, library circulation, photography, or telegraphy. See Rachel Sagner Buurma, *A Material History of Omniscience: The Critical Invention of the Victorian Novel,* unpublished typescript. On the eighteenth century, see Christina Lupton, *Knowing Books: The Consciousness of Mediation in Eighteenth-Century Britain* (Philadelphia: University of Pennsylvania Press, 2012).

3. Anna Laetitia Barbauld, ed., *The Correspondence of Samuel Richardson, Author of Pamela, Clarissa, and Sir Charles Grandison. Selected from the Original Manuscripts, Bequeathed by Him to His Family, to Which Are Prefaced a Biographical Account of That Author, and Observations on His Writings,* 6 vols. (London: Richard Phillips, 1804), 1:xi.

4. *A Collection of the Moral and Instructive Sentiments, Maxims, Cautions, and Reflexions, Contained in the Histories of Pamela, Clarissa, and Sir Charles Grandison. Digested under Proper Heads, with References to the Volume, and Page, Both in Octavo and Twelves, in the Respective Histories* (London: S. Richardson, 1755), ix.

5. *A Collection of the Moral and Instructive Sentiments,* v, vi–vii.

6. *Correspondence between the Hon. John Adams, Late President of the United States, and the Late Wm. Cunningham, Esq, Beginning in 1803 and Ending in 1812* (Boston: E. M. Cunningham, son of the late Wm. Cunningham, Esq., True and Greene, Printers, 1823), 19.

7. Barbauld's *Richardson* was a commission, at the recommendation of Maria Edgeworth, from Richard Phillips, a former bookseller and newspaperman in Leicester, who was lately out of a jail sentence for selling Paine's *The Rights of Man* in the early 1790s. The letters had been collected by Richardson himself before his death, with an eye toward their publication, and they had passed through several editors' hands before it was decided to turn the editorial authority to a person of letters outside the

Richardson family. At 200 pages, the published book was Barbauld's longest to date (though she had turned 60 the previous year), and it was her first to be reviewed in the United States. See William McCarthy, *Anna Laetita Barbauld: Voice of the Enlightenment* (Baltimore: Johns Hopkins University Press, 2008), 370, 412–419.

8. Richard Stang, *The Theory of the Novel in England, 1850–1870* (London: Routledge and Paul, 1959); Kenneth Graham, *English Criticism of the Novel, 1865–1900* (Oxford: Clarendon Press, 1965).

9. Oscar Wilde, "Portrait of Mr. W. H.," *Blackwood's Edinburgh Magazine* 146, no. 885 (July 1889): 1–21, citation at 20.

10. Qtd. in Kathleen Tillotson, *Novels of the Eighteen-Forties* (Oxford: Clarendon Press, 1954), 13.

11. C[lara]. R[eeve]., *The Progress of Romance, Through Times, Countries and Manners* (London: for the Author, 1785), 53.

12. [Walter Scott], Untitled review of Robert Southey's edition of *The Pilgrim's Progress, The Quarterly Review* 43 (1830): 469–494, citation at 487; Henry Hallam, *Introduction to the Literature of Europe in the Fifteenth, Sixteenth, and Seventeenth Centuries,* 4 vols. (London: John Murray, 1839), 4:552.

13. N. H. Keeble, "'Of Him Thousands Daily Sing and Talk': Bunyan and His Reputation," in *John Bunyan: Conventicle and Parnassus: Tercentenary Essays,* ed. N. H. Keeble (Oxford: Clarendon Press, 1988), 241–263, esp. 257–258; Isabel Hofmeyr, *The Portable Bunyan: A Transnational History of The Pilgrim's Progress* (Princeton, NJ: Princeton University Press, 2004), 217–239.

14. According to Jonathan Rose, into the nineteenth and early twentieth centuries, *Pilgrim's Progress* and *Robinson Crusoe* "probably had more working-class readers than any book except the Bible" (*The Intellectual Life of the British Working Classes* [New Haven, CT: Yale University Press, 2001], 35.

15. Charles Dickens, *The Old Curiosity Shop* [1841], ed. Norman Paige (New York: Penguin, 2000), 123.

16. Susan Warner, *The Wide, Wide World* [1851], ed. Jane Tompkins (New York: Feminist Press, 1987), 351.

17. George Eliot, *The Mill on the Floss* [1860], ed. A. S. Byatt (New York: Penguin, 2003), 252; Mark Twain, *Adventures of Huckleberry Finn* [1885] (Berkeley: University of California Press, 1985), 137.

18. Henry James, *The Aspern Papers and The Turn of the Screw,* ed. Anthony Curtis (New York: Penguin, 1984), 194–195.

19. Eric Hobsbawm, "Inventing Traditions," in *The Invention of Tradition,* ed. Eric Hobsbawm and Terence Ranger (Cambridge: Cambridge University Press, 1983), 1–14.

20. See *The Cambridge History of the Book in Britain,* vol. 6, *1830–1914,* ed. David McKitterick (Cambridge: Cambridge University Press, 2009); *A History of the Book in America,* vol. 3, *The Industrial Book, 1840–1880,* ed. Scott E. Casper, Jeffrey D. Groves, Stephen W. Nissenbaum, and Michael Winship (Chapel Hill: University of North Carolina Press, 2007).

21. The quotation comes from Richard Menke, "The End of the Three-Volume Novel System, 27 June 1894," *BRANCH: Britain, Representation and Nineteenth-Century*

History, ed. Dino Franco Felluga, http://www.branchcollective.org/?ps_articles=rich
ard-menke-the-end-of-the-three-volume-novel-system-27-june-1894. See also Troy J.
Bassett, "The Production of Three-Volume Novels in Britain, 1863–97," *Papers of
the Bibliographical Society of America* 102, no. 1 (2008): 61–75.

22. Walter Besant, "The Rise and Fall of the 'Three Decker,'" *The Dial* 17, no. 199
(October 1, 1894): 185–186; "Book Talk and Tattle," *American Bookmaker* (November 1894): 193–194, citation at 194.

23. Oscar Wilde, *The Importance of Being Earnest* [1895], in *The Portable Oscar Wilde,*
rev. ed. by Richard Aldington and Stanley Weintraub (New York: Penguin, 1981),
430–507, citation at 459.

24. Virginia Woolf, *To the Lighthouse* [1927] (San Diego: Harcourt, 1981), 98. Woolf's
joke is a bibliographically more complex one than Wilde's, because *Middlemarch* was
not a triple-decker. The first 1871–1872 edition was in eight volumes. An 1873 New
York edition (Harper and Brothers) condensed it to two, as volumes six and seven of
Novels of George Eliot, and again as a stand-alone two-volume work in 1877, while the
1873 Edinburgh edition (William Blackwood and Sons) was in four volumes, rere-
leased in three in 1874, and in a single volume of 621 pages in 1877. There is reason,
however, to suspect that Woolf is in on the joke of Minta mistaking *Middlemarch* for a
triple-decker, as Virginia and Leonard Woolf's library contained four copies of this
work: a four-volume 1872 edition, a single-volume 1891 edition, a three-volume 1913
edition, and as volumes eleven to thirteen of the 1886 *Works of George Eliot,* all published by Blackwell). See *The Library of Leonard and Virginia Woolf: A Short-Title
Catalog,* ed. Julia King and Laila Miletic-Vejzovic, introduction by Diane F. Gillespie
(Pullman: Washington State University Press, 2003).

25. Ian Watt, *The Rise of the Novel: Studies in Defoe, Richardson and Fielding* (London:
Chatto and Windus, 1957), 11.

26. Lisa Gitelman, *Always Already New: Media, History, and the Data of Culture* (Cambridge, MA: MIT Press, 2006), xi.

27. Michel Foucault, *"Society Must Be Defended": Lectures at the Collège de France 1975–
1976,* ed. Mauro Bertani and Alessandro Fontana [1997] and trans. David Macey
(New York: Picador, 2003), 7.

28. Foucault, *"Society Must Be Defended,"* 7. See also his discussion of "historical inter-
ruption" in *The Archeology of Knowledge* [1971], trans. A. M. Sheridan Smith (New
York: Vintage, 1972), 27–28.

29. Foucault, *"Society Must Be Defended,"* 8.

30. For a suggestive set of possibilities, see Meredith L. McGill, "Literary History, Book
History, and Media Studies," in *Turns of Event: American Literary Studies in Motion,*
ed. Hester Blum (Philadelphia: University of Pennsylvania Press, 2016), 23–39.

31. *A Concise Dictionary of Slang and Unconventional English,* ed. Paul Beale (New
York: Macmillan, 1990), s.v. "book."

32. On comedy and historical knowledge, see Jordan Alexander Stein, "History's Dick
Jokes: On Melville and Hawthorne," *Los Angeles Review of Books,* December 15, 2015,
https://lareviewofbooks.org/article/historys-dick-jokes-on-melville-and-hawthorne.
For a far more searching discussion of comedy in the present time, see Lauren Berlant

and Sianne Ngai, "Comedy Has Issues," *Critical Inquiry* 43, no. 2 (Winter 2017): 233–249.

33. Herman Melville, *Moby-Dick; or, The Whale* [1851], ed. Andrew Delbanco (New York: Penguin, 1992), 147.

34. Henry James, *The Portrait of a Lady* [1881], ed. Robert D. Bamberg (New York: Norton, 1975), 53.

35. Dorothy Parker, "Words, Words, Words," in *The Portable Dorothy Parker* (New York: Penguin, 1973), 540–544, citation at 541.

Acknowledgments

This work is dedicated to Teresa Toulouse, a comparativist beyond compare, for being (in no particular order) inspiring, brilliant, challenging, and true, as a teacher, scholar, colleague, and friend. She was there in my freshman year of college, teaching my first English elective, and she was there again a decade later in my first year as junior faculty, another refugee who sought higher ground. In those crucial junctures, in the time between, and in all the years since, my work and life have benefited incalculably from her fierce intelligence and her enormous heart.

More narrowly but no less meaningfully, I am fairly certain that early glimmers of what became this project emerged in conversations beginning around 2005 with Lara Cohen, Justine Murison, and Joe Rezek, friends whose interest in archives and book history piqued my curiosity and invited response. At about the same juncture, I read Meredith McGill's *American Literature and the Culture of Reprinting* and Virginia Jackson's *Dickinson's Misery: A Theory of Lyric Reading*, two works whose field-shifting brilliance I am still trying to catch up to. Whatever the present book lacks, it abounds in smart friends.

The path from inspiration to publication, more than a decade long, was very far from linear, leading me through twenty archives and rare books libraries, travel to five countries, hundreds of disorganized digital photographs, who knows how many pages of notes, and scholarship in four languages (*von denen ich schlecht spreche*). I won't also count the number of moments I thought it might not come together, but the fact that it did owes a great deal to Sharmila Sen at Harvard University Press, whose editorial alacrity and sheer enthusiasm were and remain a great gift. Also at Harvard, Heather Hughes has been a pleasure to work with, not to mention an unimaginably patient guide through the slough of despond where one acquires high-resolution image files. John Donohue and Paul Vincent have my gratitude for providing copyediting and production assistance that was astute, professional, and timely, and that spared the final copy from some of my truly careless errors.

All those years of research and writing would not have been possible without material support from the University of Colorado, in the forms of a Junior Faculty Development Award and a Dean's Fund for Excellence/ASSETT Grant, the latter of which enabled me to attend a transformative summer seminar at the American Antiquarian Society; from a National Endowment for the Humanities Postdoctoral Fellowship at the Library Company of Philadelphia; from an Andrew W. Mellon Foundation Fellowship at the New-York Historical Society; from a Fordham University Faculty Research Grant, which allowed me to undertake the final archival digging; from a Robert L. McNeil Jr. Fellowship from the Historical Society of Pennsylvania, which allowed me to follow some peripheral threads; and from the Chang Family Fellowship.

For that amazing combination of material and immaterial support that only libraries can offer, I thank the past and present staffs at the American Antiquarian Society (especially Paul Erickson, Molly O'Hagan Hardy, Tom Knowles, Marie Lamoureux, and Elizabeth Pope), the *dix-huitièmists* at the Bibliothèque Nationale in Paris, the Departments of Humanities and of Rare Books and Music at the British Library, the Deutsches Historisches Museum in Berlin, the Free Library of Philadelphia, the Walsh Family and Gerald Quinn Libraries at Fordham University (especially Kirsten Lee, patient mistress of intercampus loan), the Historical Society of Pennsylvania, the Huntington Library, the George Peabody Library at the Johns Hopkins University, the Library Company of Philadelphia (especially Jim Green, Connie King, Krystal Appiah, and Rachel D'Agostino), the Massachusetts Historical Society, the Morgan Library and Museum, the National Archives of Scotland, the New England Historic Genealogical Society, the Rose Reading Room, the Brooke Russell Astor Rare Books Room, and the mid-Manhattan branch of the New York Public Library (especially Jay Barksdale), the Bobst Library and the Fales and Adkins collections at New York University (especially Charlotte Priddle), the Patricia D. Klingenstein Library at the New-York Historical Society (especially Nina Nazionale and Henry Raine), the Rare Books and Manuscripts Collection at Princeton's Firestone Library, the Department of Special Collections at the Stanford University Archives, the Burke Library at Union Theological Seminary, the Van Pelt-Dietrich Library and the Kislak Center for Special Collections at the University of Pennsylvania (especially, warmly, John Pollack and Daniel Traister), and the Beinecke Rare Book and Manuscript Library at Yale. James Ascher, formerly of the University of Colorado's Norlin Library, performed countless acts of bibliographic and organizational magic, all while wearing a crooked smile.

At the more general level of conception, this project owes its maturation to two institutions in particular: the Library Company of Philadelphia, which took me in as a postdoc and patiently taught me an enormous amount about grounding my flights of theoretical fancy with solid empirical data; and, more foundationally, the University of California, Santa Cruz, where once upon a time a college dropout could find his way back to academe and afford (mostly) to work his way through school while receiving a world-class education. I learned so much during my college years from an outstanding roster of teachers, and it is a humbling kind of joy to finally be able to acknowledge Michael Cowan, the late John Dizikes, Sam Frost, Susan Gillman, Jody Greene, Daniel Selden, Michael Warren, and Carter Wilson. Additionally, I would be remiss not to mention that Michael Moon's professional magnanimity kept me in grad school at a decisive moment, and I'd like Jane Bennett and Bill Connolly to know that the kindnesses they showed me helped make my first year of graduate study not my last. Susan Duncan and Patrick Skinner were the first people to take me intellectually seriously—almost three decades ago, when I was still a boy—and I sometimes think they made all the difference.

As contexts go, it was my good fortune to begin my career at the University of Colorado at Boulder, an institution that provided the freedom to write a book that had nothing to do with my PhD dissertation. Thanks especially to Nan Goodman for giving me that chance. Among many colleagues who made large and small contributions, I single out David Glimp, a model colleague. Long Boulder winters were weathered in the company of Terry Toulouse, Michael Zimmerman, Lizzie Zimmerman, and Alda, who extended their home on Cornell Circle to me and mine, and made me very happy. It's a sincere delight to have occasion to thank the University of Colorado undergraduates in my spring 2008 seminar "Sex, Rights, Character, and the Novel," whose raw talent and hard work had a formative impact on this project. Several thoughtful graduate students also played a part—especially Geoffrey Bateman, Ben Beck, Kelli Towers Jasper, Mary Caton Lingold, Quentin McAndrew, Cara Shipe, and Michele Speitz. Adra Raine's talents especially fortified me—as Spencer Everett's continue to.

Outside of Boulder, portions of what became this book were presented at the Dartmouth Futures of American Studies Institute, at the Early American History and Culture seminar at the Newberry Library, at meetings of the Society of Early Americanists, the American Society for Eighteenth-Century Studies, the American Comparative Literature Association, and the Society for Novel Studies, and at the Departments of English at Cornell University, Pomona College, Fordham University, and the University of Toronto. These occasions, and the intellectual engagement they provided, were important contexts for my labors—as was an MLA interview in December 2006 with some of the wonderful folks at the University of Utah's Department of English, not least because I'm still trying to answer Barry Weller's question about whether literary criticism is a version of sexuality. (Probably?)

As I pieced together the first iteration of this book in Philadelphia, an inexhaustible schedule of seminars at the McNeil Center for Early American Studies helped me to come by my knowledge of early American history honestly, and I thank Dan Richter for inviting me to be a research associate and for years of generous collegiality ever since. Also at Penn, Peter Stallybrass's good cheer and deft programming at the Seminar on Material Texts bent my thinking into new (material) shapes.

Later, in New York, Glenn Hendler threw me a life raft, and though I cannot just now figure out how to write him a Leslie Fiedler joke, I will always owe him one. Fordham University's English Department and Comparative Literature Program abound in great colleagues, all of whom I thank, but especially Andrew Albin, Frank Boyle, John Bugg, Ed Cahill, Danny Contreras, Shonni Enelow, Anne Fernald, Beth Frost, Chris GoGwilt, James Kim, Julie Kim, Corey McEleney, Fawzia Mustafa, Tom O'Donnell, Scott Poulson-Bryant, Jackie Reich, Rebecca Sanchez, Kris Trujillo, Dennis Tyler, Vlasta Vranjes, Keri Walsh, and Sarah Zimmerman. Stuart Sherman graciously lent me his office for a year of productive writing. Bob Davis and Ben Dunning have gone above and beyond. I'm grateful as well to Eva Badowska for all that she makes possible in her role as dean of the Faculty of Arts and Sciences. Fordham students have taught me a lot, but especially Kyle Campbell, Will Fenton, Rhianna Marks-Watton, and Christy Pottroff; meanwhile, acknowledgment of Adam Fales's contributions would far exceed a single sentence. Carole Alvino, MonaLisa Torres-Bates, Chaney Matos, Labelle De La Rosa, and Kerri Maguire took care of the day-to-day, often saving me from my own incompetence. While I thank these individuals easily and often, it's more difficult to summarize my gratitude for the opportunity to work at a university whose tenure and promotion standards are rigorous yet didn't force me to rush this work to press prematurely. What I can say is how heartening it feels to be evaluated by colleagues who appreciate the laborious hours and days of work that stand behind single sentences, which become footnotes, which get deleted.

And then there's the writing help. During my sophomore year of college, I turned in a lousy paper to Sharon Kinoshita, who displayed the pedagogical fortitude to comment that I should "put more weight on [my] verbs"—enduringly excellent advice for which I remain thankful. In the summer following my first year of graduate school, Rachel Cole sat with me and my seminar paper at a Donna's in Baltimore and explained how terrible my writing was, and I have ever since been grateful for her patience. Later, I learned an enormous amount from the marvelous pedagogies of Sarah Blackwood and Sarah Mesle at *Avidly*—thanks for all this and much besides.

For engaging readings of different iterations and parts of this manuscript, I thank Rachel Buurma, Lara Cohen, Heather Dubrow, Adam Fales, Jonathan Beecher Field, Lisa Gitelman, Jim Green, Claire Jarvis, Justine Murison, Seth Perry, Joe Rezek, Sarah Rivett, Dana Seitler, Stephen Shapiro, Laura Stevens, Kathryn Stockton, and Teresa Toulouse. A late-breaking reading by Meredith Neuman saved me from some significant errors and provoked some great insights. Huge, sincere, and unqualified thanks to my two readers for Harvard, Elizabeth Maddock Dillon and Caleb Smith, who were as generous as they were motivating and, what's more extraordinary, made me feel understood. My gratitude to them is not lessened by the limitations of time, space, and intelligence that prevented me from incorporating all of their excellent suggestions. Meanwhile, when my writing and reading haven't been in English, I have been grateful to draw upon Jeff Shoulson's knowledge of Hebrew. Bob Davis checked my Latin and talked me through Augustine's later works. A handful of friends checked my French and teased me about my pronunciation. *Ils avaient tous raison.*

Some people gave more than readings. Lauren Berlant said things that were somehow both acute and magical. Amanda Claybaugh deployed her considerable gift of saying the thing I needed to hear at the moment I needed to hear it. Chris Looby made astounding feats of generosity look effortless. Rei Terada shared her unmatched appreciation of films, cats, rocks, cities, angels, and things that matter. And Donald Pease lavished his legendary generosity on me and my work, brilliantly illuminating the darkest corners of the room. I cannot thank them enough.

Further help came from friends around the profession who, being friends, may not have known that they were some of my best teachers. I'm talking about Rachel Adams, Tanya Agathocleous, Mike Allan, John Levi Barnard, Ben Bascom, Nancy Bentley, Mandy Berry, Steven Blevins, Hester Blum, Colleen Boggs, Fiona Brideoake, Erica Burleigh, Rachel Buurma, Tara Bynum, Luis Campos, Corey Capers, Tim Cassedy, Russ Castronovo, Chris Castiglia, Max Cavitch, Sarah Chinn, Michael Cobb, Brian Connolly, Colin Dayan, Jeannine DeLombard, Joe Dimuro, Marcy Dinius, Steffi Dippold, Hilary Emmett, Jonathan Beecher Field, Tom Foster, Travis Foster, Andy Franta, Kat Fredrickson, Beth Freeman, John Garcia, Geoff Gilbert, Lisa Gitelman, Jeff Glover, Miles Grier, Kirsten Gruesz, Laura Heffernan, Michael Henderson, Todd Henry, Jared Hickman, Katherine Hijar, Jason Hoppe, Carrie Hyde, Jennie Jackson, Leon Jackson, Peter Jaros, Claire Jarvis, Toni Jaudon, Colin Johnson, Keith Jones, Anna Kornbluh, Paul Lai, Kevin Lamb, Caroline Levine, Crystal L'Hôte, Eng-Beng Lim, Dana Luciano, Deidre Lynch, Tim Mackin, Stacey Margolis, Meredith McGill, Sianne Ngai, Julie Orlemanski, Catherine Osborne, Andy Parker, Amy Parsons, Jason Payton, Yvette Piggush, Lloyd Pratt, Robert Reid-Pharr, Sarah Rivett, Camille Robcis, Marty Rojas, Britt Rusert, Cannon Schmitt, Bethany Schneider, Ana Schwartz, Joan Scott, Dana Seitler, Jonathan Senchyne, Cristobal Silva, Sam Sommers, Gus Stadler, Jill Stauffer, Simon Stern, Kathryn Stockton, Dan Stout, Mina Suk, Shannon Supple, Elisa Tamarkin, Kate Thomas, Pam Thurschwell, Kyla Tompkins, Mark Vareschi, Michael Warner, Bryan Waterman, Ed Whitley, Michael Winship, Nate Wolff, Cindy Wu, and Cat Zuromskis. Oh, and Ben Wurgaft, because he's slinkster cool.

A lot of things didn't go as planned during the too many years it took to write and publish this book. In those times I came to depend on Noah Glassman's conversations, which have held me (together) in and beyond the final phases of this writing. Hilary Emmett and Dave Stewart (and monkeys), and Byron Harrison and Brian Klinksiek sheltered me for weeks (weeks!) at a time in London, proving, among other things, that they are all great supporters of the humanities. Meredith Neuman and Danny Thompson made Worcester, Massachusetts, seem like the cultural and culinary center of the universe. Brad Anderson and Robin Riley provided reliable couches in Hell's Kitchen on nights when the transitions that preoccupied me were not just historical ones. I thank them all so. Members of the greater New York City diaspora have my gratitude for years spent schooling me in the hard lessons of how to be happy: Benjamin Adam, Brad Anderson, Phil Blumenshine, Seth Carlson, Ray Cha, Phil Chong, Greg Edwards, Ian Epstein, John Havard, Peter Hill, Mark Horn, Jon Kay, Patrick Kwan, Mike Moore, Janet Neary, Michael Nedelman, Victor Ng, Frank Pasquale, Jasbir Puar, Jordy Rosenberg, Tim Stewart-Winter, James Saelee, Ian Shin, Kyla Schuller, Liam Stack, Ben Steverman, Alex Testere, Morgan Tingley, Tim Wade, and BG Wright. Big ups to Sam Draxler for, among other things, soaking cashews and teaching me to fly. Love too to the Baltimore crew who gave me shelter and whiskey and invited me to dance: Lucky Baltimore, Clyde Duplichan, and Kristen Anchor, among them. Rahne Alexander's queer magic puts the charm in Charm City, the vice in the vicious circle, and the songs in my head and heart.

Speaking of which: Lara Cohen exemplifies the phrase "everyday chicken," kept me from being a fraud, and, like Amadeus, rocks me. Peter Coviello curated intimacies and conjured joy. Justine Murison made my anxiety history. Jason Potts just wanted to be thanked in smart people's books. Joe Rezek helped me circulate and provided an elsewhere. Tim Stewart-Winter lent me his clout. Daniel Worden made me feel like a man. Heather Malcolm, Courtney Miller-Callahan, and Michael Stevens have been there since the beginning. For the life behind, around, and apart from the work, love and thanks to Elan Abrell, Becca Howes-Mischel, Geoff Watland, Delci Winders; Robin and Newton; and, especially, to Aufie. Neither this book nor its author would exist in their present forms without the myriad contributions of Robert Chang. And Edward Hui, the Louise to my Tina: I'll see you in Sault Ste. Marie. I love them all well past the point where clever sentences falter.

Index